Credit Risk Models

and the Basel Accords

Credit Risk Models

and the Basel Accords

Donald van Deventer
&
Kenji Imai

John Wiley & Sons (Asia) Pte Ltd

Copyright © 2003 by John Wiley & Sons (Asia) Pte Ltd
Published in 2003 by John Wiley & Sons (Asia) Pte Ltd
2 Clementi Loop, #02-01, Singapore 129809

This publication is designed to provide accurate and authoritative information in regard to the subject
matter covered. It is sold with the understanding that the publisher is not engaged in rendering
professional services. If professional advice or other expert assistance is required, the services of a
competent professional person should be sought.

JK

Other Wiley Editorial Offices

John Wiley & Sons, Inc., 111 River Street, Hoboken, NJ 07030, USA
John Wiley & Sons Ltd, The Atrium, Southern Gate, Chichester PO19 8SQ, England
John Wiley & Sons (Canada) Ltd, 22 Worcester Road, Rexdale, Ontario M9W 1L1, Canada
John Wiley & Sons Australia Ltd, 33 Park Road (PO Box 1226), Milton, Queensland 4064, Australia
Wiley-VCH, Pappelallee 3, 69469 Weinheim, Germany

Library of Congress Cataloging-in Publication Data:
ISBN: 0-470-82091-8

Typeset in 10.5/13 points, Times Roman by Linographic Services Pte Ltd
Printed in Singapore by Saik Wah Press Pte Ltd.
10 9 8 7 6 5 4 3 2 1

For Ella & Jinsa, Phyllis & Bob
Donald

For Yasuko, Tomoki & Anna
Kenji

Contents

Introduction   1

Chapter 1   The Objectives of the Credit Risk Process   5

Chapter 2   The Asian Crisis: Lessons for Maximizing
            Risk-adjusted Shareholder Value   17

Chapter 3   The Evolution of Credit Modeling Techniques   25

Chapter 4   Credit Risk Models: The Impact of Macro Factors
            on the Risk of Default   65

Chapter 5   Internal Ratings and Approaches to Testing
            Credit Models   85

Chapter 6   Tests of Credit Models using Historical Default Data   119

Chapter 7   Market Data Tests of Credit Models: Lessons from
            Enron and Other Case Studies   139

Chapter 8   Out of Sample Testing of Credit Models   193

Chapter 9   Implications of the Tests for the Basel Accords and
            Management of Financial Institutions   199

Chapter 10 Measuring Safety and Soundness and Capital Allocation
            Using the Merton and Reduced Form Models   215

Chapter 11 Impact of Collateral on Valuation Models   243

Chapter 12 Pricing and Valuing Revolving Credit and Other Loan
            Agreements   249

Chapter 13 Credit Derivatives and Collateralized Debt Obligations   253

Chapter 14 Future Developments in Credit Modeling   259

Index   267

Introduction

Risk management has gone through a striking evolution from its origins in the 1970s to the current state-of-the-art systems and processes. The authors, of two different generations, are typical of this evolution. Don van Deventer was a graduate student in Cambridge, Massachusetts in the middle 1970s when Fischer Black, Robert Merton, John Lintner and other 'giants' of finance were common sights on the streets of Cambridge. The Black-Scholes options model was new and revolutionizing theoretical finance, and the capital asset pricing model was increasingly well understood. In 1977, however, Don was told in an interview on Wall Street that 'nothing as academic as the Black-Scholes options model will ever be in practical use on Wall Street.' My, how times have changed! Don, like most risk managers of his vintage, spent a decade in interest rate risk management and then evolved through transitions from investment banker to market risk and credit risk.

Kenji Imai was also a graduate student in Cambridge in the late 1980s and went immediately to the trading floor, where derivatives technology was well established. Kenji's risk management evolution was to add the multi-period perspective of the asset and liability manager to his market risk perspective, and then to apply both disciplines to the credit risk arena.

Both of us have been heavily influenced by our relationship with David Shimko and Robert Jarrow. Don began working with David Shimko in the early 1990s when David was a little-known finance professor at the University of Southern California. In the intervening years, he moved to Wall Street with JP Morgan and Bankers Trust and was later named a professor at Harvard Business School and interim Chairman of the Global Association of Risk Professionals. In 1995, David introduced Don to Robert Jarrow that led to a permanent relationship at Kamakura Corporation. Kenji joined Kamakura upon learning of Bob's appointment to the firm in order to learn as much as possible about risk management.

1

Bob Jarrow wrote his Ph.D. thesis, also in Cambridge, under the direction of Robert Merton and was selected to write the appreciation for Merton's Nobel Prize in Economics for the academic community. Don and Kenji, in one of their few accurate forecasts, predicted Robert Merton would win the Nobel Prize in the introduction to their 1996 book, *Financial Risk Analytics: A Term Structure Model Approach for Banking, Insurance, and Investment Management*. Don was so impressed with the elegance and insights of the Merton model of risky debt that he secured the marketing rights for default probabilities based on the model for Japan in the very early 1990s. In 1993, David Shimko and Don collaborated with Naohiko Tejima to extend the Merton model to a random interest rates framework in 1993. Both of Don's books have chapters on the Merton model of risky debt, extolling its virtues.

Therefore, it was curious to Don that Bob Jarrow's early work on credit risk with Stuart Turnbull in 1995 was based on a completely different framework, the reduced form model framework that we discuss extensively in this book. Don asked Bob why he chose this approach rather than extending the Merton model to make it more general and more accurate. To this day, Don is still humbled by Bob's response. Bob said: "I think that's a problem that I can't solve in a tractable way," saying he felt that the simultaneity of management's choice of capital structure and credit risk of the firm were inseparably linked.

The authors have been deeply involved in both the Merton model and reduced form models as students of the technology and as commercializers of the technology. We believe in a multiple models approach and a clear-minded scientific view of the models' performance as the only way to approach the subject of risk management. Model performance is a question for scientists, and we commend the Moody's alumni who have done so much to instill the kind of scientific discipline that Basel requires in measuring model performance.

We also commend the many central bankers who have contributed to the New Basel Capital Accord. We believe that the Basel proposals are very helpful in bringing model testing out into the open as scientific discipline. We know that the participants were handicapped by the political need to make their proposals be a "lowest common denominator" kind of regulation, which may make their task impossible. We wish them better luck than the Federal Reserve Board had in the early 1990s when it sought to link bank interest rate risk to capital in a series of proposals that were never implemented.

We hope that our comments, most of which are critical of the Basel proposals, will be interpreted as a plea by two very experienced participants in the risk management business to do better than the lowest common denominator-approach. We hope this book makes a contribution in that regard.

As authors, we have faced the same challenge that the authors of the Basel proposal have faced. To be very specific, we need to be very mathematical, and yet when we do so we know that we reduce the size of the potential audience. In this book, we have restricted ourselves to plain English to the maximum degree, although it means we occasionally pull rabbits out of a hat from a mathematical point of view. We hope that more mathematical readers will go to the detailed bibliography in this book for a more detailed explanation of the mathematics.

We would like to thank a great many people for their contributions to our thinking over the last 15 years. First and foremost, we would like to thank Bob Jarrow and David Shimko for their grace, intelligence, and relentless pursuit of excellence with a passion that inspires us all. Oldrich Vasicek and Stuart Turnbull have provided humorous and insightful inspiration over the years that has been invaluable. Bob Selvaggio, formerly of Chase Manhattan and now of Ambac, has been a long time partner in assaulting the conventional wisdom and the lowest common denominator-approach to risk management. Bob's support has pushed us forward with higher speed than we would have otherwise gone. Recently, James Costa of FleetBoston has shown us the need for a dispassionate technology for evaluating model performance from a practical point of view. His insights have been very helpful and are reflected in this book.

Our colleagues at Kamakura have shared our enthusiasm for credit modeling for years, and we are grateful to all of them for their hard work and good cheer as we loaded 32 million securities prices into 500,000 lines of software code to do many of the tests in this book. We also want to thank Sudheer Chava of Cornell University for his hard work in assembling the default data base we have used in testing.

Finally, we want to thank our long-suffering wives and children. We promise that this is the last book that we will write in hotel rooms during business trips.

Don van Deventer and Kenji Imai
Honolulu
January, 2003

1

The Objectives of the Credit Risk Process

A fter a decade of calm in the 1990s, following a turbulent decade in the 1980s, defaults of public companies in the U.S. began to surge. In addition, more than 100,000 unlisted companies went bankrupt in Japan during the last decade. These developments in the capital markets are a stark reminder of what experienced investors have known for years— of all of the risks an investor can face, credit risk is the dominant risk. It is not surprising, then, that senior management at financial institutions around the world is highly focused on the most recent pronouncements of the Basel Committee for Banking Supervision, particularly those that relate to credit risk.

For most of the last thirty years, beginning with the introduction of a simplistic 'primary capital ratio', regulation by the Board of Governors of the Federal Reserve System in the U.S. has focused on utilizing quantitative methods to assess the risk management process of major financial institutions. This has been a dramatic change from the qualitative regulatory style that was more prevalent in prior years. This development has created many fortunes, because, as one wealthy arbitrageur commented, 'Tax arbitrage and regulatory arbitrage are the only ways to make money any more.'[1] More importantly, it has had a dramatic impact, both positive and negative, upon the way senior management runs financial institutions.

Financial institutions respond to regulations in a way that depends both on the culture of that particular market and on the relative sophistication of the financial institution compared to its peers. Japanese bankers view regulatory requirements as specifying exactly the risk management approach that represents 'best practice.' American bankers have tended to regard

---

[1] Private conversation with the founder of a major credit insurer, March, 2000.

5

regulatory requirements as being a lowest common denominator-approach to regulation, and they generally view them as a minimum standard that is nowhere near best practice.

The 2001 consultative papers by the Basel Committee on Banking Supervision are different in both their comprehensiveness and in their level of sophistication. Regulators have, for the first time, clearly 'raised the bar' in terms of the sophistication of risk management systems and processes that is required of bankers. This is long overdue, considering that we are obliged to obtain a government-issued license to drive our own car, but there has never previously been any need to obtain a 'license' to run a bank which would be bailed out by the taxpayers' money in times of trouble. If implemented effectively, a license or certification for the management of banks, insurance companies, securities firms and investment management firms is a sound development.

Like any large committee offering products or services, the Basel Committee's work has both strengths and weaknesses. However, its greatest strength is encapsulated in the consultative papers by acknowledging that credit risk is the major risk facing modern global financial institutions, and the models used to manage credit risk must be proven to work well for financial institutions in order to be considered best practice. Using no model at all, or worse still, using a model based on faith rather than facts, is unacceptable.

With the exception of state-owned financial institutions, the management of financial institutions works for the shareholders. The emphasis in this book is on maximizing risk-adjusted shareholder value-added within the constraints imposed by a prudent board of directors. For almost all financial institutions, these constraints will be more binding than the regulatory minimums. That is why this book takes the maximization of risk-adjusted shareholder value-added as its focus, as opposed to blind compliance with regulatory pronouncements. Compliance with regulatory pronouncements is the minimum acceptable performance, and maximizing shareholder value-added on a risk-adjusted basis is a higher standard that financial institutions should aspire to. Surprisingly, because of the sophistication of the Basel Committee's recent work, there is less contradiction between shareholder value-added maximization and regulatory requirements than there has been in the past, when quantitative regulations were so perverse that arbitrage was not only profitable, but just. The rest of this book is devoted to showing the positive developments in the management of credit risk that have emerged from state-of-the-art financial research to practical application at the best financial institutions in the world, largely encouraged, but sometimes hindered, by regulation.

The next section puts credit risk into perspective.

How Important is Credit Risk among all the Risks that Financial Institutions Face?

Because of the extremely high interest rates that prevailed in the United States during the late 1970s and early 1980s, the primary focus of regulators in the United States was on interest rate risk and the massive number of defaults among both banks and non-bank savings and loan institutions. Similar interest rate-related financial problems rippled throughout Southeast Asia during the Asian crisis that began with the fall of the Thai baht on July 2, 1997 and continued for most of the next two years. The first response of central bankers was generally to increase interest rates and to severely devalue exchange rates. Consequently, financial institutions and corporate borrowers with an interest rate 'mismatch' paid the price. In this context, it is understandable that interest rate risk has been the primary regulatory and management focus in many countries.

Relatively speaking, though, it is apparent from financial institutions' default history that credit risk is much more important as we demonstrate in Figure 1.1.

In Figure 1.1 below, the share price in Australian dollars for the ANZ Banking Group is plotted against the 3-year Australian dollar interest rate swap rate. As the trend line shows, on average, as interest rates increase, the stock price of the ANZ Banking Group decreases. This is rational, even if the bank's interest rate risk is fully hedged, because even in that event, the bank's constant net interest income has a lower present value at a higher level of interest rates. There is a much more important lesson from this

Figure 1.1 ANZ Banking Group interest rate sensitivity of common stock February 1, 1996–February 8, 2001

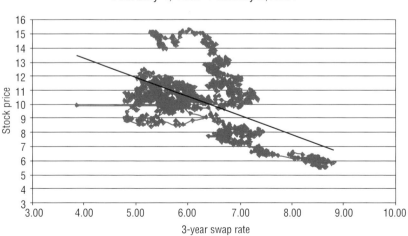

graph, however. If we draw a line to explain the change in stock price as a function of the change in interest rates, the resulting statistical relationship explains less than 1% of the total variation of the stock price of the ANZ bank. Other factors explain the 99%, and of these other factors, it is clearly credit risk that is the 'heavy weight' in this scenario.. A regulatory and managerial emphasis on credit risk is clearly consistent with the market's view of the major risks facing financial institutions.

Further confirmation comes from Japan. From the end of the second world war until the mid-1990s, no bank in Japan had ever gone into default. From the early 1990s until the present, interest rates in Japan have been on a very steady downward trend, an extremely favorable interest rate environment for banks. Nonetheless, three of the top 20 banks in Japan were nationalized by the end of 1998: Hokkaido Takushoku Bank, Long Term Credit Bank of Japan, and Nippon Credit Bank. We discuss two of these three in later chapters but the lesson is clear— of all the major factors that cause banks to default, credit risk is number one. This was confirmed in a 1995 study by the Board of Governors of the Federal Reserve, which used advanced statistical methods to create an early warning index of bank failure. The Financial Institutions Monitoring System[2] developed by the Federal Reserve Board found the following variables (all expressed as a percentage of assets) to be statistically significant predictors of bank default in the United States:

- loans past due 30-89 days;
- loans past due 90 or more days;
- non-accrual loans;
- foreclosed real estate;
- tangible capital (accounting capital, i.e. goodwill);
- net income;
- investment securities;
- percentage ranking of asset growth over last 4 quarters;
- prior management rating;
- prior composite CAMEL[3] rating.

Five of the ten variables were clearly credit-related, and none of the ten variables were interest rate risk-related.

---

[2] This system was developed to provide the Federal Reserve with estimates of the financial condition of institutions insured by the Bank Insurance Fund between on-site examinations.

[3] "Camel" is a U.S. bank regulatory acronym which refers to the index which summarizes the condition of the bank in one number.

Objectives of the Credit Risk Process

It is very important to keep the 'big picture' in mind when analyzing the objectives of the credit risk process and how to achieve it. There are a number of important objectives. Bankers have spent most of their time over the last four decades on the first two questions that the credit risk process should answer, which are:

> *Should I make this loan? Should I undertake this derivatives transaction? Should I buy this bond? Yes or no?*

Most chief investment officers and credit officers have focused on origination—i.e. what loans to make, what bonds to buy, and what derivatives transactions to undertake. The traditional credit approval process is heavily focused on supplying 'yes'; or 'no' answers to these origination questions. This question is much too simple. The right question is as follows:

Are there terms on which this transaction creates shareholder value? If so, what are they, and do the proposed terms fall within the acceptable range? If not, what counter-offer makes sense? We address these issues in more depth in the following section.

The second question that has occupied the most time in a traditional credit risk process is whether a transaction that has been originated should be disposed of:

> *Should I sell this loan? Should I close out this derivatives transaction? Should I sell this bond? Yes or no?*

In the case of a loan, this could mean an outright sale, a syndication of part of the loan, or a decline to rollover the loan. In the case of a derivative, it could mean an early termination of a particular transaction or a formal netting agreement to reduce gross exposure. In the case of a bond, the question is whether to sell it or not.

Again, these questions have preoccupied credit analysts for decades, but they are too simple. The right question is:

> *Do I create more shareholder value on a risk-adjusted basis by keeping the transaction or disposing of it?*

In order to answer this question, it is not enough to know whether or not the default probability of the counterparty has increased. We need to know whether the price of the transaction, if sold, is higher or lower than the institution's best estimate of its value. For example, even if the credit risk of a company is increasing and it has issued bonds that are trading at 60, the bond holder may well expect that the bond will be worth 70 even upon default. Selling the bond may be rational given internal politics, but it's not rational in terms of economics. Similarly, if the credit risk of a borrower has increased to the point where the correct spread on the loan is LIBOR[4] plus 100 basis points, but the loan already yields LIBOR plus 125 basis points, a rational economic decision is to renew the credit since the bank receives more than enough compensation for its risk.

Using Valuation, Pricing, and Hedging to Increase Risk-adjusted Shareholder Value

The problem with the first two questions we've posed is their simplicity and lack of context. We need to make significant changes in the way we've been approaching the credit decision. First of all, the objective is to create maximum risk-adjusted shareholder value. What this means is that we want to maximize the share price of the organization, continuously, over time. The share price reflects risk-adjusted shareholder value, taking into account the risk of bankruptcy of the institution and the significant losses to the institution's shareholders, bond holders, depositors, policy holders, and employees from default or bankruptcy.

This means that we need continuous visibility on the value of all current and potential transactions on two dimensions:

1. Their fair market value to others, and
2. Their value to our institution in particular.

Therefore credit modeling technology has to provide a lot more than just a default probability to be useful. We need a fully consistent methodology for pricing, valuation and hedging. If we have any one of these three capabilities, by definition we have the other two as well. If we know the pricing, we can calculate the value. If we can calculate the value, we can 'stress test' the value with respect to key risk factors to obtain a hedge.

Assessing the Bankruptcy Risk of Our Own Institution

The second key implication is that we need to assess the probability of bankrupty of our own institution and the cost of going bankrupt. This calculation is rare in the financial services industry, and even though it is a critical part of the credit risk process, it is rarely done and often considered politically incorrect. What credit analyst hasn't anticipated this response

---

[4] London Interbank Offered Rate

from management, when they compile an assessment of their own institution's bankruptcy risk: 'Kowalski, your job is to make sure we don't go bankrupt, so don't waste your time telling me the probability that you haven't done your job.'

Ironically, this is the primary focus of regulators and an area of the risk information market that is flourishing. Third parties are assessing and publishing the risk of our own institutions, but we don't do this ourselves, even though we have much more information than any outsiders. This has to change to give the right answers to the key credit questions. Why? Consider the following exceptions to the general rule 'Buy low, sell high.' The 'buy low, sell high' rule is the rule we should follow must of the time, but sometimes it doesn't work as the following examples of an institution experiencing financial difficulties illustrate:

- **Can't buy favorably-priced assets:** A borrower whose fair market pricing is LIBOR plus 75 basis points on a loan is willing to take a loan from our institution at LIBOR plus 100 basis points because of a 20-year banking relationship and 18 years of playing golf with our President. Any strong institution would make the loan. However, we can't because we are more concerned with rolling over the liabilities we have, let alone issuing more liabilities to fund good assets.
- **Can't sell assets at a fair price:** We want to restore liquidity so we are willing to sell assets at a fair price, or even a little worse than fair price, to avoid incurring the costs of bankruptcy. We think fair value is 98 cents on the dollar but offer the assets to the market at 95 cents on the dollar. All six major dealers know we're in trouble, they know the other five dealers know too, and the only bids we get are at 90 cents on the dollar. A strong institution would decline to sell, but a weak one may have to say yes to avoid bankruptcy. Ask the former management team at Long Term Capital Management how market prices responded to their problems.

The moral of the story is this: we need to know both the credit risk of the company we've extended credit to, and we need to know our own credit risk, in order to make the buy and sell transactions that make sense for the shareholder. Knowing the default probabilities of our counterparty and of our own bank is only the first of many steps—we need to know pricing, valuation and hedging for the transaction that our borrower has undertaken and any liabilities we might issue. We need to know the macro factors that are driving risk and creating correlation among counterparties whose credit quality depends on the same macro factors.

If we have this knowledge, we can both ask and answer more difficult and more useful questions such as the following:

*What broad classes of assets create the most shareholder value for
our institution, given our own risk situation?*

We do this by valuing the assets we have and assessing the macro factors
that drive their risk. We analyze potential transactions and understand how
much value would be derived if a strong financial institution analyzed them
on a 'buy low, sell high' basis. On this basis, if we can buy a loan for 100
cents on the dollar and if it is worth 103, we do it. If we can sell a loan for
101 cents on the dollar that is worth 99, we sell it. When our institution is
strong, decisions are simple when we have valuation capability as part of our
credit modeling tools.

When the institution is weak, the questions become more complex. Given
our own probability of default, does buying this new asset increase risk-
adjusted shareholder value (stock price)? It is entirely possible that buying
a bond, making a loan or undertaking a derivatives transaction that looks
good on a 'buy low, sell high' basis can drive down the share price of a
troubled institution by increasing the short-term risk of bankruptcy. For
example, let's assume a troubled bank is having difficulty rolling over its
certificates of deposit and at the same time a three-month Treasury bill
matures. If the bank has the opportunity to invest the proceeds of the three-
month bill maturity into a 10-year illiquid private placement worth 105 cents
on the dollar at a price of 100, it will have to decline the opportunity. The
transaction, even though it adds 5 cents on the dollar in shareholder value
for a strong institution, can destroy shareholder value for a weak institution
by making the expected costs of bankruptcy (i.e. probability of bankruptcy
multiplied by costs if bankruptcy occurs) higher.

With good credit technology, we can analyze potential transactions on
both a 'buy low, sell high' basis and from the perspective of their value to
our institution specifically. If our institution is very strong, the two
perspectives will be the same.

Regulators want us to take steps to strengthen our institution so that the
two perspectives are the same, and shareholders certainly want to keep the
risk of bankruptcy in a manageable range.

What is the market value of my portfolio?

If we have good credit modeling technology, we should be able to value the
portfolio on demand to see how a change in major risk factors (for example,
oil prices, interest rates, exchange rates, etc.) has affected us. From a
computer science perspective, this can be done at a rate of hundreds of
transactions per second. There are no computer science constraints on our
ability to do this.

What are the major risk factors driving the value of my loan, bond or derivatives portfolio?

State-of-the-art credit modeling technology does much more than just tell us what the historical migration from one credit class to another has been probabilistically over a given historical period. Historical migration tells us almost nothing about our ability to create shareholder value going forward because it gives only limited guidance on pricing and valuation and no guidance on hedging the risks of the portfolio we have. Instead, we need to understand what macro factors *caused* those correlations in the past. Once we know what the key macro risk factors are that affect our institution, we can take practical action to increase and protect risk-adjusted shareholder value.

Am I as diversified as I could be? How does a change in my current level of diversification affect my risk-adjusted shareholder value?

To answer this question, we need the valuation of all the assets and liabilities we have (including the liabilities issued by our own institution) and the potential assets we could buy. The change in risk-adjusted shareholder value depends on how a change in diversification affects our own risk of bankruptcy, as we saw in the examples above.

We need tools that can analyze both our own risk and the risk of our counterparties.

How can I hedge the risk of my portfolio?

Unless we can answer this question, almost all of the other questions lose most, if not all, of their meaning. Regulators and shareholders want management to be able to change the risk of the institution if it moves into an unacceptable range. An unacceptable range is a range outside of the 'safety zone,'[5] which is defined as the range of portfolio choices where the bankrupcty risk of an institution is very small. Once outside this zone, an increase in risk begins to destroy large amounts of shareholder value.

Therefore, a state-of-the-art credit modeling technology should allow management to manage where we are in the safety zone. Without a hedging capability, this is almost impossible. Obvious hedges with clear implications like outright non-recourse loan sales or name-by-name hedging in the credit

---

[5] See Dennis Uyemura and Donald R. van Deventer, *Financial Risk Management in Banking*, McGraw-Hill, Chicago, 1993 for more on the concept of the "safety zone."

derivatives market are not enough to make major changes in the nature of the portfolio. The hedging capability we are referring to is hedges of the macro factors which drive credit risk and determine shareholder value—i.e. interest rates, oil prices, central business district building prices, foreign exchange rates, stock indices, and so on. Hedging these macro risks is practical in large quantities, even in the case of building prices. If you have too much exposure to building price risk in the real estate loan portfolio, the bank can sell its headquarters building exactly as Security Pacific Corporation of Los Angeles did in the early 1990s (albeit it was too little, too late, given the bank's aggressiveness in real estate lending).

> *How much risk-adjusted shareholder value-added does this type of loan business (bond business, derivatives business) create for a strong institution? For my institution?*

First class credit modeling technology answers this question. This drives both asset origination and securitization strategy. If the value of a loan sector is worth more to a strong institution than it is to my institution, then we sell the portfolio or securitize it.[6]

> *Is Ms. X a good performer or a bad performer? How much risk-adjusted shareholder value did she create?*

The streets of the Hamptons on Long Island are largely populated with former traders who undertook billions of dollars of derivatives transactions that lowered the credit quality of their institutions. The traders' bonus payments, however, ignored this credit quality-related destruction of shareholder value and were grossly out of proportion to the value the traders truly generated. High-quality credit analysis avoids this by analyzing not only the 'buy low, sell high' value of a transaction but also its incremental impact on risk-adjusted shareholder value of the institution doing the transaction. This is the basis on which bonuses should be paid.

> *How should this loan (bond, derivative) be priced to create shareholder value-added for a strong institution? For my institution?*

---

[6] This being said, securitization isn't an efficient tool for most institutions; its principal use has been as an expensive form of arbitrage to avoid regulatory capital constraints. Uyemura and van Deventer's *Financial Risk Management in Banking* outlines the potential pitfalls in detail.

This is a much better question than question one. Business is not a 'yes' or 'no' business in most circumstances. It's an offer and counter-offer business. Credit committees should have the capability to say 'At the proposed pricing, we don't want the deal but at 25 basis points higher price we'll do it.' A high-quality credit modeling capability delivers this objective. Don't say no, make another offer.

> *From a credit policy perspective, how should I view the risk of the bank's loan portfolio given that economic conditions have recently changed?*

The technology exists today to give every financial institution's CEO a mark-to-market of their entire portfolio, from retail loans to credit derivatives, on a credit-adjusted and default-adjusted basis. There should be an almost instantaneous response to the question 'How did the mark-to-market value of my Japanese loan portfolio change when the yen moved from 134 to 119 per dollar?'

> *What should my loan loss reserve (i.e. reserve for credit losses on bonds, derivatives) be?*

This is one of the most important questions management, shareholders and regulators should be asking, and it is surprising how many financial institutions either cannot quickly answer the question or give the answer: 'zero, I'll cover my losses out of interest income on other transactions.' With good credit modeling technology, the answer is simple—mark-to-market the portfolio in two ways—with defaults turned off in the system (i.e. no one defaults), and then with defaults turned on. The latter calculation should reflect all possible default scenarios. The loan loss reserve should be very closely related to the mark to market value difference between the two valuations.

> *Do I have enough capital in my institution to maximize risk-adjusted shareholder value of the firm? Do I have enough in this business unit? What is the probability of default of my institution? Of this business unit?*

Financial institutions' regulators are devoting an enormous amount of time to this question after the trillion- dollar bail-out of U.S. savings and loan institutions in the 1980s. The most advanced credit modeling technologies in the world are being actively studied by U.S. bank regulators for deposit insurance pricing and 'early warning' of financial difficulty.[7] Each financial institution should be examining its own credit risk and how a change in capital structure can alter that credit risk to improve risk-adjusted shareholder value.

In Summary

Credit risk modeling is not just about deciding whether or not to make a loan. Credit risk modeling is at the heart of the creation or destruction of shareholder value. A high-quality credit risk modeling effort allows management of financial institutions to directly drive strategy and shareholder value creation by managing risk both from the top down and from the bottom up. Financial institutions which fail to use this technology skillfully will be the unwitting counterparties of those who do. As a young derivatives trader said after his first year on the trading floor, 'Arbitrage is the process by which people who are smart take money from people who are not.'[8]

The next chapter emphasizes the importance of the questions we have addressed in this chapter with lessons from economies where the credit risk-related excitement has been substantial over the past few years, that is, the Asia Pacific region.

---

[7] The Federal Deposit Insurance Corporation of the United States held a major conference on the use of "reduced form" credit models for deposit insurance pricing in September, 2002. The Office of the Comptroller of the Currency is using hazard rate modeling (related to "reduced form" credit models) to provide early warning of bank defaults.

[8] David Kuo, formerly of Lehman Brothers, private conversation, 2000.

2

The Asian Crisis: Lessons for Maximizing Risk-adjusted Shareholder Value

There are three extremely important lessons from the Asian crisis that this chapter illustrates within the context of a critical incident involving one of the most highly-skilled and most prestigious financial institutions in the world, JP Morgan Chase, then JP Morgan. The events related in this chapter are based solely on public information available at the time on the Bloomberg financial information service. We believe that the incident described below is perhaps the single most enlightening credit event of the last decade because it illustrates three key pillars of success in credit risk:

- **Fear**: No matter how good your institution is in risk management in general and credit risk in particular, bad things are going to happen. Go looking for weaknesses now and try to stop them before they happen. *Be afraid.*
- **Links**: The amount a counterparty owes you and their probability of default are almost always correlated, usually to your disadvantage.
- **Macro Risk Drivers**: Risk and large scale correlation of defaults are driven by macro economic risk factors, which means that counterparty default probabilities change with every change in these macro risk drivers. Identify macro risk drivers and understand their impact on defaults for every counterparty.

We turn now to the incident that illustrates these principles so richly.

Lessons from the JP Morgan—SK Securities Incident

Although it did not receive a significant amount of publicity at the time, perhaps the most significant credit risk incident of the last quarter of a century was the potential loss of approximately $500 million by JPMorgan on a derivatives transaction with a Korean counterparty in 1997–1998. This incident serves to clearly illustrate the importance of macro-economic risk factors on two things:

- The amount of the legally required payments under a contract with a counterparty and
- The default probability of the counterparty.

Large financial institutions today still remain heavily dependent on first- and second-generation credit models where only the first influence, the impact of macro factors on required payments, is included in the analysis. A review of the JPMorgan incident reveals the dangers of this approach.

In 1997, JP Morgan and a number of other securities firms were structuring complex derivatives transactions with payment being a function of the level of the Thai baht. SK Securities, a Korean securities firm, and a number of other Korean institutions created a special purpose vehicle in Labuan in Malaysia to invest in one of these Thai baht transactions, which effectively involved a purchase of a Thai baht forward foreign exchange contract. At the time, the Thai baht was managed by the Thai government according to the value of a currency 'basket' and there was a considerable divergence of market opinion about whether this basket pricing methodology would hold, leaving the Thai baht at its long time level of approximately 25 baht to the U.S. Dollar, or whether it would be abandoned, leading to a considerable weakening in the currency. The Korean parties' investment was essentially a bet that the basket would hold.

Within any major financial institution, the Thai baht trader would 'purchase' the transaction from the origination unit, in this case JPMorgan Hong Kong. The trader would then seek to offload the transaction to another party at a better rate, leaving the trader with a perfect 'delta hedge' with respect to the Thai baht. The delta of this purchase of the Korean transaction and the delta of the sale to a third party would, in theory, remain equal regardless of whether the Thai baht was 25, 30, 40 or 50 to the U.S. dollar. The trader would view his position as hedged and all first and second generation risk management systems would have shown that the Morgan trader was indeed hedged with respect to the Thai baht.

There was only one flaw in this view of the risk exposure. The capital in the Labuan special purpose vehicle would be completely wiped out with a movement in the Thai baht to a level slightly above 30 baht to the dollar. The 'delta' hedge of the trader's exposure to the Thai baht was not what a first or second generation credit risk system would indicate, because the default probability of the counterparty was affected by the same macro factor (the Thai baht exchange rate) that affected the pay-off on the derivative.

In this case, the delta of the position the trader purchased from Hong Kong was not the delta he thought it was, because the counterparty's capital was wiped out as the Thai baht moved above 30 baht to the dollar, settling near 50 baht by the height of the Asian crisis. The trader had lost his counterparty, but no risk management system in place world-wide using first or second generation credit risk models would have shown that the counterparty was gone! The true credit risk-adjusted delta of the Bank's exposure to the Korean counterparties was a delta that was a smaller and smaller fraction of the 'replacement value' delta (which assumes a risk free counterparty), finally reaching zero at about 30 Thai baht to the U.S. dollar.

What if the trader had been able to see his true 'credit-adjusted delta' with respect to the Thai baht?

- He would have known, even after a small weakening of the Thai baht, that his buy-side and sell-side deltas were no longer equal and that he needed additional protection from a fall in the Thai baht because one side of the transaction was less likely to be able to pay.
- He would have 'layered in' small positions with each move in the baht (which was quite rapid) as it became more and more likely that a counterparty was going to default.
- He would have substantially reduced potential losses by incrementally replacing the counterparty as the Thai baht weakened.

The technology necessary to do this incorporates scenario-specific default probabilities that recognize that the default probability of the counterparty was different at every level of the Thai baht.

The objective of third generation credit models is to be able to do this for every transaction done by a corporation or financial institution whenever necessary. The mathematics and computer science to do this are available today.

Scenario-Specific Default Probabilities: The General Problem

The JP Morgan experience with its Korean counterparties was not a unique experience. Take the example of someone owed money on an interest rate cap at 10% (if they had existed at the time) from a U.S. savings and loan institution in 1979. The trillion U.S. dollar bailout of the U.S. savings and loan industry came about because the industry's entire asset base consisted of 30-year fixed-rate home mortgages and predominately short-term liabilities. As interest rates rise, the amount of money owed on the interest rate cap increases, but so does the probability that the savings and loan institution will default. If the yield on the 30-year fixed-rate mortgage portfolio is 10%, for example, the savings and loan institution would be bankrupt at rate levels above 10% and the promise to pay on a 10% cap is literally worthless because the savings and loan institution will be unable to perform on the contract. This link between the macro-factor, interest rates, and default would have been critical to understanding counterparty credit risk in the 1980s in the United States, yet first and second generation credit models are incapable of this analysis.

Macro factors such as interest rates, exchange rates, central business district building prices, oil prices and stock prices, affect legally required payments on the loan, bond or derivative, plus they affect the probability of default of the counterparty. The delta of a financial institution's position in the transaction has to take into account both impacts to avoid the JP Morgan 'wrong way correlation' mentioned above and the associated hedging errors. It is very important to note that these are not isolated, unique examples of risk exposure. They are the rule rather than the exception. A number of typical cases where both default probabilities and the amount of exposure are affected by macro factors are common to all major banks:

- Interest rates affect the legally required payments on a home mortgage, but they also affect the value of the house. When the value of the house drops below the principal due on the loan, default becomes more likely. In the U.S. in this environment, the Federal Reserve Board has determined that the probability of default increases by a factor of five times. In Mexico, almost 50% of a major bank's mortgage portfolio was in default during the high interest rate period in the middle 1990s. The implication of this is that a traditional match-funded interest rate hedge of a fixed-rate mortgage portfolio is not correct on a credit-adjusted basis. Above a certain level of rates, the bank may own the house, not the mortgage, and the hedging vehicle has to take that into account.

Figure 2.1   Banks need hedge ratios for each macro risk factor that recognize their direct and indirect impact on portfolio value, not just VAR

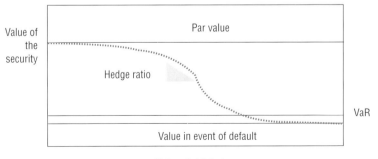

- Foreign exchange put options often have local banks as their counterparty, but the probability that the bank is in trouble is much higher if the currency is weak. That is one of the great lessons of the Asian crisis of 1997–1998.
- Stock put options and stock index put options with local financial institutions as the counterparty also have dual macro-factor impacts on both payments owed and default probability. When stock prices are low, the counterparty is more likely to be in financial difficulty, as we saw in the Asian crisis.
- Interest rate derivatives, such as a cap on interest rates, are often undertaken with local banks as counterparties. As in Malaysia or Thailand during the Asian crisis, the local banks are much more likely to be in distress when they owe the most money on the cap. In Malaysia, 21% interest rates at the height of the Asian crisis were triple the level prior to the crisis and the direct and indirect impact on bank credit quality was severe.

The dual impact of macro factors on payments owed and default probabilities can have beneficial as well as negative affects. These examples show that in either case, the impacts of macro factors on default cannot be ignored.

Managing Credit Risk to Create Shareholder Value

With scenario-specific default probabilities, a true credit-adjusted valuation can be derived as a function of any given macro-factor. This means that the entire valuation surface is available and a delta hedge can be calculated at any level of the macro-risk factor. This can be done transaction by transaction and then aggregated to obtain a macro factor hedge ratio for each macro factor affecting the portfolio of the corporation or the financial institution. Value-at-risk (i.e. VAR) is not enough because it would give a credit-adjusted value for only one level of the macro factor, and that isn't sufficient for practical hedging.

Another reason that credit-adjusted valuation is essential is that it allows benchmark performance measurement to be used even on a portfolio of illiquid bank loans. For example, the daily credit-adjusted valuation of a portfolio of auto loans can be tracked versus a benchmark (created with yield-curve 'smoothing' technology from actual traded government bonds) of matching maturity risk-free government bonds. This benchmarking analysis gives the portfolio manager of the auto loan book (and senior management) very precise feedback on the true amount of shareholder value created by the business after proper adjustment for credit risk and expenses versus a risk-free benchmark, just like the performance of a bond portfolio manager would be judged. This is a subtle but important shift away from the traditional matched maturity financial accounting-based transfer pricing that has been used in banking for more than 25 years. The excess return over the risk-free government benchmark shows the true 'plus alpha' performance of the loan book.

Credit-adjusted valuation also addresses one of the great debates in banking that has been generated by the traditional emphasis on matched maturity transfer pricing and the move toward economic value-added calculations and risk-adjusted return on capital. JP Morgan in a presentation at a meeting of the North American Asset and Liability Management Association in Toronto, October 2000, discussed a new credit-adjusted transfer pricing system being implemented at the Bank. The Bank noted that the economics of a bank loan to ABC company could be replicated by buying matching maturity U.S. Treasuries and providing credit default protection on ABC company through the credit derivatives market. The true shareholder value-added created by the Bank loan is the difference between the bank loan pricing and the pricing obtained by the replicating portfolio of Treasuries and the credit derivative. This form of shareholder value measurement is much simpler, more accurate and less controversial than the traditional combination of matched maturity funding costs (which is based on the marginal risk of the bank as a whole), expected losses, expenses, and the required risk-adjusted return on capital (which is based on the risk of the asset being financed).

Using the credit-adjusted transfer pricing approach, banks once again have an incentive to buy low-risk assets if they are priced properly. Under

Figure 2.2 Auto loan portfolio performance versus risk-free benchmark

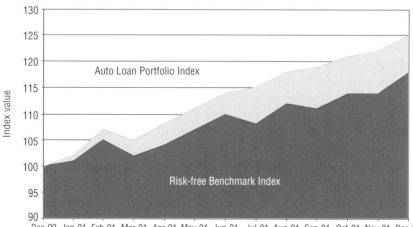

the traditional approach, bankers are discouraged from originating loans that have less risk than the bank has on average, and they are encouraged to make loans that have a higher risk level than the bank, because the bank's marginal cost of funds is the base for pricing, not the risk-free rate employed in the JP Morgan method. Proof that the JP Morgan method is conceptually superior comes from two sources, practical experience and financial theory. With regards to practical experience, all banks own government bonds even though the traditional transfer pricing methodology says they destroy shareholder value. The JP Morgan method says that if the government bonds are fairly priced, owning them neither destroys nor creates value. From a financial theory point of view, every financial theory of credit-adjusted valuation has the risk-free curve as its base, like the JP Morgan method. In no academic publication is the cost of funds curve of the buyer (i.e. the base in traditional transfer pricing) relevant to valuation.

Accurate credit-adjusted valuation is essential to making this new performance measurement methodology work, because a 'pseudo credit derivatives price' has to be calculated for all of those borrowers, large or small, for whom the credit derivatives price is not observable.

Integration of Market Risk, Credit Risk, Asset and Liability Management and Performance Measurement (Transfer Pricing)

As the previous discussion shows, there is now no analytical reason for a distinction between market risk, credit risk, asset and liability management, and performance measurement or transfer pricing. There has only been a distinction in the past because first and second generation credit models could not link the default probability (credit risk) with macro factors driving payoffs on derivatives and other bank assets and liabilities.

From a computer science point of view, there is no reason not to combine all of these functions into a single system with common database, graphical user interface, financial mathematics, and reporting.

The JP Morgan incident described in the beginning of the chapter illustrates the following issues:

- A traditional value-at-risk analysis with the Thai baht as a risk factor would have shown no special risk, because the bank's market risk system showed a hedged position.
- A credit risk stress test with respect to the Thai baht wouldn't have shown any sensitivity to Thai baht levels because no bank system showed such links.
- The measured profitability of the transaction, as calculated on origination, would have tremendously overstated the perceived profits

because nowhere in any of the bank systems was it reflected that the Korean counterparties would have no capital at a Thai baht level above 30 to the dollar.

•   A net income simulation of major risk factors would have shown no exposure to events in Thailand for the same reason.

We now turn to the kinds of credit models that can help minimize the damage from similar incidents.

3

The Evolution of Credit Modeling Techniques

Selection of the appropriate credit risk model is an important aspect of credit risk management, as the JP Morgan incident in the previous chapter illustrates. An inappropriate model contains model error, and model error introduces risk into the credit risk management process. This model risk is as 'real' in terms of profit/loss volatility as is market, credit, liquidity, or operational risk. In the JP Morgan case, the 'model error' was that the bank was not using a credit model which linked the key macro factor driving the pay-off on the transaction, the Thai baht, with the default probability of the counterparty, even though the link was very direct and recognized at the time the transaction was originated.

In another example, an $80 million loss at the New York branch of a major international bank stemmed from the activities of a derivatives dealer who believed his pricing model was better than 'the market.' The trader viewed the difference between his model's prices and market prices as a profit opportunity, and, unchecked by a third party who could spot the model risk, he dominated trading in that type of derivative for many months. External auditors ultimately called a halt to his trading activity, and the position was marked-to-market using market prices, not a flawed model. The same discipline is essential on the entire portfolio of a financial institution, not just the derivatives or bond portfolio.

The History of Credit Model Development

Historically, the first class of credit risk models adopted was the 'structural' approach. Such models include the original Merton model [1974] and the extension of this model to random interest rates by Shimko, Tejima and van Deventer [1993]. This class of models imposes assumptions on the evolution of the value of the firm's underlying assets. The liability structure of the firm, in conjunction with the firm's asset value fluctuations, determines the occurrence of bankruptcy and the payoffs (recovery rates) in the event of default. Most of this book is devoted to this approach, its implications, and its performance under the scrutiny of standard model testing procedures.

Extensions of the structural approach, assuming exogenous recovery rates, include the papers by Nielsen, Saa-Requejo and Santa Clara [1993] and Longstaff and Schwartz [1995]. The Longstaff and Schwartz paper contains some empirical results. The original Merton model, like the Black-Scholes model, assumed constant interest rates. The assumption of constant interest rates is a common assumption in derivatives modeling, but it is one that is not consistent with the lessons of the previous chapter. Default can be triggered by movements in macro factors, and models which omit them can potentially understate risk. We examine the relative importance of this issue in great detail in later chapters.

Random interest rates, from both an intuitive and a theoretical perspective, are an attractive feature of any credit risk model. Indeed, the U.S. taxpayers' trillion-dollar experience with the interest rate-induced failures of many banks and the savings and loan institutions in the mid-1980s provides anecdotal evidence for the validity of this claim. More anecdotal evidence also comes from the 1997–1998 Asian crisis where high interest rates (used to defend weak Asian currencies) triggered record bankruptcies. In recent years, random interest rates, in fact, have been a standard assumption underlying almost all of the recent models of the credit risk process.

It was the desire to include random interest rates and the discovery of the Heath, Jarrow and Morton [1992] term structure modeling technologies that led to the reduced form approach to modeling credit risk, which we also discuss in great detail in this book. Jarrow and Turnbull [1995], Duffie and Singleton [1999], and Jarrow [2001] represent just a few examples of a wide array of research being done on reduced form models in recent years.

Reduced form models impose their assumptions directly on the prices of the firm's traded liabilities, primarily its debt, and on the default-free term structure of interest rates. Intuitively, the assumptions on the firm's debt prices relate to the credit spread, which is decomposable into the probability of bankruptcy (per unit time) multiplied by the loss (per promised dollar) in the event of bankruptcy, and (in the case of the Jarrow [2001] model) a separate factor which represents the relative illiquidity of trading in debt securities compared to equities. Exogenous assumptions are imposed on these quantities (the bankruptcy and recovery rate process) directly. This procedure gives the reduced from models added flexibility in fitting market realities of debt, credit derivatives (see Jarrow and Yildirum [2002] for an example), and other securities.

Managerial Decisions about Capital Structure: An Important Distinction

One important difference between these two classes of models is the implicit assumption they make about managerial decisions regarding capital structure. The structural approach implicitly assumes that the dollar amount of debt outstanding is static, with the liability structure fixed and unchanging. For example, the Merton model (and its extension by Shimko, Tejima and van Deventer) assumes that management puts a debt structure in place and leaves it unchanged even if the value of corporate assets (and therefore equity) has doubled. This implies that the ratio of the market value of equity in a firm to the market value of its debt will vary, perhaps very significantly, as the value of company assets varies.

Reduced form models do not make this implicit assumption. In fact, they make no assumptions at all about the capital structure of the borrower, as we will see below. They are consistent with the view that management is constantly refining the capital structure, trying to maintain a steady and stable ratio of the market value of equity to the market value of debt, subject to random shocks from macro risk drivers. This relative simplicity of the reduced form models was one of the reasons why Robert Jarrow, one of the foremost researchers in the area, turned to this approach after an extensive review of the structural models. 'I believe that the interaction between capital structure and a firm's financial condition is very dynamic,' he said in 1995. 'I don't believe that one can capture this interaction accurately in a tractable way if you try to model capital structure directly. The reduced form approach, I believe, can be much more accurate and practical even though its nominal assumptions seem simpler than the structural models.'[1]

In later chapters of this book, we turn to empirical tests to see if this distinction between the models is important.

Another Distinction: Data Used for Benchmarking Credit Models

The common implementations of the Merton models use accounting data and equity prices to estimate the relevant parameters, as we shall see later in this chapter. The common implementations of the reduced form models use Treasury and corporate debt prices or credit derivatives prices to estimate model parameters. Chava and Jarrow [2002] show how historical market and accounting data can also be used to fit the parameters of a

---

[1] Private conversation with Donald van Deventer, 1995.

reduced form model. Reduced form models have been sometimes viewed with caution because corporate debt markets and credit derivatives markets (outside the top 200 names or so) are known to be less liquid than equity markets—with a scarcity of available quotes and wider bid/ask spreads. To accommodate the wider bid-offered spreads in thinly traded debt, reduced form models need to explicitly model liquidity risk, a modification introduced by Jarrow [2001].

The question of whether debt prices and credit derivatives prices contain information that improves default probability prediction is an empirical question, not a philosophical question. It is a testable proposition and we discuss those results later in this book.

Before turning to a more detailed discussion of structural and reduced form credit models, it is helpful to place them in the context of the development of derivatives models in general.

First Generation Models

First generation models, largely developed in the 1960s and 1970s, were based on a number of assumptions that were sophisticated in their day, and many of the researchers who developed them have gone on to win the Nobel Prize in Economics for their efforts. Generally speaking, they assumed for the first time that a particular variable was random and then valued securities based on the probability distribution of this random variable. This was a major step forward compared to the static earlier generation of models where all variables were deterministic. Examples of first generation models include:

- The Black-Scholes Options Model [1973];
- Single Factor Term Structure Models of Interest Rate Movements;
- Jamshidian [1989] Bond Option Model;
- Trinomial Lattice-Based American Options Models.

Each of these models also made a powerful implicit assumption—that the counterparty making the promise to pay was either default-free or the amount and timing of the amount of loss from default was known with certainty.

There are many examples of these assumptions at work:

- The Black-Scholes options model implicitly assumes that the payer on a put or call option on common stock will pay with certainty. The only uncertainty is the value of the common stock, from which we can then derive the value of the put or call.
- The term structure models of interest rates that now form the best market risk models all assume that the yield curve represents the yield curve for a risk-free counterparty. As we will see below, if the

counterparty is in fact risky, the term structure model leads to a different formula that is related to and dependent on the default-free term structure, but it is not identical to it.

- Bond option models based on models of the risk-free term structure implicitly assume not only that the underlying bond will not default but also that the payer on the bond option will not default.
- Trinomial and binomial trees are often used to value American options to call a bond or prepay a mortgage. These numerical techniques also implicitly assume either that the mortgage borrower will pay with no default risk or that the default risk is known with certainty. This is analytically identical to assuming the borrower is default-free but that the payment schedule is slightly less than the payment schedule for a borrower for whom losses will be zero.

Second Generation Models

Second generation models seek to maximize the insights in credit risk derived from first generation models with little or no modification. Examples of second generation models include the following:

- The **Merton Model of Risky Debt**: which assumes that equity is a Black-Scholes call option on the value of the assets of the firm. In this model, there is still only one risky variable, the market value of the assets of the firm. Interest rates are assumed constant as in the Black-Scholes option model.
- **Monte Carlo simulation of portfolio value**: using the first generation models to determine instrument values and then adding a separate default/no default simulation for the credit quality of the payer. This approach assumes that the default probability of the payer is known from some external source, that the default probability is uncorrelated with any of the macro factors or micro factors that may drive the market value of the underlying instruments, that models which assume the payer is risk-free can be used for valuation, and that default probabilities are constant over time. This is a common 'ad hoc' approach to counterparty credit exposure measurement on trading floors around the world.

Third Generation Models

Third generation models have two common characteristics: they include at least two random factors, not one, and they make an explicit assumption about the potential default of the counterparty and carry that in a consistent way through the calculation used to value all related instruments. There are a number of models of this type. A very limited listing includes the following models:

- The **Jarrow-Turnbull** model (1995) assumed that default was a random statistical process and interest rates were random, arriving at valuation formulas for a number of 'defaultable' security types.
- The **Jarrow-Lando-Turnbull** (1997) model allowed for random evolution of default probabilities according to a rating transition matrix.
- The **Duffie-Singleton** (1999) framework broadened the assumptions of the Jarrow-Turnbull model.
- The **Shimko-Tejima-van Deventer** (1993) credit model allowed for random interest rates in the Merton model framework.
- The **Jarrow** model (2001) greatly expands the default intensity framework to allow for interest rate-driven and market index-driven default probabilities.

We now turn to a more detailed explanation of the Merton model, the Shimko-Tejima-van Deventer (STV) model and the Jarrow reduced form model.

The Merton Model of Risky Debt[2]

In 1996, the authors of this book correctly predicted that Robert Merton would win the Nobel Prize in economics, in part because of his model of risky debt, first published in 1974. Merton was among the first academics to aggressively exploit and extend the options model of Black and Scholes, published just a year earlier in 1973.

Merton's model of risky debt starts with a set of assumptions that allow the modeler to view equity as an option on the assets of the company. From this insight, the value of debt can be derived. A number of assumptions, common to the Black-Scholes options model, have to be imposed on the model for this insight to be valid. Some of them can be relaxed and some of them cannot:

- The value of company assets is the only random variable in the model.
- The company's assets are perfectly liquid and are traded in frictionless markets. Securities identical to the company's assets can be bought or sold, including short sales, in any fractional amounts.

---

[2] An earlier version of this section was published by Jarrow and van Deventer [1998].

- Interest rates are constant.
- There is only one period in the life of the company, and at the end of the period the equity of the company trades at its liquidation value.
- The volatility of the company's assets is constant.
- The company's assets follow a 'stochastic process' that is consistent with a lognormal distribution, exactly the same assumption that Black and Scholes assumed for their options model.
- No cash flow is disposed of either by the company itself or by the assets it owns. Cash is generated by asset sales.

Merton makes some additional assumptions that make it easy to value the debt of the firm in this framework:

- There is only one payment (equal to the sum of debt plus interest, i.e. a zero-coupon bond structure) on the debt.
- Management sets the amount of debt in the firm and does not change the amount of debt outstanding until the firm is liquidated at the end of the period.
- There are no costs to bankruptcy.
- There is no 'option' for management to declare bankruptcy prior to the end of the period. Bankruptcy is not a surprise; it always occurs at the end of the single period when the value of company assets is less than the value owed on debt. Implicit in this assumption is the absolute priority of debt holders over equity holders in liquidation.
- There are no taxes that would cause net cash flow from interest to be different from that of principal, so the distinction is unimportant in the model.
- Management chooses the amount of debt outstanding at time zero and cannot modify this choice prior to maturity of the debt.
- The value of the debt plus the value of equity of the firm is equal to the market value of the company's assets (the famous Modigliani and Miller assumption).

These assumptions have a number of important implications for the model:

- The value of the firm's debt is simply the difference between the value of company assets and the value of its equity, for which we know the formula—the Black-Scholes options formula.
- The latter assumption helps insure that there is no 'cost' to bankruptcy in excess of the net liquidation values paid to debt and equity holders. In fact, bankruptcy is indistinguishable from end of period liquidation. There is never any 'going concern' value of the firm that would be destroyed by bankruptcy.

- Capital structure, in a market value sense, is highly random because the ratio of the market value of equity to market value of debt can range anywhere from zero (just before default) to infinity, as would be the case when the value of company assets rises sharply. Management has no real option to change its capital structure, no matter what happens to the value of company assets.
- The value of debt and the value of equity are both determined only by the value of company assets and other parameters that are assumed to be constant.

In more mathematical terms, the Merton model postulates that equity is an option on the assets of the firm, since equity holders receive nothing upon maturity of the debt unless the value of the firm's assets at that time is worth more than the amount owed on the debt.[3] Under Modigliani and Miller [1958] assumptions, the value of the assets of the firm V equals the sum of the value of equity E and the value of debt D. Merton therefore concludes that the value of debt D is $D(V) = V - E(V)$. The formula for E is the well-known Black Scholes [1973] options formula. In the Merton model, V is the only random variable, so it is natural to assume that the value of debt D would be hedged with a position in V. The Merton model assumes that a debt holder can sell short all or part of V.

If the borrower was a bank in the U.S., the assumption that one could sell short all or part of V is not a bad assumption, since such a high percentage of the assets of a commercial bank in the U.S. are freely traded.[4] For that reason, it is ironic that most of the commercial applications of the Merton model have been for non-bank corporations where this assumption is less plausible. We certainly cannot sell short a fraction of a Ford motor assembly plant to hedge a position in a loan to Ford, for example. In practice, however, it is easier to assume that hedging takes place by replicating the value of debt with a position in the firm's equity, since equity depends on the same random variable V and we know the precise specification of the reliance on V. The hedge ratio is calculated by solving for that amount of common shares of the bank or the corporation that would exactly offset changes in the value of risky debt due to random changes in V. The hedge ratio is related to, but different from, the well-known Black Scholes delta

---

[3] Although the Merton model assumes only one issue of zero-coupon debt, common cross default provisions of typical bond indentures link all outstanding issues together from a legal perspective in most major financial centers.

[4] U.S. Treasury securities, municipal bonds, commercial paper (a near perfect substitute for corporate commercial loans), and securitized consumer loans like mortgages and credit cards are concrete examples.

since $D = V - E(V)$, not the call option $E(V)$ itself. See Jarrow and Turnbull [1995] for formulas regarding the calculation and use of delta hedges.

Note however, that even though the Merton model implies that debt can be hedged by selling short equity, this hedge is possible only over narrow ranges of company asset values. Once the value of company assets falls below a certain level, the number of shares that one would need to sell short exceeds the total number of shares outstanding. The reason is that, as the company approaches bankruptcy, the value of assets and the value of debt can continue to fall long after the value of the company's shares has gone to zero (and therefore provide no further gain from a short sale).

The Merton model assumes that interest rates are constant, but this assumption is clearly incorrect. We discuss how to relax this assumption in the next section.

Inputs to the Merton Model

The Merton model requires as inputs the current market value of corporate assets and the volatility of those assets, along with the estimated amount of principal and interest that will be due (i.e. the principal amount of a zero-coupon bond) at the maturity of the debt. To calculate this amount, the amount of corporate liabilities and their average yield can be taken from financial statements and compounded to get the estimated amount of the zero-coupon principal amount. Note, however, that the analyst is immediately presented with a dilemma with multiple dimensions:

- What 'maturity' should we assume for analysis if the company has a rich array of debt outstanding over many years with staggered interest payments and maturities?
- If current debt is repaid before maturity, will it be replaced? What will be the terms of the replacement debt?
- What do we do about debt with different levels of seniority and subordination?
- How do we deal with revolving lines of credit, which may or may not be drawn?

In practice, analysts make a number of 'ad hoc' assumptions to 'bend' the model's simplifying assumptions to be more consistent with a multi-period world where the management team dynamically adjusts the capital structure. The best analysts choose their 'ad hoc' assumptions because of statistical testing that we discuss in later chapters.

The values for the market value of company assets and their volatility can be computed so that the theoretical value of company equity and its volatility are consistent with observed values.

Risk-neutral Versus Empirical Probabilities of Default in the Merton Model

From Merton's risky debt model, one can infer the implied *pseudo* default probabilities. These probabilities are not those revealed by actual default experience, but those needed to do valuation. They are sometimes called *martingale* or *risk-adjusted* probabilities because they are the probabilities, after an adjustment for risk, used for valuation purposes. If we are to compare implied default probabilities from Merton's model with historical default experience, we need to remove this adjustment. Note that in the discussion of the Merton model so far, we have assumed nothing about the expected returns on the value of company assets or the relationship between the expected returns on the value of the assets of ABC company and the expected returns on the value of the assets of XYZ company. Like the Black-Scholes options model on which it is based, the value of risky debt in the Merton model *does not depend* on the expected return on the assets of the company.

In order to derive default probabilities that are consistent with actual default experience, we essentially have to insert expected returns back into the valuation procedure. If we don't do this, the only default probabilities that we can derive are the 'risk neutral' probabilities, which are based on the assumption that the drift over time (subject to random shocks) in the assets of all companies depends only on the risk-free rate of interest, just as in the Black-Scholes options model. There is no impact on the expected return of the assets of any two companies of the benefits of diversification, because we are 'risk neutral' and indifferent to risk—in the risk neutral world, only the expected value of the outcome affects valuation, pricing and hedging. This means that the only risk-free interest rate drives the 'distance from default' that we can expect company assets to have just prior to maturity, other than the shocks that come randomly, impact company asset values—there is no adjustment to expected return from the benefits from diversification.

To show the benefits from diversification and estimate the actual statistical probabilities of default, we need a continuous-time equilibrium model of asset returns consistent with the Merton risky debt structure. Merton's [1973] intertemporal capital asset pricing model provides such a structure. We now show how to make this adjustment for the mathematically-inclined readers. Those who prefer plain English can skip the next few paragraphs.

Let the value of the ith firm's assets at time t be denoted by $V_i(t)$ with its expected return per unit time denoted by a_i and its volatility per unit time denoted by σ_i. This is the Merton assumption that the value of company assets is lognormally distributed, and there are a few implications of this from a mathematical point of view:

Under the Merton [1974] structure, we have that:

$$V_i(t) = V_i(0)e^{\mu_i t + \sigma_i Z_i(t)}$$

where $\mu_i = a_i - \sigma_i^2/2$ and $Z_i(t)$ is a normally-distributed random variable with mean 0 and variance t.

The evolution of $V_i(t)$ above is under the statistical or empirical probabilities.[5] In Merton's [1973] equilibrium asset pricing model, when interest rates and the investment opportunity set[6] are constant, the expected return on the ith asset is equal to:

$$a_i = r + \frac{\sigma_i \rho_{iM}}{\sigma_M}(a_M - r)$$

where r is the risk-free rate,[7] the subscript M refers to the 'market' portfolio or equivalently, the portfolio consisting of all assets of all companies in the economy, and ρ_{iM} denotes the correlation between the return on firm i's asset value and the market portfolio. This is reminiscent of the capital asset pricing model, except that it is a multi-period, continuous time version, rather than a single period model like the capital asset pricing model. Note that this relationship becomes more complex when interest rates are random, as Merton assumed in his 1973 model.

Using this equilibrium relationship for the pricing of the assets of all companies, the drift term on the ith company's assets can be written as:

$$\mu_i = -\frac{1}{2}\sigma_i^2 + (1 - b_i)r + b_i a_M$$

where $b_i = \frac{\sigma_i \rho_{iM}}{\sigma_M}$ is the ith firm's beta.

For expositional purposes, we can think of the expected return on the market a_M as equal to a constant k times the risk-free interest rate r, i.e:

$$a_M = kr.$$

This is without loss of generality. Using this relation, we have that:

---

[5] Under the risk neutral probabilities, .

[6] The investment opportunity set is the means and covariances of all the assets' returns. This implies that the mean and covariances with the market return are also deterministic.

[7] In this structure, this is the spot rate of interest on default free debt.

$$\mu_i = -\frac{1}{2}\sigma_i^2 + (1 - b_i + b_i k)r.$$

In Merton's risky debt model, the firm defaults at the maturity of the debt if the firm's asset value is below the face value of the debt. We can now compute the probability that this event occurs, using the true statistical probabilities rather than the risk-neutral probabilities.

The Empirical Probability of Default in the Merton Model

Let t be the maturity of the discount bond and let B be its face value. Jarrow and van Deventer [1998] show that bankruptcy occurs when $V_i(t) < B$, expressed mathematically:

$$\text{Probability(Default)} = \text{Probability}(V_i(t) < B) = N\left(\frac{\ln(B/V_i(0)) - \mu_i t}{\sigma_i \sqrt{t}}\right)$$

where $N(.)$ represents the cumulative normal distribution function.

We see from this expression that default probabilities are determined given the values of the parameters $(B, V_i(0), \sigma_i, r, \sigma_M, \rho_{iM}, k)$.

We discuss the estimation of these parameters later in this book. Please note that the difficulties we will face in that exercise are fairly daunting:

- The correlation between the assets of company i and the assets of all companies is not only unobservable, but it is also the correlation of two variables which themselves are unobservable. We need the correlation of two objects that are statistically invisible.
- Secondly, we need the expected return on the assets of all companies, which we capture as a ratio to risk-free rates, k. This is the same problem faced by users of the capital asset pricing model, which depends on the expected return on the equities of all companies. This is one of the great unsolved problems in finance over the last 40 years.

If we are lucky, these estimation questions will have a minor impact on our estimated default probabilities. If we are unlucky, these uncertain parameters will play a large role in setting the level of default probabilities.

Finally, it is important to note that this basic single factor version of the Merton model, and all other single factors variations, have the following attributes in common:

- When the value of company assets rises, the value of the company stock price rises.
- When the value of company assets rises, the value of company debt also rises.

- When the value of company assets falls, the value of the company stock price falls.
- When the value of company assets falls, the value of the company debt falls.
- No estimate of the probability of default is needed for valuing risky debt. We only need the value of company assets and its volatility, along with the other constant parameters in the basic Merton model, to value debt.
- The same is true for pricing and hedging using the Merton model—the other parameters are all we need—we don't need the default probability, because it is implied by the value of company assets and the volatility of those assets.
- Also, because there is total priority for debtors over equity holders, the recovery rate upon default is also 'endogenous' or built into the Merton model. If we are true to the Merton model's assumptions, we don't need third party estimates of the recovery rate because it is implied by the model. The recovery rate will be different for every level of company assets at the maturity of risky debt, but we can calculate its average value. Of course the same is true for the loss given default.
- Finally, the correlation of the value of the assets of company i with the assets of all companies is not needed for valuation, pricing, hedging and recovery rate estimation. The same is true for the expected return on the assets of all companies.

We turn now to an extension of the Merton model to deal with random interest rates, perhaps the most important macro-risk factor driving default.

The Merton Model with Random Interest Rates[8]

In the previous section, we used the Merton [1974] model of risky debt for pricing, valuation, hedging and default probability estimation. We test the model extensively in later chapters, as it is in wide commercial application in its single factor form, where the sole random factor is the value of company assets. Nonetheless, it is important, to incorporate random interest rates in any valuation formula where the primary focus is the valuation of debt securities. Term structure interest rate models provide the foundation for making the Merton model more realistic and comprehensive. Term structure models have an important history in the fixed income markets

---

[8] An earlier version of this section was published by Shimko, Tejima and van Deventer [1993].

(Vasicek [1977], Cox, Ingersoll and Ross [1985], and Longstaff and Schwartz [1992] represent a short list, and van Deventer and Imai [1996] include a survey of the analytical techniques that can be built on a random interest rates framework).

The credit component of the cost of debt capital, however, hasn't been studied as intensively as the movements of the risk-free yield curve that drives all other markets. This section generalizes Merton's risky debt pricing model to allow for stochastic interest rates. We examine the combined effect of term structure variables and credit variables on debt pricing.

In this section, we retain the structure of Merton's model, but generalize it to allow for stochastic interest rates as in Vasicek [1977] term structure model. In the Vasicek model, interest rates follow a mean-reverting random process with constant interest rate volatility, that is, interest rate volatility that does not change as interest rates rise and fall. Surprisingly, Merton's [1973] valuation of options with stochastic interest rates and time-varying volatility can then be applied to find a closed-form expression for the value of risky debt when interest rates are random. Given that this is a straightforward combination of two important works by Robert Merton, it is curious that the random interest rates version of his model of risky debt hasn't been more widely applied in practice.

We can use this model, which we name STV for its authors Shimko, Tejima and van Deventer [1993], to examine the drivers of default probabilities and credit spreads with greater sophistication than the constant interest rate version of the Merton model. The STV bond pricing equation yields comparatively static results that are consistent with Merton's results. The credit premium increases with increases in the face value of the debt and the volatility of the assets. STV find that the credit spread is an increasing function of the (risk-free) term structure volatility for reasonable parameter values; however, term structure effects can cause the sign of the derivative to change. STV also find that changes in the correlation between interest rates and asset value may have a positive or negative impact on the credit spread; the comparative statistics are parameter-sensitive. For reasonable parameter values, as the correlation increases, the credit spread increases.

In addition to the pricing issues mentioned above, this analysis allows us to explore a series of critical issues faced by managers of financial institutions and by financial managers of corporations. The following questions are fundamental to their task:

- How does the correlation between a bank's credit risk and interest rate movements affect its borrowing cost?
- What maturity debt (or face value) should a corporate treasurer issue to minimize fluctuations in the value of the corporation's stock price?

- How much capital should be allocated to activities within a banking company which vary both in the absolute degree of credit risk and in the correlation of that risk with movements in interest rate risks?

We explore those issues briefly in this section and return to them in greater detail in later chapters.

Options Theory and the Valuation of Risky Debt: Merton's Model

STV start by looking at a simplified case of a bank or a corporation with assets that have a market value V, as in the original Merton model. Like Merton, STV assume that the returns on the company's assets are instantaneously normal, i.e. that the return on the company's assets follows the stochastic process

$$\frac{dV}{V} = \alpha dt + \sigma_v dZ_1$$

where α and σ are the constant drift and volatility of asset values. This assumption is the same as that made by Black and Scholes in their options model. This assumption is not realistic if the borrower is a bank, for example; a bank's own fixed income portfolio does not follow a return-generating process like equities—bank loans have lots of downside risk but little upside risk, unlike returns on equity securities. STV initially assume that the risk-free interest rate is constant in order to compare the results from the Merton and STV models. STV assume that the bank's assets are financed at time t by the issuance of zero-coupon bonds with principal B that is due to mature at time T. Like Merton, STV also assume there are no cash distributions to equity until time T. Given the risk inherent in the company's or bank's balance sheet, what should be the pricing on this risky debt? In the words of a corporate treasurer, what should be the spread to treasuries (the risk-free rate) on the company's debt?

STV match the Merton environment, assuming perfect markets, free of transaction costs, taxes and informational differences among participants. In this Modigliani-Miller [1958] environment, the market value of the firm is the sum of debt and equity values i.e. the value of the firm is independent of the capital structure. STV and Merton assume that all of the firm's assets can be or will be converted, at no cost, to cash at time T. If the value of the firm's assets at time T is greater than the principal value of the zero-coupon debt B, then the bonds will be paid off in full; otherwise, debtors receive the firm's assets. The value of equity at time T is therefore:

$$E = \text{Max}[V_T - B, 0]$$

The equity of the firm is equivalent to a call option on the assets of the firm as in the Merton case.

Assuming V can be traded or perfectly replicated, the well-known Black-Scholes call option pricing formula on an asset with value V, volatility σ, time to maturity τ, strike price B, and riskless rate of interest r is:

$$\text{Equity Value} = VN(d_1) - Be^{-r\tau}N(d_2)$$

where

$$d_1 = \frac{\ln(V/B) + (r + 0.5\sigma^2)\tau}{\sigma\sqrt{\tau}}$$

$$d_2 = d_1 - \sigma\sqrt{\tau}$$

where $N(z)$ is the cumulative normal density evaluated at z. Since the value of the firm consists only of debt and equity, the value of the risky debt is equal to the value of company assets V less the value of equity. Rearranging that equation gives the following formula for risky debt:

$$D = VN(h_1) - Be^{-r\tau}N(h_2)$$

where

$$h_1 = \frac{\ln(Be^{-r\tau}/V) - 0.5\sigma^2\tau}{\sigma\sqrt{\tau}}$$

$$h_2 = h_1 - \sigma\sqrt{\tau}$$

The required rate of return on debt, the continuous yield, is given by:

$$r_D = -\frac{1}{\tau}\ln\left(\frac{D}{B}\right)$$

It is well known that the credit spread, $r_D - r$, increases as the face value of the debt and the volatility of the assets increase, and that the credit spread decreases when the value of assets increases. For a more detailed derivation and discussion of this topic, see Ingersoll [1987] or Uyemura and van Deventer [1992]. The next section extends the analysis to the case where the risk-free interest rate is stochastic and is correlated with fluctuations in the value of this underlying asset.

Adding Random Interest Rates to the Merton Model

By making use of Merton's [1973] model for the pricing of options with stochastic interest rates, STV extend the pricing of risky debt to the case of random risk-free interest rates. Merton's valuation formula for options when interest rates are stochastic assumes that the instantaneous variance of the return on a risk-free zero-coupon bond depends only on time to maturity and 'is otherwise assumed to be non-stochastic and independent of the level of P', the price of a risk-free bond. STV note that this requirement is consistent with the term structure model of Vasicek [1977], but not the models of Cox, Ingersoll and Ross [1985] or Longstaff and Schwartz [1992], for example.

In order to take advantage of Merton's work, STV assume that the risk-free term structure is consistent with the Vasicek model. The Vasicek model assumes that the short-term risk-free interest rate is mean—reverting to the long-term mean level of interest rates γ at with a 'speed of mean reversion' k, and that its instantaneous interest rate volatility (σ_r) is constant:

$$dr = k(\gamma - r)dt + \sigma_r dz_2$$

Van Deventer and Imai [1996] provide an extensive review of the use of the Vasicek and related models for risk management purposes. The Vasicek model suffers from the implicit assumption that at any given time, the future instantaneous interest rates are normally distributed. While this implies the possibility of negative interest rates in future time periods, this liability is offset by the Hull and White [1992] observation, that the modified Vasicek model can be used to fit any observable term structure. It is this property that has made the Vasicek model and its close relatives the standard for valuation of fixed income derivatives, and it is at the foundation of the reduced form models that we discuss later in this chapter. When movements in the short-term interest rate take the Vasicek form, the zero-coupon bond is priced according to the Vasicek formula:

$$P(\tau) = \exp\left[\frac{1 - e^{-k\tau}}{k}(R(\infty) - r) - \tau R(\infty) - \frac{\sigma_r^2}{4k^3}(1 - e^{-k\tau})^2\right]$$

where:

$$R(\infty) = \gamma + \frac{\sigma_r}{k}\lambda - \frac{1}{2}\frac{\sigma_r^2}{k^2}$$

Note that lambda is the 'market price of risk for such risk-free bonds' and must be independent of the bond maturity for no-arbitrage assumptions to prevail. In the extended Vasicek model, the market price of risk lambda is absorbed by terms involving the yield curve itself. STV also assume that the stochastic factors driving the instantaneous returns on company (or bank) assets and movements in the instantaneous risk-free interest rates are correlated:

$$dz_1 dz_2 = \rho dt$$

Using the same logic as the Merton model, the value of risky debt when interest rates are stochastic can be written:

$$F = V - VN(h_1) + BP(\tau)N(h_2)$$

where:

$$\delta(s) = -\frac{1 - e^{-ks}}{k}\sigma_r$$

$$v^2(s) = \sigma_v^2 + \delta(s)^2 - 2\rho\sigma_v\delta(s)$$

$$T = \int_0^\tau v(s)^2 \, ds$$

$$= \tau\left(\sigma_v^2 + \frac{\sigma_r^2}{k^2} + \frac{2\rho\sigma_v\sigma_r}{k}\right) + (e^{-k\tau} - 1)\left(\frac{2\sigma_r^2}{k^3} + \frac{2\rho\sigma_r\sigma_v}{k^2}\right) - \frac{\sigma_r^2}{2k^3}(e^{-2k\tau} - 1)$$

and:

$$h_1 = \frac{\ln\left(\dfrac{V}{P(\tau)B}\right) + \dfrac{1}{2}T}{\sqrt{T}}$$

$$h_2 = h_1 - \sqrt{T}$$

In the STV formula for the valuation of risky debt, $N(z)$ is the cumulative normal distribution function. $\delta(s)^2$ is the instantaneous variance of the Vasicek model risk-free zero-coupon bond with maturity s, $v(s)^2$ is the instantaneous variance of the risky debt function F, and T is the integrated instantaneous variance of the risky debt function F over the life of the risky bond.

Implications of the Merton Model with Random Interest Rates

The STV model, because of its realistic assumptions about interest rates, provides much more guidance to a corporate treasurer or bank finance manager on corporate financing strategies. The following are a number of strategy questions the model can help with:

- How does an increase in the debt level impact the 'credit spread', i.e. the difference between the yield on the firm's risky debt and the corresponding maturity risk-free bond?
- How does the volatility of interest rates impact this credit spread?
- How does the riskiness of the underlying assets impact this credit spread?

- How does the correlation of credit risk with interest rate risk impact financing costs?
- What maturity debt should be selected to minimize the volatility of the firm's equity?
- How much capital should be allocated to finance assets of different riskiness so that the cost of debt financing for each asset class will be equal?

In this section, we will address each of these issues in turn. For exposition purposes, we are going to stay true to the strict assumptions of the STV model. We assume that the debt being issued by this hypothetical bank or corporation is zero-coupon debt with no covenants that would allow the debt holder to trigger bankruptcy no matter what value the assets may have prior to the maturity of the debt. STV assume that the value of assets V is initially 100 and that debt policy is set by analyzing a dollar amount of debt financing amount F at different maturities, which means that the principal amount B (which effectively includes the future value of interest as well as the up-front amount of 'principal' F) will be different for each maturity. The yield on risky debt and the yield on risk-free debt are calculated on a continuous basis, as is the 'credit spread', which is equal to the difference between the two rates. The credit spread is algebraically defined as the difference between the continuously compounded (promised) debt yield, and the comparable yield on a zero-coupon bond of the same maturity:

$$\text{Credit Spread} = r_D - r_P$$
$$= -\frac{\ln(D/B)}{\tau} + \frac{\ln(P)}{\tau}$$
$$= \frac{\ln(PB/D)}{\tau}$$

The Impact of Leverage in the STV Model

Figure 3.1 from STV shows the increase in the credit spread that results when leverage (the borrowing amount F) is increased from 50% of assets to 95% of assets assuming σ_r is 0.06, σ_v is 0.11, and the correlation between interest rate movements and the asset returns is 0.3. Given these assumptions, the credit spread is monotonically upward sloping with maturity and with the amount of leverage.

The assertion that the credit spread increases with the face value of debt is correct regardless of parameter choice. However, for some parameter choices, the credit spread decreases with debt maturity.

Figure 3.1   Credit spread as a function of the amount of debt financing, F

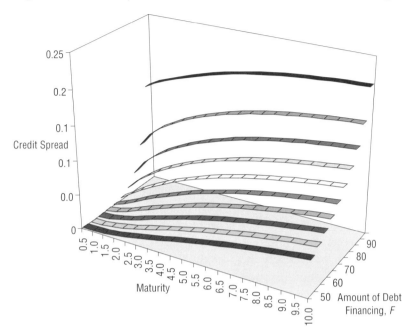

The Impact of Interest Rate Volatility

Given the same base case assumptions and a financing amount F equal to 95, increases in the volatility of the instantaneous risk-free interest rate dramatically increase the credit spread shown in Figure 3.2. This directional result is not universally correct. Changes in interest rate volatility affect the volatility of bond returns through changes in the slope of the term structure and through the correlation of interest rate changes with asset value changes. Of course, for prespecified parameter values, the sign of the partial derivative can be determined.

An important insight of the STV model is critical to note: interest rates have a significant impact on credit risk, both via their absolute level and via the volatility of interest rates. Occasionally advocates of the Merton model can be heard to argue that defaults are not correlated with interest rates, but that is not the Merton conclusion. His intertemporal capital asset pricing model [1973] shows explicitly that the expected return on the assets of the ith company depends on interest rates and various interest rate-related correlations. This means that the 'distance from default' and the default probability are in turn influenced by the level of interest rates and these

Figure 3.2 Credit spread as a function of interest rate volatility when $F = 95$

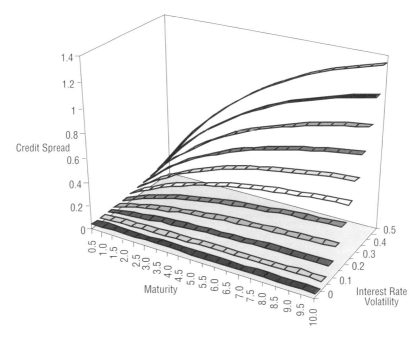

correlations. The STV valuation formula for risky debt reflects the level of interest rates, the volatility of interest rates, and the correlation between the value of the ith company's assets and interest rates. The STV default probability derivation is slightly more complex than in the constant interest rate Merton model, but when that derivation is done, it is very clear that interest rates play a major role in determining the probability. We present empirical evidence in this regard in later chapters.

The Impact of Asset Volatility

Figures 3.3 and 3.4 in STV show the impact of increasing asset volatility on the credit spread. Figure 3.3 shows the kind of monotonic increase in credit spread one might expect, both with respect to maturity and the amount of asset volatility. Figure 3.4 shows clearly, however, that the credit spread may well decrease with maturity if asset volatility is high enough and leverage (represented by F) is also high. This is a common finding of Merton models—if a highly risky company survives the near term, it is likely to have very valuable assets and therefore much lower credit spreads. We can call this the 'Amazon.com effect.'

Figure 3.3   Credit spread as a function of asset volatility when $F = 50$

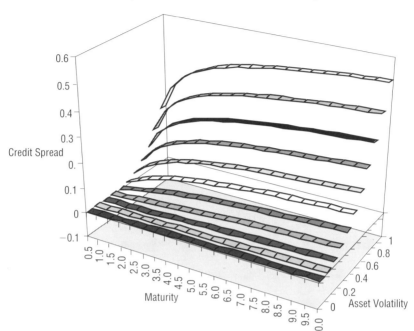

Figure 3.4   Credit spread as a function of asset volatility when $F = 95$

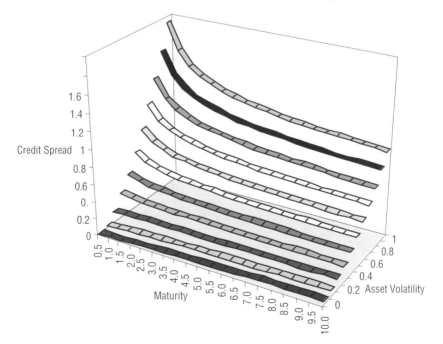

Correlation between Asset Returns and Interest Rates

Figure 3.5 from STV confirms that the impact of correlation between asset returns and the instantaneous interest rate increases the credit spread for the base case assumptions as correlation increases, but it also demonstrates that the credit spread need not increase with maturity if the correlation is strongly negative. Interest rate correlation matters, and in some cases, it can become a very important determinant of credit spreads and default probabilities.

Implications for the Minimum Risk Funding Strategy

A commonly held assumption among corporate treasurers and bank managers is that the 'zero risk' funding strategy is for the maturity of the liability issued to be matched in a maturity sense to the maturity of the asset being financed. This seems obvious on its face value, but the STV model shows it is not exactly correct. In the context of our model, what does 'zero risk' mean? STV take the zero risk funding strategy to be the funding strategy that eliminates short-term interest rate volatility from the equity return. This leaves the part of asset volatility that is uncorrelated with interest rates unhedged. We can use Ito's lemma to write the formulas for the change in the value of company assets and the value of the company's debt. We can solve for the minimum

Figure 3.5 Credit spread as a function of the correlation between asset returns and interest rates when $F = 95$

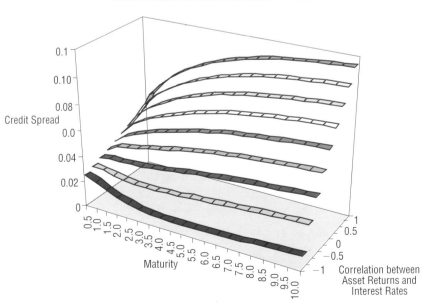

risk point by solving for the point at which the asset and debt sensitivities to interest rate changes are identical in dollar terms:

$$B = \frac{[1 - N(h_1)]\sigma_v \rho kV}{P\sigma_r N(h_2)(1 - e^{-k\tau})}$$

This formula says there is a continuum of combinations of face value and maturity for the debt that eliminates interest rate risk for equity holders. If we set B by specifying the amount of money that has to be raised, F, we can solve for the maturity that we need to issue.

This formula shows that the minimum risk funding strategy depends on the correlation between 'credit risk' and the risk-free interest rate, as well as other parameters of the model. In general, that means that a strategy of matching maturities will *not* produce the minimum risk funding strategy.

Using the Risky Debt Formula for Capital Allocation and Capital Adequacy

Capital allocation is a classic technique for examining the potential shareholder value-added generated from each business unit of a financial institution or corporation. Its use as a business tool is as widespread as the number of techniques that companies employ for this purpose. The implications of capital allocation for asset selection also vary widely with the model chosen, so there is definitely a need to improve the formulas used for capital allocation so that they more accurately reflect the market reality that interest rate risk and credit risk are correlated. The STV model helps us do this. We devote an entire chapter to this later in this book, but we can summarize the use of the STV model for capital allocation as follows:

There are five steps in the process:

- Select the time frame for the analysis (say, one year);
- Choose B, the face amount of zero-coupon debt in the model, and F so that the continuous yield on cash proceeds of F to earn B in one year is the same as the bank's marginal cost of funds for a one year horizon;
- Select the volatility of interest rates;
- Determine the underlying volatility of the asset class and its correlation with movements in the risk-free interest rate;
- Solve for V, the value of assets.

The amount of capital that would be allocated to this asset class would be $(V - F)/V$ as a ratio to the value of assets. All asset classes would have the same marginal cost of debt with a one-year maturity, and in this sense, the capital ratios are 'risk-adjusted' and properly consider credit risk, interest rate risk, and the correlation between them. We will explore the implications of this approach in much greater detail later in the book.

Comparing the Merton and STV Models

The Merton credit model and the STV model are very closely related and yet there are important differences between them. We can summarize them briefly in this way:

- The Merton risky debt model is a special case of the STV model.
- The STV model is derived by using Merton's random interest rate options model with the Vasicek (or extended Vasicek) term structure model for the random interest rate process. The STV model in this sense is a 'pure' Merton model. All the major insights were originally Robert Merton's, and Shimko Tejima and van Deventer combine them in a way that, with 20/20 hindsight, is obvious to students of Robert Merton's work.
- The Merton model of risky debt assumes interest rates are constant and the STV model assumes they are random.
- The Merton model ignores interest rate volatility as a factor determining default, while the STV model incorporates it explicitly.
- The Merton model ignores the correlation between the value of company assets and interest rates as a factor determining default, while the STV model incorporates it explicitly.

The conclusions from this summary are obvious. If one believes that the Merton model is a robust framework for credit risk modeling and that interest rates are an important determinant of default, then one would chose the STV model. If one believes that interest rates have no impact on the probability of default, then one would use the Merton model. As the $1 trillion interest rate-related bailout of the savings and loan industry in the U.S. illustrates, the view that interest rates don't impact the probability isn't consistent with most international experience. We present empirical confirmation of that fact in later chapters.

References

John C. Cox, Jonathan E. Ingersoll, Jr., and Stephen A. Ross, 1985, 'A Theory of the Term Structure of Interest Rates', *Econometrica* 53, 385–407.

L. Uri Dothan, 1978, 'On the Term Structure of Interest Rates', *Journal of Financial Economics* 6, 59–69.

H. Gifford Fong and Oldrich A. Vasicek, 1991, 'Fixed-Income Volatility Management: A New Approach to Return and Risk Analyses in Fixed-Income Management', *Journal of Portfolio Management* 17, 41–46.

D. Heath, R. Jarrow, and A. Morton, 1992, 'Bond Pricing and the Term Structure of Interest Rates: A New Methodology for Contingent Claims Valuation', *Econometrica* 60, 77–105.

F. B. Hildebrand, 1987, Introduction to Numerical Analysis (Dover Publications Inc., New York).

Thomas S. Y. Ho and Sang-Bin Lee, 1986, 'Term Structure Movements and Pricing Interest Rate Contingent Claims' *Journal of Finance* 41, 1011–1029.

Jonathan Ingersoll, 1987, Theory of Modern Financial Decision Making (Rowman & Littlefield Publishers, Inc., New York).

Robert C. Merton, 1973, 'Theory of Rational Option Pricing', *Bell Journal of Economics and Management Science* 4, 141–183.

———, 1974, 'On the Pricing of Corporate Debt: The Risk Structure of Interest Rates', *Journal of Finance* 29, 449–470.

———, 1977, 'An Analytic Derivation of the Cost of Deposit Insurance and Loan Guarantees: An Application of Modern Option Pricing Theory', *Journal of Banking and Finance* 1, 3–11.

———, 1978, 'On the Cost of Deposit Insurance When There are Surveillance Costs', *Journal of Business* 51, 439–452.

———, 1990, Continuous Time Finance (Basil Blackwell Inc., Cambridge, Massachusetts).

Dennis G. Uyemura and Donald R. van Deventer, 1992, Financial Risk Management in Banking (Probus Publishing, Chicago).

Oldrich A. Vasicek, 1977, 'An Equilibrium Characterization of the Term Structure', *Journal of Financial Economics* 5, 177–188.

Reduced Form Credit Models

In the first section of this chapter, we introduced the reduced form model approach to credit risk management. We then summarized some of the principal advantages of this alternative to the structural models such as the Merton and Shimko-Tejima-van Deventer models. Reduced form models are a variation on the "hazard rate" modeling technology which began significantly influencing financial practice in the 1980s. It is now used in disciplines as diverse as mortgage prepayment modeling, retail credit authorization, and corporate credit modeling. The hazard rate modeling approach takes advantage of the statistics used in medicine to predict the incidence of disease and the stochastic process mathematics which moved from physics to finance in the 1970s. The hazard rate modeling approach has a number of very important advantages:

- **Flexibility**: Hazard rate modeling is a general modeling approach that is flexible enough to take different inputs about borrowers who are so diverse that we know different things about them. Hazard rate modeling takes advantage of all information available: credit derivatives prices and bond prices in the case of IBM, or "years at current residence" and "credit card balances outstanding versus the credit card limit" in the case of a small business CEO.

- **Simplicity**: As we quoted Professor Jarrow as saying previously in this book, the capital structure strategy of management is deeply intertwined with the financial health of the company in a very complex way. Hazard rate modeling reduces the default problem to its very essence, bringing enormous practical benefits, without having to model the full dynamics of capital structure in all scenarios.
- **Power**: Hazard rate modeling results in a full no-arbitrage pricing, valuation and hedging approach to credit risk.

Reduced form models are called "reduced form" models because they reduce the complex mechanics of default to a simple expression which allows the model to both fit observable market data and to produce no arbitrage pricing, valuation and hedging. The default "intensity" in these models is the hazard rate. There are many variations of this modeling approach. In this section, we concentrate on the models of Robert Jarrow because of his prolific work in this area. For many other excellent references on reduced form models, the authors recommend the web site *www.defaultrisk.com.*

An Introduction to the Jarrow Reduced Form Model

The Jarrow [1999–2001] model is an extension of the Jarrow-Turnbull [1995] model, which was perhaps the first reduced form model to experience widespread commercial acceptance. In the early days of the credit derivatives markets, dealers relied on the Merton model for pricing purposes. Dealers soon realized that the credit default swap market prices were consistently different from those indicated by the Merton model for many of the reasons we have discussed in the two previous sections. Dealers were under considerable pressure from both senior manageers, risk managers, and external auditors to adopt a modeling technology with better pricing accuracy. Dealers' instinct for self-preservation was an added incentive. The Jarrow-Turnbull model was the first model which allowed the matching of market prices and provided a rational economic basis for the evolution of market prices of everything from corporate debt to credit derivatives.

The original Jarrow-Turnbull model [1995] assumes that default is random but that default probabilities are non-random, time dependent functions. The Jarrow [1999–2001] model extends the Jarrow-Turnbull model in a large number of significant respects. First, default probabilities are assumed to be random, with explicit dependence of default probabilities on random interest rates and an arbitrary number of lognormally distributed risk factors. Jarrow also explicitly incorporates a liquidity factor that affects the prices of bonds, but not equity. This liquidity factor can be random and is different for each bond issuer. In addition, the liquidity parameter can be a function of the same macro risk drivers that determine the default intensity.

The Jarrow model also allows for the calculation of the implied recovery given default δ_i. This parameter, which can be random and driven by other risk factors, is defined by Jarrow as the fractional recovery $= \delta_i(t)v(\tau-, T: i)$ where v is the value of risky debt a fraction of an instant before bankruptcy at time τ and the subscript i denotes the seniority level of the debt. Duffie and Singleton [1999] were the first to use this specification for the recovery rate. They recognized that the traditional bankers' thinking on the recovery rate, expressed as percentage of 'principal,' made the mathematical derivation of bond and credit derivatives prices more difficult. They also recognized that thinking of recovery as a percentage of principal was too narrow—what is the principal on an "in the money" interest rate cap? On a foreign exchange option? On an undrawn loan commitment? Expressing recovery as a percentage of value one instant before bankruptcy is both more powerful and more general. We can easily convert it back to the traditional 'recovery rate as a percentage of principal' to maximize user-friendliness of the concept.

The hazard rate, or 'default intensity', in the Jarrow model is given by a simple linear combination of three terms:

$$\lambda(t) = \lambda_0 + \lambda_1 r(t) + \lambda_2 Z(t)$$

This is a much simpler expression than the default probability we discussed above in the derivation of the Merton credit model. The term $Z(t)$ is the 'shock' term with mean zero and standard deviation of one which creates random movements in the macro factor (like oil prices, in the case of Exxon), which drives default for that particular company.[9] Movements in this macro factor are generally written in this form:

$$dM(t) = M(t)[r(t)dt + \sigma_m dZ(t)]$$

The change in the macro factor, for example oil prices, is proportional to its value and increases at the random risk-free interest rate $r(t)$, subject to random shocks from changes in $Z(t)$, multiplied by the volatility of the macro factor, σ_m. While the default intensity in the Jarrow model, as we have

---

[9] In more mathematical terms, $Z(t)$ is standard Brownian motion under a risk neutral probability distribution Q with initial value 0 that drives the movements[9] of the market index $M(t)$.

written it, describes interest rates and one macro factor as drivers of default, it is easy to extend the model to an arbitrary number of macro factors. This is because the sum of a linear combination of normally distributed variables such as $Z(t)$ is still normally distributed. In this book, we will use the one factor notation for expositional purposes.

In the Jarrow model, interest rates are random, but if one prefers a constant interest rate model, we can simply set interest rate volatility to zero in the Jarrow model. The term structure model assumed for the risk-free rate of interest is a special case of the Heath Jarrow Morton [1992] framework commonly known as the Hull-White or Extended Vasicek model. In our prior discussion of the STV model, we used the original Vasicek [1977] model. This is the easiest model to manipulate, and it has the virtue of being so straightforward that a good spreadsheet analyst can implement the model. For practical use, though, it is critical that the risk-free interest rate assumptions are completely consistent with the current observable yield curve (and any other interest rate derivatives on that yield curve). The Extended Vasicek model contains an 'extension' from the original Vasicek model that allows the theoretical yield curve to exactly match the actual yield curve. In this model, the short-term rate of interest $r(t)$ drifts over time in a way consistent with interest rate cycles, subject to random shocks from the Brownian motion $W(t)$, which, like $Z(t)$ has a mean of zero and a standard deviation of 1.[10]

$$dr(t) = a[\bar{r}(t) - r(t)]dt + \sigma_r dW(t).$$

Dealing with the Issue of Liquidity in the Bond Market

One of the many virtues of reduced form models is the ability to fit parameters to the model from a wide variety of securities prices. Of course, the type of data most directly related to the interests of lenders is bond prices or credit derivatives prices. Since a large company such as IBM has only one type of common stock outstanding, but could have 10, 20 or 30 bond issues outstanding, it is logical to expect that there is less liquidity in the bond market than in the market for common stock (i.e. the equity market). Jarrow makes an explicit adjustment for this in his model by introducing a very general formulation for the impact of liquidity on bond market prices. We won't go into the details of that formulation here, but it is a very powerful feature of the model that reduces the question of bond market liquidity to a

---

[10] The expression for random movements in the short rate is again written under a risk neutral probability distribution.

scientific question (how best to fit a parameter which captures the liquidity impact) rather than a philosophical or religious question of whether bond prices can be used to calculate the parameters of a credit model. Note that there can be either a liquidity discount or liquidity premium on the bonds of a given issuer, and there is no implicit assumption by Jarrow that the liquidity discount is constant-it can be random and is flexible in its specifications.

Jarrow's original [2001] model shows how the Jarrow credit model can be fitted to bond prices and equity prices simultaneously, or it can be fitted to bond prices alone. Jarrow and Yildirum [2002] show how the model can be fitted to credit derivatives prices, and Chava and Jarrow [2002a, 2002b] fit the model to historical data on defaults.

Fitting the Jarrow Model for Small Business and Retail Credits

Later in this book, we discuss how to use 'hazard rate modeling' to test credit models in a consistent and scientific way. Hazard rate modeling, first used in economics by Kiefer [1988], is a powerful technology that is a logical and significant improvement on traditional credit scoring that has become the main tool in pricing and estimating the default probability of small business and retail clients.

With the merger of pure wholesale banks like JP Morgan, Continental Illinois, and Industrial Bank of Japan with retail institutions, almost all banks have 99.9% of their transactions with retail or small business borrowers. One of the virtues of the Jarrow approach to credit modeling is that it is general enough to fit exceptionally well with retail and small business data. The Merton model, by contrast, is constrained by the assumption that 'equity' in a company is an option on the assets of the firm—the only input the model allows is restricted by this structure. As Chava and Jarrow show, we can fit the Jarrow model to an advanced credit-scoring framework that allows the use of a wide range of variables with strong explanatory power. Shumway [2001] was the first to use the advanced hazard rate modeling technology to predict default. Hazard rate modeling differs from credit scoring in a significant way. Traditional credit scoring merges two sets of data to draw its conclusions: data on companies or individuals who defaulted, in the period before they defaulted, and the most recently available data on a wide variety of companies or individuals who did not default. Hazard rate modeling recognizes that we have a long history of information on Enron, for example, above and beyond the quarter prior to default. By using all observations on Enron, not just the last observation, we get more accurate estimates of default probabilities and the factors that drive default. Similarly, rather than using only the most recent data on a company which did not default, we can use all of its history that we have.

For small businesses, some of the more popular variables used to predict default in a hazard modeling context include:

- Charge card balance of the CEO;
- Revenues;
- Bank account overdrafts;
- Retail credit quality of the CEO;
- Small business credit ratings;
- Age of company;
- Size of company.

The Jarrow model, because it can use these well-known drivers of small business defaults, performs better than the Merton model, which cannot accept these variables as input. For retail credits, there is still another list of information that lenders have that go way beyond the inputs to the Merton model:

- Income;
- Education;
- Years at current residence;
- Home-owner, yes or no?
- Retail "credit score" from third party provider;
- Age.

Again, the Chava-Jarrow framework can accept these variables and therefore has a considerable "head start" on the Merton model in its generality.

Hedging the Impact of Interest Rate and Macro Movements on the Value of Defaultable Debt

At the beginning of this book, we argued that one of the key objectives of the credit risk process is practical action—the effective hedging of credit risk. In the Merton model, the single risk driver of default is the value of company assets. For portfolio hedging, we need to know the value of company assets for all companies and how they are correlated, what macro risk drivers affect them, and what the mathematical link is between these macro factors and the value of company assets. None of these links between macro factors and the value of company assets is specified in the Merton credit model, although there are various ways one can use other work of Robert Merton to build this framework.

In the Shimko-Tejima-van Deventer model, interest rates and the value of company assets are the two random macro factors driving the default of each company. Within a given country, interest rates are a common macro factor driving default across all borrowers, so we can come up with a 'macro hedge' for the impact of interest rates on default in the STV model. This is much more efficient than 'name by name' hedging in the credit derivatives market, because the whole portfolio is covered and because the bid-offered spread in interest rate derivatives is much lower than it is in the credit derivatives market.

The Jarrow model is even better suited to hedging credit risk on a portfolio level than the Merton and STV models because the link between the (N) macro factor(s) M and the default intensity is explicitly incorporated in the model. Take the example of Exxon, whose probability of default is driven by interest rates and oil prices, among other things. If $M(t)$ is the macro factor oil prices, it can be shown that the size of the hedge that needs to be bought or sold to hedge one dollar of risky, zero-coupon debt with market value v under the Jarrow model is given by:

$$\frac{\partial v(t,T:i)}{\partial M(t)} = -\left[\frac{\partial \gamma_i(t,T)}{\partial M(t)} + \frac{\lambda_2(1-\delta_i)(T-t)}{\sigma_m M(t)}\right] v_l(t,T:i)$$

The variable v is the value of risky, zero-coupon debt and gamma is the liquidity discount function representing the illiquidities often observed in the debt market. There are similar formulas in the Jarrow model for hedging coupon-bearing bonds, defaultable caps, floors, credit derivatives and so on.

That means that the steps in hedging the macro factor risk for any portfolio are identical to the steps that a trader of options has been taking for 30 years (hedging his net position with a long or short position in the common stock underlying the options):

1. Calculate the change in the value (including the impact of interest rates on default) of all retail credits with respect to interest rates.
2. Calculate the change in the value (including the impact of interest rates on default) of all small business credits with respect to interest rates.
3. Calculate the change in the value (including the impact of interest rates on default) of all major corporate credits with respect to interest rates.
4. Calculate the change in the value (including the impact of interest rates on default) of all bonds, derivatives, and other instruments.
5. Add these 'delta' amounts together.
6. The result is the global portfolio 'delta,' on a default-adjusted basis, of interest rates for the entire portfolio.
7. Choose the position in interest rate derivatives with the opposite delta.
8. This eliminates interest rate risk from the portfolio on a default-adjusted basis.

We can replicate this process for any macro factor that impacts default, such as exchange rates, stock price indices, oil prices, the value of class A office buildings in the central business district of key cities, etc. Let's take the example of office building prices. The steps in hedging are identical:

1. Calculate the change in the value (including the impact of building prices on default) of all retail credits with respect to building prices (probably very small).
2. Calculate the change in the value (including the impact of building prices on default) of all small business credits with respect to building prices.
3. Calculate the change in the value (including the impact of building prices on default) of all major corporate credits with respect to building prices.
4. Calculate the change in the value (including the impact of building prices on default) of all bonds, derivatives, and other instruments with respect to building prices.
5. Add these "delta" amounts together.
6. The result is the global portfolio 'delta,' on a default-adjusted basis, of building prices for the entire portfolio.
7. Choose the hedge of building prices with the opposite delta.
8. This eliminates building price risk from the portfolio on a default-adjusted basis.

Step 7 is more difficult in the case of building prices than it is in the case of interest rates, but it is still possible. Security Pacific Corporation of Los Angeles, suffering from a gross over-lending position in commercial real estate, sold its headquarters office building to reduce its exposure in the early 1990s. This 'hedge' was in the right direction although it was 'too little, too late' for Security Pacific to stave off the need for a BankAmerica Corporation rescue soon after. For almost all macro factors that we discuss in the next chapter, there is a practical hedge.

Most importantly:

- We can measure the default-adjusted transaction level and portfolio risk exposure with respect to each macro factor.
- We can set exposure limits on the default-adjusted transaction level and portfolio risk exposure with respect to each macro factor.
- We know how much of a hedge would eliminate some or all of this risk.

It can be shown that all other risk, other than that driven by macro factors, can be diversified away. This hedging and diversification capability is a powerful step forward from where most financial institutions found themselves at the close of the 20th century.

Credit Risk: Transaction Level versus Portfolio Level

The previous section illustrated a key point in credit risk analytics. There should be no difference in approach between transaction level pricing, valuation and hedging on a credit-adjusted basis and the same calculations on a portfolio level basis. There is no mathematical or computer science reason not to calculate portfolio pricing, valuation and hedging on a transaction level, the sum of which equates to the portfolio exposures. Portfolio level analytics that use simplifying assumptions have an unknown level of error and therefore a very high degree of model risk. Moody's Investors Service "diversity score" concept and portfolio analytics which assume an arbitrary probability distribution for transaction values (normal or lognormal are the most common) are examples of portfolio approaches which can not be taken to the transaction level with accuracy. Because they don't work at the transaction level, they are only approximations at the portfolio level and can't be a high quality guide to valuation, pricing or hedging.

In the rest of this book we explain how to use credit models in a way that they are accurate at both the transaction level and at the portfolio level.

In Summary: Comparing the Reduced Form and Structural Approaches

We have covered a lot of ground in this chapter. The rest of the book illustrates practical application of the models and testing of the models in an intuitive way. Because we have covered so much ground, this section summarizes some of the major differences among the three models discussed. We break these differences into two classes—differences in assumptions and differences in implications.

Differences in Assumptions for Structural and Reduced Form Models

The principal differences in assumptions among the three models that we have discussed in this chapter can be summarized as follows:

Assumptions about interest rates:

- Merton model: interest rates are constant;
- Shimko, Tejima and van Deventer model: interest rates are random (Vasicek or Extended Vasicek term structure model);
- Jarrow model: interest rates are random (Vasicek or Extended Vasicek term structure model).

Assumptions about drivers of default:

- Merton model: value of company assets;

- Shimko, Tejima and van Deventer model: value of company assets and interest rates;
- Jarrow model: interest rates and 1 to N macro risk factors.

Assumptions about capital structure:

- Merton model: company has one debt issue, a zero-coupon bond, outstanding;
- Shimko, Tejima and van Deventer model: company has one debt issue, a zero-coupon bond, outstanding;
- Jarrow model: no restrictions on capital structure.

Assumptions about the number of periods:

- Merton model: one period;
- Shimko, Tejima and van Deventer model: one period;
- Jarrow model: multi-period model.

Assumptions about recovery in event of default:

- Merton model: implied by model;
- Shimko, Tejima and van Deventer model: implied by model;
- Jarrow model: random recovery in the event of default.

Assumptions about liquidity of bond market:

- Merton model: no liquidity adjustment;
- Shimko, Tejima and van Deventer model: no liquidity adjustment;
- Jarrow model: flexible specification of random liquidity adjustment.

Assumptions about different seniority of debt outstanding:

- Merton model: only one debt issue assumed;
- Shimko, Tejima and van Deventer model: only one debt issue assumed;
- Jarrow model: various levels of seniority are consistent with the model.

Assumptions about number of payments on debt outstanding:

- Merton model: only one payment at maturity assumed;
- Shimko, Tejima and van Deventer model: only one payment at maturity assumed;
- Jarrow model: N payments.

The next section summarizes some of the many implications of the three models discussed:

Differences in Implications of Structural and Reduced Form Models

Because of the assumptions of the two classes of models, they have a number of implications. These implications are testable, as we will see in later chapters:

Implications for timing of bankruptcy:

- Merton model: no "surprise" bankruptcy; occurs only at maturity;
- Shimko, Tejima and van Deventer model: no "surprise" bankruptcy, occurs only at maturity;
- Jarrow model: bankruptcy can occur at any time.

Implications for the relationship between stock prices and debt prices:

- Merton model: when stock prices go up, debt prices go up, and vice versa;
- Shimko, Tejima and van Deventer model: all other things (interest rates) being equal, when stock prices go up, debt prices go up, and vice versa;
- Jarrow model: even when stock price is made a "macro factor" in the Jarrow model, there is no restriction on the joint movement of stock prices and debt prices. Model is fit to observable data.

Implications for pricing of zero-coupon bonds:

- Merton model: model prices one zero-coupon bond;
- Shimko, Tejima and van Deventer model: model prices one zero-coupon bond;
- Jarrow model: model prices N zero-coupon bonds.

Implications for pricing of coupon-bearing bonds:

- Merton model: not consistent with coupon-bearing bonds without significant expansion of assumptions;
- Shimko, Tejima and van Deventer model: not consistent with coupon bearing bonds without significant expansion of assumptions;
- Jarrow model: consistent with observable market prices for coupon bearing bonds, subject to minimization of squared error or modest extension of model.

Implications for pricing of credit derivatives:

- Merton model: not consistent with single period nature of model;
- Shimko, Tejima and van Deventer model: not consistent with single period nature of model;

- Jarrow model: provides closed form solution for pricing of credit derivatives.

Implications for hedging:

- Merton model: has hedging formula for use of value of company assets or stock price as hedging tool;
- Shimko, Tejima and van Deventer model: has hedging formula for use of value of company assets or stock price as hedging tool;
- Jarrow model: has hedging formula for credit-adjusted hedging with respect to interest rates and the 1 to N macro factors driving default.

Implications for small business credit evaluation:

- Merton model: can't use many of the available known drivers of small business default because of functional form of model;
- Shimko, Tejima and van Deventer model: can't use many of the available known drivers of small business default because of functional form of model;
- Jarrow model: using Chava-Jarrow framework and logistic regression, all relevant drivers of small business default can be incorporated in the Jarrow model.

Implications for retail credit evaluation:

- Merton model: can't use many of the available known drivers of retail default because of functional form of model;
- Shimko, Tejima and van Deventer model: can't use many of the available known drivers of retail default because of functional form of model;
- Jarrow model: using Chava-Jarrow framework and logistic regression, all relevant drivers of retail default can be incorporated in the Jarrow model.

Implications for interest rate risk management:

- Merton model: None, since interest rates are constant;
- Shimko, Tejima and van Deventer model: Credit-adjusted interest rate risk hedges can be derived;
- Jarrow model: Credit-adjusted interest rate risk hedges can be derived.

Implications for the capital structure:

- Merton model: Since the face amount of debt is set at time zero and remains constant until maturity, the capital structure (i.e. the ratio of market value of equity to market value of debt), is highly random. This becomes very important in later chapters.

- Shimko, Tejima and van Deventer model: Since the face amount of debt is set at time zero and remains constant until maturity, the capital structure (i.e. the ratio of market value of equity to market value of debt) is highly random.
- Jarrow model: There are no explicit implications for capital structure, but the model is consistent with a relatively stable capital structure that is subject to random market shocks.

We explore the impact of these assumptions and model implications on practical credit risk management in the remainder of this book.

Selected References on Credit Risk

K. Amin and R. Jarrow, 1991, 'Pricing Foreign Currency Options Under Stochastic Interest Rates,' *Journal of Money and Finance*, 10, 310–329.

K. Amin and R. Jarrow, 1992, 'Pricing Options on Risky Assets in a Stochastic Interest Rate Economy,' *Mathematical Finance*, 2(4), 217–237.

R. Battig and R. Jarrow, 1999, 'The Second Fundamental Theorem of Asset Pricing-A New Approach,' *Review of Financial Studies*, 12(5), 1219–1235.

D. Duffie, M. Schroder and C. Skiadas, 1995, 'Recursive Valuation of Defaultable Securities and the Timing of Resolution of Uncertainty,' working paper, Stanford University.

D. Duffie and K. Singleton, 1999, 'Modeling Term Structures of Defaultable Bonds,' *Review of Financial Studies*, 12(4), 197–226.

D. Heath, R. Jarrow and A. Morton, 1992, 'Bond Pricing and the Term Structure of Interest Rates: A New Methodology for Contingent Claim Valuation,' *Econometrica*, 60(1), 77–105.

R. Hogg, and A. Craig, 1970, Introduction to Mathematical Statistics, 3rd edition, Macmillan Pub. Co.: New York.

L. Hughston, 1997, 'Pricing Models for Credit Derivatives,' Presentation at AIC Conference on Credit Derivatives, London.

R. Jarrow, 2001, 'Default Parameter Estimation using Market Prices,' (September/October), *Financial Analysts Journal*, .

R. Jarrow, D. Lando and S. Turnbull, 1997, 'A Markov Model for the Term Structure of Credit Risk Spreads,' *The Review of Financial Studies*, 10(2), 481–523.

R. Jarrow, D. Lando and F. Yu, 1999, "Default Risk and Diversification: Theory and Applications," working paper, Cornell University.

R. Jarrow and D. Madan, 1995, "Option Pricing using the Term Structure of Interest Rates to Hedge Systematic Discontinuities in Asset Returns," *Mathematical Finance*, 5(4).

R. Jarrow and D. Madan, 1999, 'Arbitrage, Martingales and Private Monetary Value,' (forthcoming), *Journal of Risk*.

R. Jarrow and S. Turnbull, 1995, 'Pricing Derivatives on Financial Securities Subject to Credit Risk,' *Journal of Finance*, 50(1), 53–85.

R. Jarrow and S. Turnbull, 2000, Derivative Securities, 2nd edition, South-Western College Publishing: Cincinnati, Ohio.

R. Jarrow and S. Turnbull, 1997, 'An Integrated Approach to the Hedging and Pricing of Eurodollar Derivatives', *The Journal of Risk and Insurance*, 64(2), 271–299.

R. Jarrow and S. Turnbull, 1999, 'The Intersection of Market and Credit Risk,' (forthcoming), *Journal of Banking and Finance*.

D. Lando, 1998, 'On Cox Processes and Credit Risky Securities', (forthcoming), *The Review of Derivatives Research*, 2, 99–120.

E. Parzen, 1962, Stochastic Processes, Holden-Day, Inc.: San Francisco, California.

P. Protter, 1990, Stochastic Integration and Differential Equations, Springer-Verlag: New York, N.Y.

M. Rooney, 1998, 'Credit Default Swaps (Transferring Corporate and Sovereign Credit Risk)', *Merrill Lynch, Global Fixed Income Research*, October.

T. Schwartz, 1998, 'Estimating the Term Structures of Corporate Debt,' (forthcoming), *The Review of Derivatives Research*, 2, 193–230.

A. Warga, 1999, Fixed Income Data Base, University of Houston, College of Business Administration (www.uh.edu/~awarga/lb.html).

4

Credit Risk Models:
The Impact of Macro Factors
on the Risk of Default

In the first three chapters of this book, we outlined the key objectives of the credit risk process. We saw how macro factors affected JP Morgan in the derivatives-related incident with SK Securities of Korea. In Chapter 3, we outlined three different approaches to model credit risk. From this chapter onward, we turn to the practical implementation of credit models, which includes, above all else, an understanding of how well they perform in a real world environment. Chapter 5 introduces the testing process for credit models from a statistical perspective, but it is very important to look at some data before getting too scientific.

The first question we need to ask before testing credit model performance is as follows:

Is there any evidence that macro economic factors are key drivers of default risk?

If not, then we can focus on company specific 'micro factors' as the sole determinants of credit risk. On the other hand, if the 'casual' cascx empiricism of this chapter makes it highly likely that macro factors are key drivers, we can feel confident that testing for their influence more formally in Chapter 5 will be informative.

The United States versus the Rest of the World

In testing credit models, data availability is one of the first practical problems we encounter. The U.S., on the one hand, is the 'Disneyland' of data. There is lots of it, although there is never as much as credit modelers would like. However, since the exciting times of the late 1970s and the defaults that followed over the next decade, the U.S. market has been relatively calm—Enron and Worldcom bankruptcies notwithstanding—compared to many other markets. In the relative calm of the late 1990s, the economic environment in the U.S. was benign and defaults were significantly fewer in number than in the late 1980s. Although that has changed since 1998, it has a heavy influence on statistical testing of credit models using U.S. data.

When markets are very calm and there are few defaults, like in the 1960s and early 1970s in the U.S., all that a researcher can see is 'white noise.' The authors have been told, with complete sincerity, that tests of credit models on U.S. data show that interest rates are not correlated with default. How quickly we forget the $1 trillion savings and loan crisis that resulted from high interest rates and plunging commercial real estate prices!

The reason for the sincere, but inaccurate, statement that interest rates are not correlated with defaults is data selection. We need to identify key periods in history and key countries that have suffered large enough movements in key risk drivers that a good statistician can measure their impact. Studying only periods filled with 'white noise' can significantly underestimate credit risk, in the same way as the previous comment we highlighted about interest rates and default. The speaker was sincere and honest, but he studied the wrong data.

For that reason, as we are looking at real world examples, we tend to focus on countries where there have been dramatic changes in fortunes, wide swings in macro factors, and dramatic numbers of defaults. In these circumstances, the truth is more obvious. Similarly, in benign environments, we have to be skeptical and look for confirmation in other markets. In 1989, there had been no bank defaults in Japan since the end of the Second World War. A wise credit risk analyst in the Japanese market could have used U.S. data to get a more accurate estimate of what the 1990s would bring the Japanese market than he would have obtained on 45 years of local history.

For that reason, in this chapter, we analyze data from all over the world and then seek to confirm that the typical international experience applies in our own country. One Japanese banker, who argued that only a 'Japanese' credit model was useful to his bank, now works at an American financial institution because his Japanese bank failed from credit losses. We can only benefit from knowing the hazards of a myopic view of the world.

Australia: Typical Macro Factors for Leading Banks

Since our focus in this chapter is unashamedly casual empiricism, we first do a quick test to determine whether or not macro factors may affect major banks in Australia. One approach is to take each macro factor one at a time and run a simple linear regression to determine if the macro factor is statistically significant in explaining the banks' stock price movements. If the answer is no, then we will probably find a very low percentage of stock price variation explained by the macro factor.

The chart below shows such analysis for seven of the largest banks in Australia: Bank of Western Australia, ANZ Banking Group (ANZ), Commonwealth Bank of Australia (CBA), National Australia Bank (NAB), Westpac, Suncorp Metway, and St. George Bank. We ran a regression for three home price data series, four interest rates, three commodity prices, and three exchange rates for each of the banks, linking their stock price to the macro factors one at a time. The 'Adjusted R^2' shows the percentage of stock price variation explained by each of the factors for each of the banks, done one by one. The results are surprisingly high almost across the board.

Our 'quick and dirty' analysis confirms the importance of home prices in macro factor exposure at the major Australian banks; this is no surprise since the banks are very large mortgage lenders in a country where the secondary market in mortgage loans is just beginning to reach large size.

At this point, we can turn the problem over to the econometricians to do a multiple regression in various functional forms that takes into account the correlation between the macro factors, lags in their influence, and possible accidental correlation. For the typical bank, 9 to 12 of these macro factors are statistically significant in a multiple linear regression linking the absolute level of the stock price to the absolute level of the macro factor. The explanatory power of the regressions ranges from 80% to 97% (on an adjusted R^2 basis) for the banks listed above.

What does this mean for our casual empiricism? Just as in the JP Morgan-SK Securities case, macro factors are drivers of risk as reflected in the stock market value of Australian banks. The macro factors that are key drivers of risk are logical, given the nature of the banking business in Australia, and there are a lot of them that are key drivers.

Let us now turn to Japan.

Bank of Tokyo-Mitsubishi

Japan is one of the most interesting markets in the world for the study of credit risk. As we noted above, 10 years ago no one in Japan believed there was credit risk in the country. A large number of the big banks were rated AAA/Aaa by the major international rating agencies. Now Japan is one of the most troubled economies in the world. Of all the major banks in Japan, Bank of Tokyo-Mitsubishi has probably emerged, at least to date, as the least damaged by the decade-long recession in Japan. We can use Bank of Tokyo-

Figure 4.1 Macro Factor Correlations for Australian Banks

Single Macro Factor Correlations (Adjusted R²) for Australian Banks	BankWest	ANZ	CBA	NAB	Westpac	Suncorp Metway	St. George	Average
Perth Mediam Home Prices	0.844	0.738	0.866	0.725	0.804	0.801	0.316	0.728
Sydney Median Home Prices	0.863	0.726	0.870	0.713	0.795	0.809	0.292	0.724
Melbourne Median Home Prices	0.856	0.720	0.853	0.694	0.766	0.789	0.296	0.711
USD/AUD	0.711	0.688	0.806	0.710	0.816	0.756	0.410	0.700
Perth CBD Rentals	0.299	0.799	0.907	0.869	0.863	0.902	0.212	0.693
JPY/AUD	0.636	0.333	0.509	0.315	0.427	0.399	0.440	0.437
3 Year Rate	0.187	0.509	0.416	0.584	0.488	0.485	0.044	0.388
90 Day Rate	0.173	0.414	0.364	0.522	0.370	0.443	0.002	0.327
SGD/AUD	0.266	0.279	0.281	0.224	0.330	0.242	0.315	0.277
1 Year Rate	0.122	0.413	0.320	0.495	0.154	0.399	0.004	0.272
180 Day Rate	0.133	0.392	0.322	0.489	0.130	0.402	0.001	0.267
Iron Ore	0.000	0.354	0.384	0.323	0.343	0.428	0.002	0.262
Wool	0.069	0.005	0.095	0.038	0.048	0.087	0.074	0.059
Oil	0.046	0.036	0.032	0.003	0.027	0.015	0.043	0.029
Above Average is in Bold								
Below Average is in Bold Italic								

Source: Kamakura Corporation, 2001.

Mitsubishi's credit spread as a 'lower bound' on the credit spread for the other Japanese banks. The credit spread here is based on comparing yields on observable U.S. dollar bonds for Bank of Tokyo-Mitsubishi with yields on risk-free U.S. Treasury securities.

When we run a simple linear regression seeking to explain movements in the bank's credit spread over 652 days of data, we find the following results:

Table 4.1   Regression Analysis for Bank
of Tokyo-Mitsubishi

Regression Statistics	
Multiple R	0.51467
R Square	0.26489
Adjusted R Square	0.26262
Standard Error	8.56356
Observations	652

	Coefficients	*Standard Error*	*t Stat*
Intercept	−31.85	4.12	−7.73
3 Month Yen Rates	7.89	2.24	3.53
Yen/Dollar FX	0.48	0.04	13.35

3-month yen interest rates and the yen-dollar foreign exchange rate explain 26% of the variation of Bank of Tokyo-Mitsubishi's credit spread to a statistically significant degree. When interest rates rise by 1%, Bank of Tokyo-Mitsubishi's credit spread rises. When the yen weakens, the credit spread rises as well. Macro factors drive credit spreads for the Bank, and within the credit spread is the market's estimate of the Bank's probability of default.

This finding parallels the findings for Japanese retailer Daiei and the Korean Development Bank, as explained below.

Daiei, Ltd., Japanese Retailer

The case of the Japanese retailer, Daiei, illustrates a number of crucial principles about credit analytics. Figure 4.2 below shows the price histories of three Daiei yen bond issues versus the Daiei equity price at the bottom of the graph.

In chapter 3, we saw that the Merton model of risky debt predicts that equity prices and debt prices are positively correlated, because an increase in the value of company assets should increase the price of both debt and equity. As this graph of the Daiei experience shows, however, this is not the case in many real world situations.

Figure 4.2   Daiei equity and bond price history

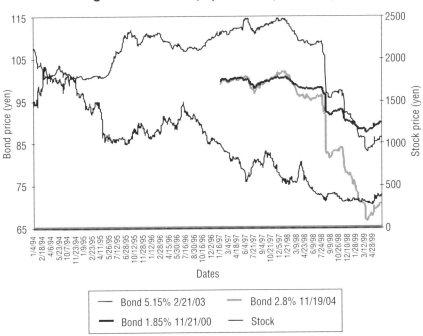

Toward the right hand side of the graph, a restructuring of Daiei debt was announced, resulting in very large decreases in the Daiei bond prices. Equity prices, however, increased as a result of the announcement. This was not irrationality on the part of either debt holders or equity holders,. The restructuring transferred wealth from the debt holders to the equity holders by staving off bankruptcy. This is typical of the restructurings observed in Asia in the last half of the 1990s, and it seems to apply almost universally in a restructuring context. The reduced form models can handle this dichotomy, but it is not consistent with the implications of the Merton assumptions. This is a cautionary 'yellow flag' that we may want to test more formally in later chapters.

Figure 4.3 shows a frequency distribution of Daiei yen bond prices, and this illustrates another important point, as we will see below.

Prices of risky debt do not have a simple normal or lognormal distribution. As credit analysts, it is fun to assume that these popular probability distributions apply, because it makes the mathematics of credit risk much easier. Unfortunately, however, they don't apply and the mathematics that results is therefore incorrect. As the Daiei case illustrates, when times are good, an analyst can erroneously conclude that bond prices are normally distributed based on the clustering of Daiei bond values on the

Figure 4.3   Frequency distribution

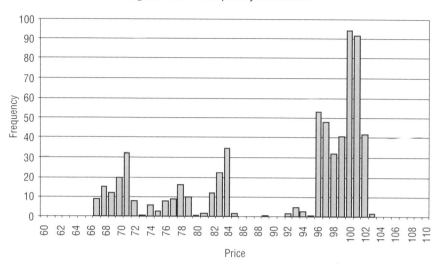

right-hand side of this graph. If the analyst committed to a value-at-risk number based on this distribution, however, they would be mistaken.

Once Daiei's financial problems became well known, bond prices clustered at a level much lower than any reasonable value-at-risk level that would have been derived from prices in normal times. This is absolutely

Figure 4.4   Daily history of credit spreads and stock price, Daiei, Ltd. 1996–99

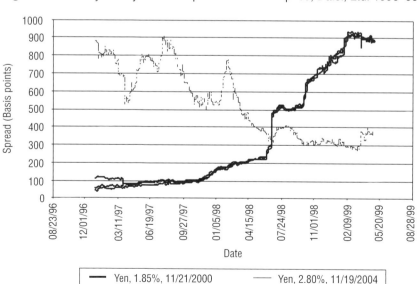

typical and an excellent illustration of why value-at-risk should only be calculated on the basis of a true simulation of default, not historical variability in bond prices on a set of issuers who have not defaulted. We deal with this issue in much greater detail in later chapters.

When Daiei's equity price is graphed against the credit spreads for the three Daiei bond issues, we see behavior that again is much different from that predicted by the Merton model. The Merton model predicts that credit spreads will decline when equity prices rise and vice versa. Yet, in the Daiei case, we see equity prices seesawing up and down during a period when Daiei credit spreads were steadily rising. This is consistent with the findings in Janosi, Jarrow, and Yildirum [2001] that equity contains a 'bubble' component that is not captured by the state-of-the-art Fama and French [2001]-style equity estimation procedures. While it is often argued that equity prices predict fault better than debt prices, we can see in the case of Daiei that 'data mining' leads you to opposite conclusions about the relationship between equity prices and credit spreads, depending on the period chosen. This is another 'yellow flag' that indicates the need for more scientific testing.

Table 4.2 below shows that we can explain 66% of the variation in the Daiei credit spread over 389 days with only two variables, short-term yen interest rates and the yen dollar foreign exchange rate.

Table 4.2 Regression Analysis for Daiei

Regression Statistics			
Multiple R	0.81719		
R Square	0.66781		
Adjusted R Square	0.66608		
Standard Error	37.27056		
Observations	389		

	Coefficients	Standard Error	t Stat
Intercept	−772.67	33.38	−23.15
3 Month Yen Rates	48.27	10.76	4.48
Yen/Dollar FX	6.96	0.28	24.96

This is confirmation of the phenomenon we have noted throughout this chapter—macro factors are powerful contributors to movements in default intensities and credit spreads. The yen-dollar exchange rate's extraordinary *t*-score of nearly 25 is easy to explain. Daiei is a retailer in a high-cost country. Nearly everything it sells is imported. If the yen weakens, all of Daiei's goods become more expensive, revenue drops, and so does profitability. Risk increases. This is something lenders to Daiei would have benefitted from knowing before the yen dropped from its peak of 79 to the dollar to the 120–130 range in the late 1990s and the early years of this century.

Exxon Capital

We now examine a commodity-driven U.S.-based multinational company. We would expect Exxon Capital, like the example of Petronas given below, to have credit spreads (and default probabilities) that are very sensitive to oil price levels.

A simple x-y graph shows what we expect even more simply than the linear relationship we have plotted on this scatter diagram. As the price of oil rises, the credit spreads on Exxon Capital decline. The company becomes a higher quality borrower because the increased value of its reserves provides a higher degree of collateralization to the unsecured creditors of the company. Again, this is something a lender needs to know.

Goldman, Sachs & Co. and Merrill Lynch

Another issue that a credit model should help address is the issue of diversification. One very basic method for estimating the degree of diversification that is achieved by splitting exposure between two credits in the same industry is the Moody's 'diversity score' concept. Even in a chapter

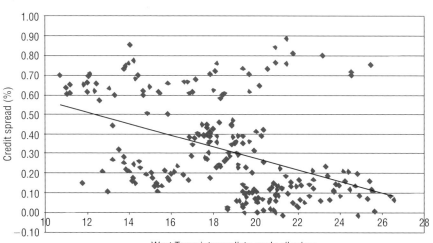

Figure 4.5   Credit spreads on Exxon Capital

Figure 4.6   Credit spread correlation

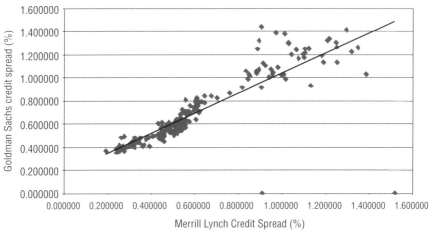

on casual empiricism, though, we can be much more precise than that. Credit spreads are powerful tools for measuring the potential diversification from holding fixed income investments in two firms in an industry rather than an investment in one firm. Consider Merrill Lynch and Goldman Sachs & Co., two common U.S. derivatives counterparties for financial institutions and corporations around the world. Is it beneficial to split exposure between those two firms? Obviously yes, but diversification is minimal, as Figure 4.6 shows.

The credit spread of Merrill Lynch and the credit spread of Goldman, Sachs & Co. have a 95% correlation. While the credit spread reflects bond market liquidity as well as default likelihood, this correlation coefficient shows that we have to do much more in seeking diversification than purely intra-industry diversification in order to have much impact on risk reduction.

Korean Development Bank

The Korean Development Bank (KDB) case is an extraordinarily interesting study of performance during the Asian crisis that began on July 2, 1997 and lasted through most of 1999. While the prices for some bond issues were unreliable, for the most part credit spreads clearly indicated the stress that KDB was under during the Asian crisis.

Credit spreads on substantially all KDB issues widened from less than 100 basis points to almost 900 basis points on some issues during the height of the Asian crisis. The graph below shows the movements in KDB credit spread plotted versus the Korean won/U.S. Dollar exchange rate.

When the won weakened, there was a dramatic increase in the credit spreads on the U.S. Dollar 8.09% bonds due 10/6/2004. The same phenomenon can be seen for credit spreads on a separate KDB issue.

The 6.50% KDB bonds due 11/15/2002 show slightly more dispersion around the trend line. When we run a regression to explain the movements in the credit spreads on 1192 days of the 8.09% bonds due in 2004, we find the following:

Figure 4.7   Credit spreads for KDB

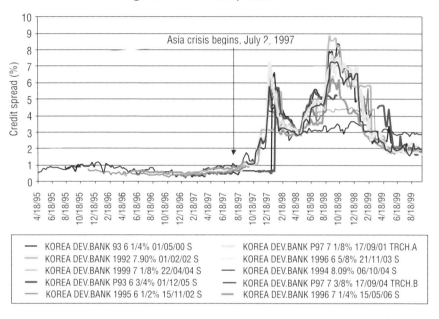

Figure 4.8   Credit spreads on KDB bond due 2004

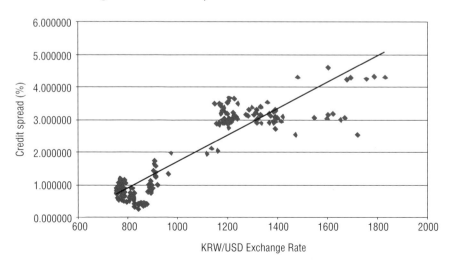

Figure 4.9   Credit spreads on KDB bond

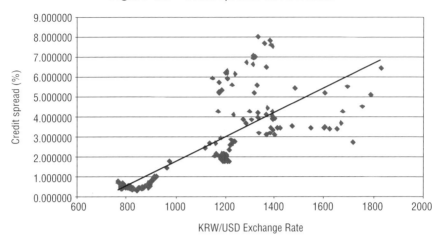

KRW/USD Exchange Rate

Table 4.3   Regression Analysis for KDB

Regression Statistics	
Multiple R	0.86085
R Square	0.74107
Adjusted R Square	0.74064
Standard Error	106.36214
Observations	1192

	Coefficients	Standard Error	t Stat
Intercept	96.04	63.24	1.52
3 Month USD Rates	−90.44	10.22	−8.85
KRW/Dollar FX	0.62	0.01	51.11

    A simple linear regression with 3 month dollar rates and the won/dollar exchange rate as an explanatory variable explains 74% of the movement in KDB credit spread, with a very high t-score of 51 on the won as an explanatory macro factor. A U.S. dollar-based investor who bought U.S. dollar bonds of the KDB would have been mistaken if they concluded that they had no foreign exchange risk because the credit spread on KDB was directly linked to the Korean won exchange rate, an excellent proxy for government credit quality, among other things.

Long Term Credit Bank of Japan

We now turn back to Japan to examine another fascinating case study in bank failure. Long Term Credit Bank of Japan (LTCB) was one of the two biggest bank failures of the twentieth century, with Nippon Credit Bank (see below) being the other. LTCB was a monthly issuer of five-year yen bonds, so there were more than 60 yen bond issues of LTCB outstanding as its credit quality deteriorated. This data set is extremely useful in understanding the dynamics of credit modeling.

There was a high degree of variation in yen bond yields for LTCB during the last 3 years of its existence. For the most part, the yield variation was due solely to changes in perceived credit risk as government bond yields in Japan were very stable (but not risk-free) during this period. Figure 4.11 on the next page plots the yield on one of the LTCB bonds versus the bank's equity price. The Merton model of risky debt, which we discussed in Chapter 3, implies that bond yields and equity prices move in opposite directions, but the chart below shows that equity prices and bond yields were positively correlated for much of the period prior to the bank's seizure by regulators in Japan.

The Merton model predicts that a rise in stock price should be accompanied by a decline in bond yields. Figure 4.12 below graphs the yield to maturity on LTCB bonds as a function of stock price. Instead of a downward sloping line that the Merton model predicts, we have a U-shaped curve.

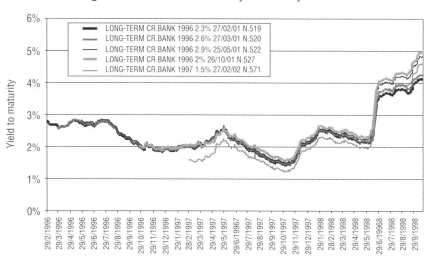

Figure 4.10 Yield to maturity on LTCB yen bonds

Figure 4.11   LTCB price and yield history

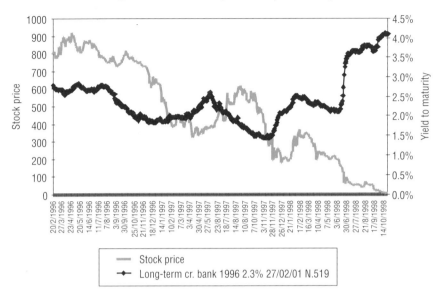

Figure 4.12   Yield to maturity on LTCB bonds

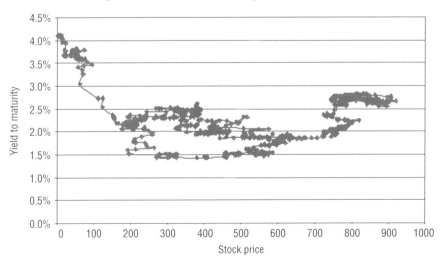

When we supplement this graph with regression analysis that seeks to explain bond yield as a linear function of stock price, we do get a negative coefficient on stock price as predicted by the Merton model.

Table 4.4 Regression Analysis for LTCB

Long Term Credit Bank of Japan
Yield to Maurity on 2.3% Yen Bonds due 2/27/2001
As a Function of Stock Price
2/29/96 to 10/23/98

Regression Statistics	
Multiple R	34.484%
R Square	11.892%
Adjusted R Square	11.764%
Standard Error	0.005947675
Observations	692

	Coefficients	*Standard Error*	*t Stat*
Intercept	0.0276876	0.0004503	61.4927107
Stock Price	−0.0000082	0.0000008	−9.6502496

The t-statistic is normally considered statistically significant if it has an absolute value greater than 2, so at 9.65 one would say the Merton-based relationship is statistically significant. This is good news for those of us who are long-time fans of the Merton model.

Unfortunately, however, if one picks a subset of the data that covers 80% of the sample period, the opposite conclusion results:

Table 4.5 Regression Analysis for LTCB

Long Term Credit Bank of Japan
Yield to Maurity on 2.3% Yen Bonds due 2/27/2001
As a Function of Stock Price
2/29/96 to 2/28/98

Regression Statistics	
Multiple R	48.499%
R Square	23.522%
Adjusted R Square	23.374%
Standard Error	0.003421561
Observations	522

	Coefficients	*Standard Error*	*t Stat*
Intercept	0.0166914	0.0004290	38.9084089
Stock Price	0.0000090	0.0000008	12.6463380

The sign is positive instead of negative, and the *t*-statistic is even more significant than it was over the full sample period. We can't avoid this conclusion—we can prove either that the bond yield/stock price relationship is consistent with Merton or inconsistent with Merton with only a slight variation in the data set used. The impact of data selection is a major modeling risk that we need to be sensitive to.

These inconsistencies of the LTCB experience with the Merton model is a cause for concern given that the LTCB failure was one of the two largest bank failures in the last 100 years. We turn next to the case of Nippon Credit Bank to see if the same concerns are evident there.

Nippon Credit Bank

Like Long Term Credit Bank of Japan, Nippon Credit Bank (NCB) was seized by Japanese bank regulators and nationalized in October 1998. NCB was also a monthly issuer of five-year yen bonds, and its data reflects the rich array of maturities for which prices were observable.

The Merton model predicts that bond yields should fall when equity prices rise. The graph of the NCB experience, however, shows long periods of positive as well as negative correlation.

When one plots the bond yield against stock price, instead of the downward sloping relationship predicted by the Merton model, we get a scattering of data points:

Figure 4.13   Yield to maturity on Nippon Credit Bank bonds

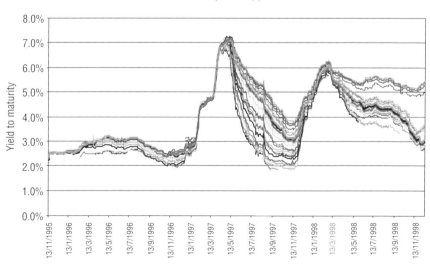

Figure 4.14　Stock price and bond yield history for NCB

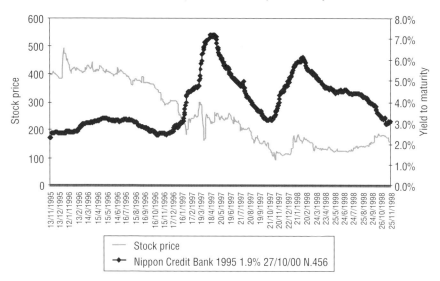

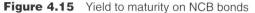

Figure 4.15　Yield to maturity on NCB bonds

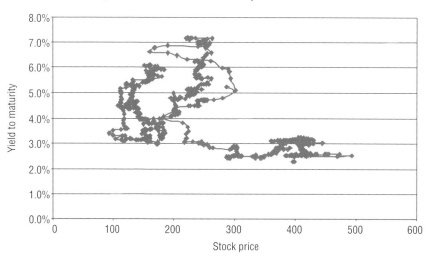

When we run a regression of the long-term bond yield on stock price over the entire sample period, we do indeed get the negative sign as predicted by the Merton model:

Table 4.6 Regression Analysis for NCB

Nippon Credit Bank
Yield to Maurity on 1.9% Yen Bonds due October 27, 2000
As a Function of Stock Price
November 13, 1995 to December 14, 1998

Regression Statistics	
Multiple R	57.554%
R Square	33.124%
Adjusted R Square	33.041%
Standard Error	0.010071347
Observations	806

	Coefficients	Standard Error	t Stat
Intercept	0.0556562	0.0008766	63.4902455
Stock Price	−0.0000630	0.0000032	−19.9557193

The *t*-score is almost 20, indicating a high degree of statistical significance. However if we choose a data set consisting of the last 18 months before nationalization of the bank, when the Merton model should have been most powerful, we get the opposite result:

Table 4.7 Regression Analysis for NCB

Nippon Credit Bank
Yield to Maurity on 1.9% Yen Bonds due October 27, 2000
As a Function of Stock Price
June 1, 1997 to December 14, 1998

Regression Statistics	
Multiple R	25.3888%
R Square	6.4459%
Adjusted R Square	6.2114%
Standard Error	0.008033704
Observations	401

	Coefficients	Standard Error	t Stat
Intercept	0.0360963	0.0017253	20.9215789
Stock Price	0.0000558	0.0000106	5.2432007

The coefficient on stock price is now positive, the opposite of the Merton model prediction, and the t-score is statistically significant.

We now have two very large sized yellow flags, associated with the two biggest bank failures of the twentieth century, regarding the implications of the Merton model. The reduced form models do not necessarily have the same implications—the relationship between debt and equity prices in the reduced form models depends on the value of the coefficients estimated. At this point, we will note a potential concern about the implications of the Merton model's assumptions—it may well be that the simplicity and power of the model comes at a high price. We've learned from casual empiricism that more formal testing is necessary. We use the case of Enron to do that in later chapters.

Petronas, Malaysian State Oil Company

The Malaysian state oil company, Petronas, provides another fascinating case study of the impact of macro factors on credit spreads and default probabilities. Credit spreads on the U.S. dollar bonds issued by Petronas widened to over 600 basis points during the Asian crisis.

Regression analysis allows us to sort out the contributors to this deterioration in credit quality.

The results of a regression on 654 days of data show that four macro variables and a dummy variable were able to explain 90% of the variation in the credit spread of Petronas.

Figure 4.16   Petronas Credit Spread as a function of the Malaysian Ringgit

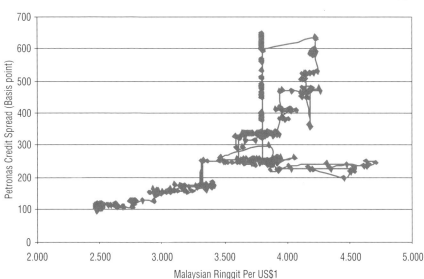

Table 4.8   Regression Analysis for Petronas

Regression Statistics	
Multiple R	0.95234
R Square	0.90696
Adjusted R Square	0.90624
Standard Error	58.60388
Observations	654

	Coefficients	Standard Error	t Stat
Intercept	1823.876	98.793	18.462
US Treasury	−19114.454	1074.101	−17.796
KL Stock Exchange	−0.128	0.062	−2.057
$/Barrel	−15.092	1.124	−13.427
MYR/$	−45.158	14.138	−3.194
Pegged FX	32.609	10.621	3.070

The macro factors were U.S. Treasury yields, Kuala Lumpur stock price levels, the U.S. Dollar price of oil, the Malaysian ringgit exchange rate, and a dummy variable for the part of the data set during which the Malaysian ringgit exchange rate was pegged at 3.80 ringgit to the U.S. Dollar. Again, macro factors are powerfully useful in understanding the market's perceptions of changes in Petronas's credit spread. We know this is closely (but not exactly) linked to the probability of default.

Implications for Credit Modeling

The casual empirism illustrated in this chapter has emphasized two key points:

- Firstly, macro factors seem to drive credit spreads, and by implication credit risk, in every one of the counterparty names that we have looked at, in Australia, Japan, Korea and the U.S.
- Secondly and perhaps more importantly, it appears that some of the implications of the Merton model (the relationship between stock prices and bond prices) are worthy of further testing. We now turn to an introduction to that testing process.

5

Internal Ratings and Approaches to Testing Credit Models[1]

In Chapters 1–3 we described three popular approaches to the modeling of credit risk:

- the Merton model;
- the Merton model with random interest rates (the Shimko, Tejima and van Deventer model) and;
- the Jarrow reduced form model.

In addition to these modeling approaches, every major financial institution has its own 'internal models' and some of the institutional counterparties to the financial institution have ratings from the major international rating agencies.

We have three basic practical questions that we need to answer:

- Are any of these methodologies better than random chance in ranking credit worthiness?
- If so, which method is the 'best'?
- More importantly, can we combine two or more approaches and get better results than using any one approach by itself?

The testing of the internal ratings approach used by major international banks will be required under the New Capital Accord proposed by the Basel Committee, therefore these three questions are important not only from a shareholder value perspective but also from a regulatory perspective. The ability to rapidly and accurate test the performance of a credit model

---

[1] This chapter is a substantially revised and expanded version of 'The New Capital Accord and Internal Bank Ratings,' by Donald R. van Deventer and Jaqueline Outram, Chapter 18, Credit Ratings: Methodologies, Rationale, and Default Risk, Michael Ong, editor, Risk Waters Group, London 2002.

substantially speeds up the process of achieving the objectives of credit risk management that we outlined in Chapter 1.

Purpose of Internal Ratings

Early in this book, we summarized the objectives of the credit risk process in a number of questions for which we need the answer:

(a) Should I make this loan? Undertake this derivatives transaction? Buy this bond? Yes or no?

(b) Should I sell this loan? Should I close out this derivatives transaction? Should I sell this bond? Yes or no?

(c) What broad classes of assets create the most shareholder value for our institution, given our own risk situation?

(d) What is the market value of my portfolio?

(e) What are the major risk factors driving the value of my loan, bond or derivatives portfolio?

(f) Am I as diversified as I could be? What change in risk-adjusted shareholder value-added results from a change in my current level of diversification?

(g) How can I hedge the risk of my portfolio?

(h) How much risk-adjusted value-added does this type of loan business (bond business, derivatives business) create for a strong institution? For my institution?

(i) Is Ms. X a good performer or a bad performer? How much risk-adjusted shareholder value did she create?

(j) How should this loan (bond, derivative) be priced to create shareholder value added for a strong institution? For my institution?

(k) From a credit policy perspective, how should I view the risk of the bank's loan portfolio given that economic conditions have recently changed?

(l) What should my loan loss reserve (reserve for credit losses on bonds, derivatives) be?

(m) Do I have enough capital in my institution to mazimize risk-adjusted shareholder value of the firm? Do I have enough in this business unit? What is the probability of default of my institution? Of this business unit?

As we noted in Chapter 1, the traditional financial institution's credit analysis has focused on questions (a) and, to a lesser extent, a proxy for (d), the value or current credit quality of the portfolio. Even if we restrict our interest only to these two issues, we need a concrete measure of the performance of all types of credit models that may be employed for these objectives. To a surprising degree, the same testing methodology can be used no matter what type of ratings technology the financial institution may be using.

Types of Internal Ratings

There are two basic categories of internal ratings used at major financial institutions:

- Ordinal rankings of risk without a valuation framework;
- Relative rankings of risk within a full (or partial) valuation framework.

The models we reviewed in Chapter 3 fall into the second category. The Merton and Shimko-Tejima-van Deventer structural models of credit risk provide relative credit rankings (the estimate of the default probability) within a partial valuation framework, because the models' assumptions restrict their applicability to zero-coupon bonds.[2] The Jarrow and other reduced form models provide relative rankings (the default intensity and related probability of default) within a full valuation framework applicable to a wide array of instruments.

Traditional credit risk analysis has emphasized ordinal rankings of risk using a ratings system that is not part of a general framework for valuation, pricing and hedging. These objectives can only be achieved by mapping the ordinal ranking to historical default probabilities in order to be useful in valuation, pricing and hedging. One of the difficulties in doing this is that the probabilities of default for companies within each ratings category are not stable over time, and they tend to differ across instruments despite the best efforts of financial institutions to apply a consistent risk definition to the rating. For instance, a retail borrower rated a '5' is likely to have a different default probability than a small business which is rated a '5'.

The three models we presented in Chapter 3 can be used as internal ratings. They produce default probabilities that provide ordinal rankings of risk, relative rankings of risk, and at least a partial framework for valuation, pricing and hedging. A relative ranking of risk does more than simply establish that Company A is riskier as a counterparty than Company B. A relative risk rating also shows how great the difference in risk is. We illustrate the differences in approach below.

---

[2] In practical application, we can 'stretch' the theory in an ad hoc way to use the model more widely. For instance, we could assume that the amount of debt that triggers bankruptcy is different at each maturity and use a series of Merton model zero-coupon bonds to model a coupon-bearing bond. This isn't good finance theory but it is a frequently committed sin in practice.

Ordinal Scale Credit Ratings

A representative of one of the world's largest banks stated recently that the most important issue in credit risk management was how many categories a bank should have in its internal modeling system. While the authors feel this is a mistaken emphasis on form over content, the comment is confirmation of the perceived importance of Ordinal Scale Credit Ratings in traditional bank ratings systems. A sample of such a ratings scale is given in Table 5.1 below:

Table 5.1 Ordinal Scale Credit Ratings

Rating	Explanation
1	In default with very little chance of recovery
2	In default with poor chance of recovery
3	In default with moderate chance of recovery
4	In default with good chance of recovery
5	Near default
6	Poor credit quality
7	Average credit quality
8	Good credit quality
9	Excellent credit quality normally only observed in the highest quality of large corporate borrowers
10	Highest possible credit quality normally only observed in high quality sovereign counterparties

The most important question about ordinal scale credit ratings is whether or not they work. Ordinal scale credit ratings have a number of conceptual virtues:

- They have a long history of practical application at most large banks;
- There is a large database of the migration of both individual credits and portfolio composition according to these ordinal credit ratings;
- The system is easy to understand and well understood by management.

Nonetheless, ordinal credit ratings have a number of liabilities:

- Regardless of the number of ratings categories, the bulk of bank counterparties are compressed into a small number of categories. In the example above, most bankers would lump their borrowers in credit ratings 6, 7 and 8, resulting in a scale that effectively has only three grades;
- The ratings are expensive to create;
- The ratings are time-consuming to create;

- The ratings are updated infrequently because of the high expense of credit review;
- The ratings are applied with varying strictness over time as personnel change-there is no 'grading on the curve' that insures a continuous percentile of borrowers in each category;
- The ratings provide no information on relative risk, pricing, hedging or valuation unless combined with some other information, using historical information on defaults;
- Even if the financial institution has a transition matrix consistent with these ordinal ratings, they provide no visibility on the macro risk drivers that are causing a correlated migration from one rating to another for a wide array of borrowers. We know from the examples in this chapter that understanding these macro risk drivers is probably the single most important issue in credit risk management, and ordinal credit ratings fail on that score.

In spite of these liabilities, ordinal scale credit ratings are more common than any other system in financial institutions around the world. They are very commonly used by third party credit information providers.

Do such ratings work in practice? The authors recently completed a study that covered more than one million small businesses over a 17-year period. More than 100,000 defaults occurred, and there was a total of 15.7 million observations in the sample. The authors found that the 20 ratings grades used by a major financial institution had very high statistical significance, with t-score equivalents of more than 40 for each ratings category. Normally, a t-score equivalent of 2 or more would be considered statistically significant by most analysts. Ordinal ratings are very effective in classifying risk levels—but they are not as helpful as other tools in dealing with the resulting credit risk. We have illustrated this in this chapter.

Rating Agency Ratings

Moody's Investors Service, Standard and Poor's Corporation and other well-known rating agencies around the world have been assigning credit ratings to major borrowers for decades. Table 4.6 summarizes the description of ratings and their interpretations at Standard and Poor's Corporation:

Table 5.2 Standard & Poor's Long-term Issuer Credit Ratings

AAA	An obligor rated 'AAA' has EXTREMELY STRONG capacity to meet its financial commitments. 'AAA' is the highest Issuer Credit Rating assigned by Standard & Poor's.
AA	An obligor rated 'AA' has VERY STRONG capacity to meet its financial commitments. It differs from the highest rated obligors only in small degree.
A	An obligor rated 'A' has STRONG capacity to meet its financial commitments but is somewhat more susceptible to the adverse effects of changes in circumstances and economic conditions than obligors in higher-rated categories.
BBB	An obligor rated 'BBB' has ADEQUATE capacity to meet its financial commitments. However, adverse economic conditions or changing circumstances are more likely to lead to a weakened capacity of the obligor to meet its financial commitments.
	Obligors rated 'BB', 'B', 'CCC', and 'CC' are regarded as having significant speculative characteristics. 'BB' indicates the least degree of speculation and 'CC' the highest. While such obligors will likely have some quality and protective characteristics, these may be outweighed by large uncertainties or major exposures to adverse conditions.
BB	An obligor rated 'BB' is LESS VULNERABLE in the near term than other lower-rated obligors. However, it faces major ongoing uncertainties and exposure to adverse business, financial, or economic conditions which could lead to the obligor's inadequate capacity to meet its financial commitments. B An obligor rated 'B' is MORE VULNERABLE than the obligors rated 'BB', but the obligor currently has the capacity to meet its financial commitments. Adverse business, financial, or economic conditions will likely impair the obligor's capacity or willingness to meet its financial commitments.
B	An obligation rated 'B' is more vulnerable to nonpayment than obligations rated 'BB', but the obligor currently has the capacity to meet its financial commitment on the obligation. Adverse business, financial, or economic conditions will likely impair the obligor's capacity or willingness to meet its financial commitment on the obligation.
CCC	An obligor rated 'CCC' is CURRENTLY VULNERABLE, and is dependent upon favorable business, financial, and economic conditions to meet its financial commitments.
CC	An obligor rated 'CC' is CURRENTLY HIGHLY-VULNERABLE. Plus (+) or minus(-) The ratings from 'AA' to 'CCC' may be modified by the addition of a plus or minus sign to show relative standing within the major rating categories.
C	A subordinated debt or preferred stock obligation rated 'C' is CURRENTLY HIGHLY VULNERABLE to nonpayment. The 'C' rating may be used to cover a situation where a bankruptcy petition has been filed or similar action taken, but payments on this obligation are being continued. A 'C' also will be assigned to a preferred stock issue in arrears on dividends or sinking fund payments, but that is currently paying.
R	An obligor rated 'R' is under regulatory supervision owing to its financial condition. During the pendency of the regulatory supervision the regulators may have the power to favor one class of obligations over others or pay some obligations and not others. Please see Standard & Poor's issue credit ratings for a more detailed description of the effects of regulatory supervision on specific issues or classes of obligations.
SD and D	An obligor rated 'SD' (Selective Default) or 'D' has failed to pay one or more of its financial obligations (rated or unrated) when it came due. A 'D' rating is assigned when Standard & Poor's believes that the default will be a general default and that the obligor will fail to pay all or substantially all of its obligations as they come due. An 'SD' rating is assigned when Standard & Poor's believes that the obligor has selectively defaulted on a specific issue or class of obligations but it will continue to meet its payment obligations on other issues or classes of obligations in a timely manner. Please see Standard & Poor's issue credit ratings for a more detailed description of the effects of a default on specific issues or classes of obligations.
N.R.	An issuer designated N.R. is not rated.

Van Deventer and Outram [2002] note that rating agency ratings are another form of ordinal scale ratings. They have the same virtues and vices of the ordinal scale ratings discussed in the previous section, plus these additional virtues:

- They cover a larger range of the major corporate market than most banks have in their portfolios, allowing risk analysis on potential as well as actual borrowers at the bank.
- They typically cover a longer history for each borrower than most banks would maintain for each borrower.
- They have international credibility because of the history of the rating agencies and extensive testing of their relative performance.
- They are derived independently of the conflicts of interest that may exist within an internal ratings process at a bank.

The liabilities of a rating agency ordinal rating in addition to those given in the prior section are important:

- Most of the bank counterparties will not have agency ratings because the bank counterparty is either too small or does not regularly issue the fixed income securities that require rating agency ratings.
- The bank has only limited visibility on the reasons for the ratings and the process by which they were derived.
- Most importantly, even the rating agency ratings provide no information on relative risk, pricing, hedging or valuation unless combined with some other information, using historical information on defaults.
- As noted above, rating agency ratings also provide no visibility on the macro risk drivers that cause default probabilities to change over time. They provide no visibility on the macro factors that cause correlated defaults and correlated movements in default probabilities prior to default.

We now turn to more quantitative measures of relative risk, which represent a significant supplement to traditional bank credit ratings.

Structural Models of Risky Debt

We can use the Merton and Shimko-Tejima-van Deventer model of risky debt discussed in Chapter 3 as internal ratings. The use of the default probabilities derived from these two models has a number of benefits compared to ordinal credit ratings long in use in the banking industry, as van Deventer and Outram [2002] note:

- Structural model default probabilities are much more 'precise' than ordinal credit rankings in that N borrowers will have N different credit ratings (except if the default probabilities of two or more companies are the same by coincidence) instead of the effective three or four credit grades from most banks' internal ordinal credit ranking systems. Precision and accuracy, however, are not necessarily the same, and we need to measure the difference.

- Structural model default probabilities are changed monthly by most institutions, on average much more frequently than banks would revise a traditional ordinal credit rating. The best financial institutions are using daily default probabilities for this purpose, recognizing that the higher frequency introduces some 'noise' in the process.

- Structural model default probabilities have a much lower marginal production cost than traditional ordinal credit ratings.

- Structural model default probabilities can be derived for all listed companies, a much larger universe of similarly sized companies than that for which a bank normally derives internal ordinal credit ratings (since the bank is typically lending to a small fraction of the listed company universe).

- The model for structural model default probability calculation is more likely to be used consistently over time than the consistency we can expect in the derivation of ordinal bank credit ratings, which have a much higher subjective component.

- The "rating" itself is intuitively understandable and clear—what could be a better rating than the probability of default itself?

- The structural model ratings are both ordinal (ranking borrowers from most risky to least risky) and relative, since knowing the default probability for companies A and B tells you both whether company A is more risky than company B and how much more risky one company is than the other. Ordinal credit ratings cannot make the amount of relative risk clear.

There are a number of concerns and potential concerns with the use of structural models, the magnitude for which must be determined. The methodology for doing this is the main purpose of this chapter. The potential concerns to be explored include the following:

- Accuracy needs to be measured objectively so that third parties (regulators, the audit committee of the Board of Directors, external auditors, etc.) can confirm.

- The single period nature of the Merton and STV models and the Merton assumption of constant interest rates are clearly approximations the significance of which needs to be measured. In

Chapter 4, we saw a number of cases where random interest rates are statistically significant determinants of the movements in bond credit spreads. In Chapter 7, we show that Enron credit spreads over a nine-year period also have interest rates as an important determining factor, therefore this source of potential inaccuracy is important.

- The macro factors driving the Merton and STV value of company assets and therefore default probabilities are not specified, nor is the formula by which they influence the value of company assets. This leaves a large gap in the model that needs to be addressed for practical pricing, hedging and valuation.

- As we mentioned earlier, both the Merton and STV models are single period pricing models that require considerable extension to realistically model most financial institutions credit products such as multi-payment loans, credit derivatives, lines of credit, callable debt, floating rate debt, etc.

We will use the tests in this chapter to determine whether these problems are a practical problem or merely a theoretical concern with no relevance in practice.

Reduced Form Models of Risky Debt

The Jarrow reduced form model and many closely related reduced form models by other authors can be used for internal ratings purposes as well. Reduced form credit rating models share many advantages with structural models used for rating purposes and they have some benefits unique to the reduced form modeling approach, as van Deventer and Outram; [2002] point out:

- Reduced form model default probabilities can be derived from credit derivatives prices and debt prices, perhaps the market sectors most sensitive to the risk of default and to the economic payoffs to debt holders in the event of default. Jarrow [2001] and Jarrow and Yildirum [2002] show how these derivations can be done.

- Reduced form model parameters can be fully derived from observable market prices. Reduced form models have much less parameter estimation risk (see Jarrow and van Deventer [1998, 1999]) than structural models, which have default probability estimates that depend on two parameters whose values cannot be derived from observable market prices. We discuss this issue in detail in later chapters.

- Reduced form models produce the same precision benefits in estimating default probabilities for use as ratings as structural models.

- Reduced form models can be used to estimate daily default probabilities.
- Reduced form model default probabilities have a much lower marginal cost than traditional ordinal credit ratings.
- Reduced form model default probabilities can be derived for all companies with traded debt or credit derivatives and using the Chava-Jarrow approach discussed below, for all companies with traded equity. This is a much larger universe than that for which a financial institution normally derives internal ordinal credit ratings.
- The model for reduced model default probability calculation is also more likely to be used consistently over time than the consistency we can expect in the derivation of ordinal bank credit ratings, which have a much higher subjective component.
- The "rating" itself is intuitively understandable and clear—again, the default probability is a rating with intuitive appeal.
- Like structural models of risky debt, reduced form models produce ratings that are both ordinal and relative ratings. We know from the default probabilities for companies A and B, which company is riskier and by what amount its risk is higher.
- Interest rates are random in the reduced form models, not constant.
- Reduced form models are multi-period models by definition.
- Reduced form models are part of a full valuation framework applicable to any capital structure and any number of payments
- Reduced form models imply hedging, pricing and valuation formulas.
- Reduced form models have an explicit formula by which macro factors such as interest rates and other factors (foreign exchange rates, oil prices) affect default probabilities.

On the negative side, reduced form models also have some drawbacks:

- As in the structural model case, we need to prove whether or not reduced form models have sufficient accuracy (in contrast to precision) for practical risk management at a performance level high enough to satisfy management, the Board of Directors, shareholders, and regulators
- Reduced form models are the most modern models making them less well known than either structural models or ordinal credit rating models.
- Reduced form model derivation is more powerful but more complex than other models.

Up until now, we have been discussing the kind of ratings technology that is usually applied to large entities, usually public for-profit corporations or government-related entities which are frequent bond issuers. We recognize, though, that retail borrowers and small business borrowers dominate the balance sheets of many financial institutions. We now turn to the kind of ratings technology that is usually applied to these small borrowers.

Credit Scoring and Hazard Rate Estimation and Their Implications for Retail and Small Business Ratings

Van Deventer and Outram [2002] note that structural models and reduced form models for the derivation of default probabilities depend on a small number of well-defined inputs: equity prices, bond prices, and credit derivatives prices. For small business and retail lending however, these inputs are not available but many other variables useful in predicting defaults are available. We noted earlier that the charge card balance of the president of a small business is the single best predictor of small business default. Credit scoring has the flexibility and power to combine diverse information about the borrower into a coherent and practical framework that results in a default probability estimate.

Van Deventer and Outram [2002] explain that credit scoring is a type of 'explicit estimation' of default probabilities from historical data on defaults and the explanatory variables. Reduced form and structural models use 'implicit estimation' from observable market prices to estimate default probabilities. In the derivation of a credit score, the ''best'' model is chosen to predict whether the borrower will default (default flag = 1) or not default (default flag = 0). The model must produce a probability, a number that must be greater than or equal to zero and less than or equal to one. In deriving the parameters of the equation to do this, the challenge is that the residuals or errors from this fitting process are not normally distributed. If the estimated probability of default for a particular counterparty is p, the error from this estimate will either be $0 - p$ (if the counterparty did not default) or $1 - p$ (if the counterparty did default). This is a binomial distribution of the error terms, not the normally distributed error terms that one normally assumes when fitting a traditional linear regression.

The most advanced formula that is currently used for this probability estimation is the logistic formula, which guarantees output will range in magnitude from zero to one. Maximum likelihood estimation is used to calculate the coefficients on each explanatory variable and its statistical significance. The 'maximum likelihood' parameters are those parameters that make the formula derived ''most likely'' to be consistent with the observable data.

This approach is used to do 'credit scoring' for retail clients and small business clients at most large financial institutions. Van Deventer and Outram [2002] explain that commercial vendors of credit scores often "scale" the default probability estimates by multiplying the default probability by a constant and adding an adjustment factor. In essence, the vendor is disguising the default probability just estimated.

Chava and Jarrow [2001a, 2001b] show, following Shumway [2001], how logistic regression can be used to refine estimates of reduced form default probabilities by combining observable market stock price data (relative stock price performance and stock price volatility) and accounting data over a data set containing all listed companies in the United States over a forty year period. The results of the Chava Jarrow exercise are reduced form default probabilities that can be used for pricing, hedging and valuation just like the Jarrow model default probability estimates implied from observable market prices for debt or credit derivatives.

Credit scoring and the logistic regression approach is a perfect complement to either the structural approach to credit ratings or the reduced form approach but it is most consistent with the reduced form modeling technique because the output of a credit scoring model can be used for pricing, valuation and hedging like any other reduced form default probability.

The key point in this section is that there is no reason to restrict our application of quantitative credit models to the large corporate and government entities that are the usual subjects of quantitative credit analysis. Advanced credit scoring and hazard rate modeling can be used and are being used at the retail and small business level as well. Therefore the credit model performance measurement that we are discussing in this chapter is relevant to borrowers of all sizes and descriptions.

Tests of Credit Models

Van Deventer and Outram [2002] have explained that the testing of credit models is in its early stages, but the statistical methodology that should be applied is well established. Almost of the testing methodology that is best applied to credit models comes from medical science, with a lesser amount coming from physics and electronics. In medicine, researchers seek to find the most likely causes of disease (and methods of disease prevention) based on a sample of M subjects, of which N are later infected. In the credit risk arena, there are a number of variables that may or may not explain default, and we need to determine which are the most powerful and whether there is value to using them in combination.

In this section, we use an expanded version of the hypothetical internal ratings discussed by van Deventer and Outram. We assume that a financial institution has compiled the following sample of companies, some of whom defaulted, and four types of ratings of those companies one year prior to default. The first type of rating is an internal bank rating, where 10 is the highest credit quality and 1 is the lowest. The second type of rating is a rating agency rating with AAA being the highest credit quality. The bank has converted the rating agency rankings to a numerical scale from 10 (best) to 1 (worst). Two other statistical ratings methodologies have been compiled, model 1 and model 2. Both models produce credit ratings in the form of default probabilities. The financial institution is facing the three questions we posed at the beginning of this chapter:

- Are any of these methodologies better than random chance in ranking credit worthiness?
- If so, which method is the 'best'?
- More importantly, can we combine two or more approaches and get better results than using any one approach by itself?

We will use this hypothetical data to show how credit models can be measured.

Table 5.3 below summarizes these hypothetical ratings methodologies for 30 companies in the sample. Nine defaulted and have a default index of 1. Twenty-one did not default and have a default index of zero.

Testing Methodologies Using Historical Defaults

The first test for determining the relative merit of the four methodologies is a test against the null hypothesis that each method has no explanatory power. As we have stated earlier, the first step is to prove that each of the internal ratings methodologies at least beats tossing a coin. A common test for this type of hypothesis on a relatively small sample is the chi-squared test, which is so commonly used that it is available in popular spreadsheet software.

Do Any of the Ratings Beat Random Chance: Chi-squared Test of Internal Bank Ratings

We first apply the test to internal bank ratings. The null hypothesis is that internal bank ratings are no better than random chance, which means that (if this hypothesis was true) the number of defaults in each ratings class would be the same percentage as default percentage in the sample as a whole, 9/30. We group the companies by internal rating and calculate the number of defaults we should expect in each ratings class if the internal ratings were merely random. This calculation is shown in Table 5.4 below:

Table 5.3 Hypothetical Ratings Methodologies

Number	Company	Bankruptcy Index	Internal Rating	Rating Agency	Rating Agency Numerical Rating	Model 1 Default Probability	Model 2 Default Probability
1	a	0	9	A-	9	0.140	0.450
2	b	0	9	A-	9	0.850	0.650
3	c	0	9	A-	9	0.160	0.260
4	d	0	9	A-	9	0.270	0.330
5	e	1	9	A-	9	3.560	1.790
6	f	0	9	BBB	8	0.790	0.650
7	g	0	9	BBB	8	0.390	0.430
8	h	0	8	BBB	8	0.460	0.590
9	I	0	8	BBB	8	0.570	0.750
10	j	1	8	BBB	8	4.250	2.540
11	k	0	9	A-	9	0.180	0.162
12	l	0	8	A-	9	0.230	0.207
13	m	0	8	BBB	8	0.350	0.315
14	n	0	8	BBB	8	0.360	0.324
15	o	0	7	BBB	8	0.340	0.306
16	p	0	7	BB	7	0.550	0.495
17	q	1	7	B	6	0.980	0.882
18	r	0	7	BB	7	1.060	0.954
19	s	0	7	BB	7	0.700	0.630
20	t	0	6	BB	7	0.760	0.684
21	v	1	6	BB	7	0.800	0.720
22	w	1	6	B	6	1.560	1.923
23	x	0	6	B	6	2.030	1.827
24	y	1	6	B	6	3.450	4.290
25	z	0	5	B	6	3.200	2.880
26	aa	0	5	Not rated	Not rated	4.030	3.627
27	ab	0	5	Not rated	Not rated	2.790	2.511
28	ac	1	5	Not rated	Not rated	3.650	5.782
29	ad	1	5	Not rated	Not rated	5.120	4.608
30	ae	1	5	Not rated	Not rated	6.780	6.102
	Defaults	9					

Table 5.4 Chi-Squared Test of Internal Ratings

Class Name	Defaults	Members	Expected Defaults
9	1	7	2.1
8	1	7	2.1
7	1	5	1.5
6	3	5	1.5
5	3	6	1.8
Total	9	30	9.0
Chi Squared Test			0.4600
Chi Squared Probability			0.9773

Chi-Squared Test of Internal Bank Ratings

There are seven companies rated 9, seven companies rated 8 and so on. Nine of the thirty companies defaulted. If the ratings system was the same as random chance, the number of defaults we would have expected in the "9-rated" class of companies is the number of firms in the class (seven) times 9/30, or 2.1 defaults. We apply this ratio to each class to get the number of defaults we would expect in each class.. The chi-squared statistic is the sum of the actual defaults in each class less the expected defaults in each class, squared and divided by the expected number of defaults. This total is 0.4600 for the internal bank ratings system, and this is better than random chance at a statistical significance level of 97.73%.

We repeat this test for the other methodologies.

Table 5.5 Chi-Squared Test of Rating Agency Ratings

Class Name	Defaults	Members	Expected Defaults
A-	1	7	2.1
BBB	1	8	2.4
BB	1	5	1.5
B	3	5	1.5
Not Rated	3	5	1.5
Total	9	30	9.0
Chi Squared Test			0.3355
Chi Squared Probability			0.9874

Rating agency ratings were better than the null hypothesis of randomness at the 98.74% level of statistical significance.

Model 1 is tested in the same way, but since we don't have ratings 'classes,' we create them by ranking the companies by riskiness and dividing the companies into quintiles (with more data, deciles are a more common choice).

Table 5.6 Chi-squared Test of Model 1

Class Name	Defaults	Members	Expected Defaults
Quintile 1	0	6	1.8
Quintile 2	0	6	1.8
Quintile 3	2	6	1.8
Quintile 4	2	6	1.8
Quintile 5	5	6	1.8
Total	9	30	9.0
Chi Squared Test			0.0533
Chi Squared Probability			0.9997

Model 1 is better than random chance with a statistical significance of 99.97%.

Model 2 is tested in the same way and is better than random chance with a statistical significance of 99.80%.

Table 5.7 Chi-squared Test of Model 2

Class Name	Defaults	Members	Expected Defaults
Quintile 1	0	6	1.8
Quintile 2	0	6	1.8
Quintile 3	2	6	1.8
Quintile 4	3	6	1.8
Quintile 5	4	6	1.8
Total	9	30	9.0
Chi Squared Test			0.1301
Chi Squared Probability			0.9980

We have succeeded in answering the first of the three questions posed at the beginning of the chapter:

> *Are any of these methodologies better than random chance in ranking credit worthiness?*

The answer is definitive: Yes, they are all better than random chance. We can now turn to the second question we posed initially:

> *If so, which method is the 'best'?*

Which Model is Best?

One common credit ranking method is to rank the credit models by the statistical significance with which they perform better than the null hypothesis of randomness. By this criteria, Model 1 is the superior methodology but by a narrow margin. It is better than random chance at the 0.03% level. All of the methodologies beat random chance at the commonly selected 5% level of statistical significance.

We now turn to another important method for ranking the performance of credit models.

Table 5.8 Ranking by Statistical Significance

Rating Technique	Chi-squared Value	Statistical Significance	P-Test
Model 1	0.0533	99.97%	0.03%
Model 2	0.1301	99.80%	0.20%
Rating Agency Ratings	0.3355	98.74%	1.26%
Internal Ratings	0.4600	97.73%	2.27%

Mann-Whitney U Test/ROC Accuracy Ratio Test of Internal Bank Ratings

Another popular methodology for testing rankings goes by two different names but in fact the concepts are closely related. The Mann-Whitney U test and the receiver operating characteristic (ROC) accuracy ratio are common ways of comparing models in medical science and they have been used more and more frequently in finance. 'Receiver operating characteristic' curves were originally developed to better understand the signal to noise ratio in radio receivers. The ROC accuracy ratio is usually depicted as the area under the 'ROC curve.' We will use the term ROC curve throughout this book, because that is the standard term in statistics. More informal names that are sometimes used in finance are the 'power curve' or the 'cumulative accuracy profile.' The latter concept is closely related but slightly different from the ROC accuracy ratio.

Later in this section, we show how to calculate the ROC accuracy ratio based on the area under the ROC curve. There is a more intuitive explanation, however, that we will illustrate first. This method and measuring the area under the curve produce identical results:[3]

The ROC accuracy ratio results are based on a comparison of performance that works like this:

1. Take all possible pairs of companies, one of which defaulted and one of which did not default;
2. Compare the rating of the two companies in the pair;
3. Give one point if the company which did not default is rated as the better credit, one half point if the two companies are rated the same, and zero points if the defaulted company is rated as the better credit;
4. Add up all the possible points;
5. Divide by the maximum number of points possible (which is equal to the number of pairs).

---

[3] For a more detailed explanation of why these methods are equivalent, see Chapter 5 of *Applied Logistic Regression* by Hosmer and Lemeshow.

This intuitively appealing method of model testing has the following implications:

- A perfect model will have a score of 100;
- A model which is no better than random chance will have a score of 50, because someone tossing a coin could earn a score of 50.

The 'best model' is the model that has the highest ROC score. Note the power of this technique-it involves the use of every single data point or credit rating available in the study. There is no data wasted and there is no data mining. In the study, the authors mentioned earlier, default probabilities were estimated for a sample that included observations on approximately 1 million small businesses annually for more than 15 years, and there were approximately 100,000 defaults during that period. The total number of observations (or credit ratings) was 15.7 million. Calculating the ROC curve in that case (which we do religiously in every model study) involves making 1.56 trillion (i.e. $100,000 \times 15.6$ million) pairs of default probabilities.[4] While this sounds tedious, in modern software it is a standard feature and the total calculation time on a high quality personal computer at the time of writing is less than 30 minutes.

The following section illustrates how the ROC accuracy ratio for internal bank ratings is calculated using our sample data.

Table 5.8 above shows how to calculate the ROC ratio for the internal bank ratings. Each row represents one of the bankrupt companies in our sample data set, 9 in all. Each column represents one of the 21 companies that did not go bankrupt. The intersection of each row and column contains the number of points for that pair. For instance, the first column combines company *a* (which did not go bankrupt) with company *e* (which did go bankrupt). Both companies had an internal rating of 9, so we give that pair 0.5 points for a 'tie.' In the second row, but still in the first column, we pair companies *a* and *j*. Company *a* was rated a 9 and company *j* was rated an 8. Since company *j* defaulted and it correctly had a weaker credit rating than company a, we give 1.0 points for that pair. We repeat this for all $9 \times 21 = 189$ pairs. The total number of points is 136.5 out of a possible 189 points, for an ROC accuracy ratio of 72.22. This falls into the 'pretty good' category.

We repeat this for the rating agency ratings, which we have converted to a numerical ranking to ease the comparison.

---

[4] 15.6 million is the total number of observations 15.7 million less the number of defaults (100,000), giving the number of observations which were non-defaulting companies at the time the default probability was calculated.

Table 5.8 ROC Ratio for Internal Bank Ratings

		ROC Accuracy Ratio/Mann-Whitney U Test for Internal Ratings Approach Companies that Did Not Go Bankrupt																				
Bankrupt Companies		Company	a	b	c	d	f	g	h	i	k	l	m	n	o	p	r	s	t	x	z	aa	ab
		Internal Rating	9	9	9	9	9	9	8	8	9	8	8	8	7	7	7	7	6	6	5	5	5
Company	Internal Rating	Count of Pairs for Which Rating Was More Risky for Company Which Went Bankrupt																				
e	9		0.5	0.5	0.5	0.5	0.5	0.5	0.0	0.0	0.5	0.0	0.0	0.0	0.0	0.0	0.0	0.0	0.0	0.0	0.0	0.0	0.0
j	8		1.0	1.0	1.0	1.0	1.0	1.0	0.5	0.5	1.0	0.5	0.5	0.5	0.0	0.0	0.0	0.0	0.0	0.0	0.0	0.0	0.0
q	7		1.0	1.0	1.0	1.0	1.0	1.0	1.0	1.0	1.0	1.0	1.0	1.0	0.5	0.5	0.5	0.5	0.0	0.0	0.0	0.0	0.0
v	6		1.0	1.0	1.0	1.0	1.0	1.0	1.0	1.0	1.0	1.0	1.0	1.0	1.0	1.0	1.0	1.0	0.5	0.5	0.0	0.0	0.0
w	6		1.0	1.0	1.0	1.0	1.0	1.0	1.0	1.0	1.0	1.0	1.0	1.0	1.0	1.0	1.0	1.0	0.5	0.5	0.0	0.0	0.0
y	6		1.0	1.0	1.0	1.0	1.0	1.0	1.0	1.0	1.0	1.0	1.0	1.0	1.0	1.0	1.0	1.0	0.5	0.5	0.0	0.0	0.0
ac	5		1.0	1.0	1.0	1.0	1.0	1.0	1.0	1.0	1.0	1.0	1.0	1.0	1.0	1.0	1.0	1.0	1.0	1.0	0.5	0.5	0.5
ad	5		1.0	1.0	1.0	1.0	1.0	1.0	1.0	1.0	1.0	1.0	1.0	1.0	1.0	1.0	1.0	1.0	1.0	1.0	0.5	0.5	0.5
ae	5		1.0	1.0	1.0	1.0	1.0	1.0	1.0	1.0	1.0	1.0	1.0	1.0	1.0	1.0	1.0	1.0	1.0	1.0	0.5	0.5	0.5
Subtotal			8.5	8.5	8.5	8.5	8.5	8.5	7.5	7.5	8.5	7.5	7.5	7.5	6.5	6.5	6.5	6.5	4.5	4.5	1.5	1.5	1.5

Total Count 136.50
ROC Percentage 0.7222
Number of Pairs 189.00

Table 5.9 ROC Ratio for Rating Agency Ratings

		ROC Accuracy Ratio/Mann-Whitney U Test for Rating Agency Ratings — Companies that Did Not Go Bankrupt																				
Bankrupt Companies		Company	a	b	c	d	f	g	h	i	k	l	m	n	o	p	r	s	t	x	z	aa	ab
		Rating	9	9	9	9	8	8	8	8	9	9	8	8	8	7	7	7	7	6	6	Not rated	Not rated
Company	Rating	Count of Pairs for Which Rating Was More Risky for Company Which Went Bankrupt																				
e	9		0.5	0.5	0.5	0.5	0.5	0.5	0.0	0.0	0.5	0.0	0.0	0.0	0.0	0.0	0.0	0.0	0.0	0.0	0.0	0.0	0.0
e	9		0.5	0.5	0.5	0.5	0.0	0.0	0.0	0.0	0.5	0.5	0.0	0.0	0.0	0.0	0.0	0.0	0.0	0.0	0.0	0.0	0.0
j	8		1.0	1.0	1.0	1.0	0.5	0.5	0.5	0.5	1.0	1.0	0.5	0.5	0.5	0.0	0.0	0.0	0.0	0.0	0.5	0.0	0.0
q	6		1.0	1.0	1.0	1.0	1.0	1.0	1.0	1.0	1.0	1.0	1.0	1.0	1.0	1.0	1.0	1.0	1.0	0.5	0.0	0.0	0.0
v	7		1.0	1.0	1.0	1.0	1.0	1.0	1.0	1.0	1.0	1.0	1.0	1.0	1.0	0.5	0.5	0.5	0.5	0.0	0.5	0.0	0.0
w	6		1.0	1.0	1.0	1.0	1.0	1.0	1.0	1.0	1.0	1.0	1.0	1.0	1.0	1.0	1.0	1.0	1.0	0.5	0.5	0.0	0.0
y	6		1.0	1.0	1.0	1.0	1.0	1.0	1.0	1.0	1.0	1.0	1.0	1.0	1.0	1.0	1.0	1.0	1.0	0.5	0.5	0.0	0.0
ac	Not rated		0.0	0.0	0.0	0.0	0.0	0.0	0.0	0.0	0.0	0.0	0.0	0.0	0.0	0.0	0.0	0.0	0.0	0.0	0.0	0.0	0.0
ad	Not rated		0.0	0.0	0.0	0.0	0.0	0.0	0.0	0.0	0.0	0.0	0.0	0.0	0.0	0.0	0.0	0.0	0.0	0.0	0.0	0.0	0.0
ae	Not rated		0.0	0.0	0.0	0.0	0.0	0.0	0.0	0.0	0.0	0.0	0.0	0.0	0.0	0.0	0.0	0.0	0.0	0.0	0.0	0.0	0.0
Subtotal			5.5	5.5	5.5	5.5	4.5	4.5	4.5	4.5	5.5	5.5	4.5	4.5	4.5	3.5	3.5	3.5	3.5	1.5	1.5	0.0	0.0

Total Count   81.50
ROC Percentage   0.7149
Number of Pairs   114.00

Table 5.9 shows the calculation of the ROC accuracy ratio for rating agency ratings, which are analyzed in their numerical ordinal ranking equivalent. Note that we only had $6 \times 19 = 114$ pairs because 3 of the 9 defaulting companies were not rated and 2 of the 21 non-defaulting companies were not rated. The accuracy ratio is 71.49% for this hypothetical rating agency example.

Table 5.10 shows that Model 1 has an ROC accuracy ratio of 90.48, scoring 171 points out of a possible $9 \times 21 = 189$ pairs. Table 5.11 shows that Model 2 produces an ROC accuracy ratio of 89.42%.

Table 5.12 summarizes the performance of all four approaches to internal bank ratings. Model 1 is the best performer by a narrow margin over Model 2. The internal bank ratings and rating agency ratings lag behind.

When doing historical studies of default and testing on that basis, the Mann-Whitney U Test/ROC accuracy ratio comparison of models is very powerful. The test uses every single rating produced for all companies for all periods as the basis for the test. There is no data mining and there is no bias from the data selected. The pair-wise calculation of the ratio itself has an intuitive appeal and a simplicity that even senior management can understand. For that reason, the accuracy ratio deserves to be elevated to senior management's attention as the primary historically based test of credit model performance for the Basel II accord. There are other tests using market data that are also very powerful. We discuss then in later chapters.

Graphical Depiction of ROC Accuracy Ratios

The receiver operating characteristics curve and the area under it (the ROC ratio) are rapidly making their way from medical statistics to finance. Their use in finance has been hindered by the lack of a plain English explanation of what the curves represent and compounded by frequent errors in explanation. The authors believe that the presentation of the calculation of ROC accuracy ratios in the previous section is very simple to do and simple to explain. We believe the graphical depiction of the same phenomenon 'becomes intuitive' only over longer time frame, and we don't recommend this means of exposition to anyone but those who have seen the curves over and over. Finally, we believe that a depiction of the curve without a revelation of the accuracy ratio is indicative that the analyst has something to hide. Caveat emptor!

With that cautionary paragraph out of the way, let's examine a common way of depicting the ROC accuracy ratios and the associated ROC curves that we discussed in the previous section. Figure 5.1 shows a typical ROC curve that might be used in ROC analysis.

Table 5.10 ROC Ratio for Model 1

ROC Accuracy Ratio/Mann-Whitney U Test for Model 1
Companies that Did Not Go Bankrupt

Company	a	b	c	d	f	g	h	i	k	l	m	n	o	p	r	s	t	x	z	aa	ab
Model 1	0.14	0.85	0.16	0.27	0.79	0.39	0.46	0.57	0.18	0.23	0.35	0.36	0.34	0.55	1.06	0.70	0.76	2.03	3.20	4.03	2.79

Count of Pairs for Which Rating Was More Risky for Company Which Went Bankrupt

Company (Bankrupt)	Model 1	a	b	c	d	f	g	h	i	k	l	m	n	o	p	r	s	t	x	z	aa	ab
e	3.56	1.0	1.0	1.0	1.0	1.0	1.0	1.0	1.0	1.0	1.0	1.0	1.0	1.0	1.0	1.0	1.0	1.0	1.0	1.0	0.0	1.0
j	4.25	1.0	1.0	1.0	1.0	1.0	1.0	1.0	1.0	1.0	1.0	1.0	1.0	1.0	1.0	1.0	1.0	1.0	1.0	1.0	1.0	1.0
q	0.98	1.0	1.0	1.0	1.0	1.0	1.0	1.0	1.0	1.0	1.0	1.0	1.0	1.0	1.0	0.0	1.0	1.0	0.0	0.0	0.0	0.0
v	0.80	1.0	0.0	1.0	1.0	1.0	1.0	1.0	1.0	1.0	1.0	1.0	1.0	1.0	1.0	0.0	1.0	1.0	0.0	0.0	0.0	0.0
w	1.56	1.0	1.0	1.0	1.0	1.0	1.0	1.0	1.0	1.0	1.0	1.0	1.0	1.0	1.0	1.0	1.0	1.0	0.0	0.0	0.0	0.0
y	3.45	1.0	1.0	1.0	1.0	1.0	1.0	1.0	1.0	1.0	1.0	1.0	1.0	1.0	1.0	1.0	1.0	1.0	1.0	1.0	0.0	1.0
ac	3.65	1.0	1.0	1.0	1.0	1.0	1.0	1.0	1.0	1.0	1.0	1.0	1.0	1.0	1.0	1.0	1.0	1.0	1.0	1.0	0.0	1.0
ad	5.12	1.0	1.0	1.0	1.0	1.0	1.0	1.0	1.0	1.0	1.0	1.0	1.0	1.0	1.0	1.0	1.0	1.0	1.0	1.0	1.0	1.0
ae	6.78	1.0	1.0	1.0	1.0	1.0	1.0	1.0	1.0	1.0	1.0	1.0	1.0	1.0	1.0	1.0	1.0	1.0	1.0	1.0	1.0	1.0
Subtotal		9.0	8.0	9.0	9.0	9.0	9.0	9.0	9.0	9.0	9.0	9.0	9.0	9.0	9.0	7.0	9.0	9.0	6.0	6.0	3.0	6.0

Total Count	171.00
ROC Percentage	0.9048
Number of Pairs	189.00

Table 5.11 ROC Ratio for Model 2

ROC Accuracy Ratio/Mann-Whitney U Test for Model 2
Companies that Did Not Go Bankrupt

Company	a	b	c	d	f	g	h	i	k	l	m	n	o	p	r	s	t	x	z	aa	ab
Model 2	0.45	0.65	0.26	0.33	0.65	0.43	0.59	0.75	0.16	0.21	0.32	0.32	0.31	0.50	0.95	0.63	0.68	1.83	2.88	3.63	2.51

Count of Pairs for Which Rating Was More Risky for Company Which Went Bankrupt

Bankrupt Companies — Company	Model 2	a	b	c	d	f	g	h	i	k	l	m	n	o	p	r	s	t	x	z	aa	ab
e	1.79	1.0	1.0	1.0	1.0	1.0	1.0	1.0	1.0	1.0	1.0	1.0	1.0	1.0	1.0	1.0	1.0	1.0	0.0	0.0	0.0	0.0
j	2.54	1.0	1.0	1.0	1.0	1.0	1.0	1.0	1.0	1.0	1.0	1.0	1.0	1.0	1.0	1.0	1.0	1.0	1.0	0.0	0.0	1.0
q	0.88	1.0	1.0	1.0	1.0	1.0	1.0	1.0	1.0	1.0	1.0	1.0	1.0	1.0	1.0	1.0	1.0	1.0	0.0	0.0	0.0	0.0
v	0.72	1.0	1.0	1.0	1.0	1.0	1.0	1.0	1.0	1.0	1.0	1.0	1.0	1.0	1.0	1.0	1.0	1.0	0.0	0.0	0.0	0.0
w	1.92	1.0	1.0	1.0	1.0	1.0	1.0	1.0	0.0	1.0	1.0	1.0	1.0	1.0	1.0	0.0	1.0	1.0	1.0	0.0	0.0	0.0
y	4.29	1.0	1.0	1.0	1.0	1.0	1.0	1.0	1.0	1.0	1.0	1.0	1.0	1.0	1.0	0.0	1.0	1.0	1.0	1.0	1.0	1.0
ac	5.78	1.0	1.0	1.0	1.0	1.0	1.0	1.0	1.0	1.0	1.0	1.0	1.0	1.0	1.0	1.0	1.0	1.0	1.0	1.0	1.0	1.0
ad	4.61	1.0	1.0	1.0	1.0	1.0	1.0	1.0	1.0	1.0	1.0	1.0	1.0	1.0	1.0	1.0	1.0	1.0	1.0	1.0	1.0	1.0
ae	6.10	1.0	1.0	1.0	1.0	1.0	1.0	1.0	1.0	1.0	1.0	1.0	1.0	1.0	1.0	1.0	1.0	1.0	1.0	1.0	1.0	1.0
Subtotal		9.0	9.0	9.0	9.0	9.0	9.0	9.0	8.0	9.0	9.0	9.0	9.0	9.0	9.0	7.0	9.0	9.0	6.0	4.0	4.0	5.0

Total Count	169.00
ROC Percentage	0.8942
Number of Pairs	189.00

Table 5.12 Ranking of models by ROC ratio

Credit Modeling Technique	ROC Accuracy Ratio
Model 1	0.9048
Model 2	0.8942
Internal Ratings	0.7222
Rating Agency	0.7149

Figure 5.1 ROC curve

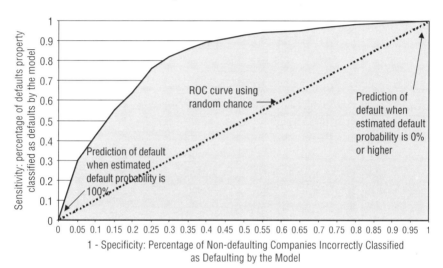

The left hand side of the graph is the proportion of defaults that are correctly 'predicted' as defaults by the ratings technology. The statisticians call this 'sensitivity'—the percentage of the 'positive' (i.e. default occurring, or the bankruptcy index = 1) results that we correctly classify. The horizontal axis is the percentage of the 'non-defaulting' companies that we incorrectly predict to default. To statisticians, 'specificity' is the percentage of the 'negative' results (i.e. default not occurring, or the bankruptcy index = 0) that we correctly classify. Here we want to know 1-specificity: the percentage of non-defaulting companies that we mistakenly forecast to default.

How do we get each point on the ROC curve? It's easiest to see using a specific example, illustrated in Table 5.13 below.

In Table 5.13 above we have created what is called a 'classification table.' The steps involved are as follows:

- Step 1 in creating a classification table is taking your credit rating model, in this case Model 1 from our hypothetical example, and

Table 5.13 Calculating One Point on the ROC Curve

Number	Company	Bankruptcy Index	Model 1 Default Probability
1	a	0	0.140
3	c	0	0.160
11	k	0	0.180
12	l	0	0.230
4	d	0	0.270
15	o	0	0.340
13	m	0	0.350
14	n	0	0.360
7	g	0	0.390
8	h	0	0.460
16	p	0	0.550
9	l	0	0.570
19	s	0	0.700
20	t	0	0.760
6	f	0	0.790
2	b	0	0.850
18	r	0	1.060
23	x	0	2.030
27	ab	0	2.790
25	z	0	3.200
26	aa	0	4.030
21	v	1	0.800
17	q	1	0.980
22	w	1	1.560
24	y	1	3.450
5	e	1	3.560
28	ac	1	3.650
10	j	1	4.250
29	ad	1	5.120
30	ae	1	6.780

Analysis of "Predicted Defaults"

Total Number of Non-Defaulters	21
Total Number of Defaults:	9
Cut-off for "Predicting Default":	1.000
Number of Companies Predicted To Default	
Among Non-Defaulters:	5
Among Actual Defaulters:	7
Total Predicted to Default	12
% of Defaulters Correctly Predicted:	**77.78%**
% of Non-Defaulters Predicted to Default	**23.81%**

ranking the data in order by both the bankruptcy index (0 = non default, 1 = default) and by the estimated credit ranking, in this case the Model 1 default probability.

- The next step is to choose a 'cutoff,' a ratings level which draws the line between those companies we believe will not default and those companies we believe will default. In this example, we have chosen a default probability of 1.0% as the cutoff.

- Next, we segment the data into four groups: The companies which defaulted and had default probabilities greater than one (correct predictions of default), companies which defaulted and had default probabilities less than one (incorrect predictions of non-default), companies which did not default and had default probabilities less than one (correct predictions of non-default), and companies which did not default and had default probabilities of more than one (incorrect predictions of default)

- We then know that we correctly predicted 7 of the 9 companies that did default. This gives us 7/9 = 77.78% on the vertical axis.

- We also know that we incorrectly predicted that 5 of the 21 non-defaulters would default, giving us 23.81% on the horizontal axis.

- This gives us one point on the ROC curve, the x, y pair of (23.81, 77.78)

- We draw the entire curve by varying the cutoff from zero (which is the upper right hand corner of the ROC curve) to 100% default probability (which gives us the lower left hand corner of the graph).

The area under the ROC curve, in blue, is the ROC accuracy ratio. In the authors' opinion, this is a much more convoluted way to get the accuracy ratio than the pair-wise comparison of the previous section. Once you understand the intuition of the curve, it becomes more sensible. We want the ratings model with the most area under the curve. The more the curve bends toward the upper left hand corner of the graph, the better the model is.[5]

There are a few more properties of the ROC curve that are worth summarizing:

- A model no better than random chance has an ROC curve which is identical to the straight line running from the lower left hand corner of the graph to the upper right hand corner.

- The ROC accuracy ratio is the blue area, not the blue area above this 45-degree line as is sometimes argued.

---

[5] Hosmer and Lemeshow, *Applied Logistic Regression*, have an excellent explanation of this approach in Chapter 5.

The ROC curve must always be monotonically increasing (i.e. it never declines) as you move from left to right. Again, ROC curves are sometimes mistakenly depicted as wavering, due to a misunderstanding of the concept. We can see this by moving the cut-off from 1% to a higher number. The number of defaults we correctly classify can only decline when we do this, and the number of non-defaults that we incorrectly classify can only decrease. If we had started with a zero cutoff, in the upper right hand corner of the curve, we would move steadily downward, finally reaching the lower left hand corner, by raising the cutoff in steps to 100%.

Now that we have mastered the basics, we will use the ROC curve and the ROC accuracy ratio frequently in the following chapters.

Are the Models in Combination More Powerful than any Single Model?

The previous section was focused on the simplest type of credit model testing: Is Model A better than Model B, based on a historical sample of defaulted and non-defaulted companies? There are many other more sophisticated questions that can be answered with state-of-the-art credit model testing technology. The following are the kinds of questions that analysts can definitively answer, as van Deventer and Outram [2002] pointed out:

- Does the use of Model 2 default probabilities with accounting data improve our ability to predict default?
- How do we combine rating agency ratings, internal ordinal ratings, and a default probability model to produce maximum accuracy in predicting default?
- Does market data, when combined with various credit models, improve our ability to predict default?
- Is it more accurate to use a combination of credit models for default prediction or to use just one?
- How can I convert an ordinal credit rating to a default probability?

The tool for answering these kinds of questions is logistic regression. Logistic regression was introduced above as a methodology for forecasting defaults using consumer or small business data, but it is equally powerful as a testing tool. There are two tests that are common outputs of logistic regression.

Likelihood Ratio Test Statistic

The likelihood ratio test statistic, sometimes called deviance, is somewhat like comparing the adjusted R^2, the most common measure of explanatory power, of two linear regressions. The likelihood ratio test statistic compares two logistic regressions. We call the first logistic regression the base regression, which we denote by the subscript 0. The second logistic regression considers the addition of variable j to the set of variables already represented in the base regression 0. In logistic regression, all common logistic regressions produce a number which represents the 'likelihood' that the observed data is consistent with the parameters fitted in that model. To calculate whether variable j adds explanatory power to our ability to explain default, we calculate as follows:

$$D = -2[\ln(\text{likelihood of base regression 0})$$
$$- \ln(\text{likelihood of new regression with variable } j \text{ added})]$$

The statistic D has a chi-squared distribution with 1 degree of freedom if the new variable is continuous (like a series of default probabilities) or $k - 1$ degrees of freedom if the variable is ordinal like a rating agency rating or an internal rating. For example, if an internal rating has 10 categories, there would be 9 degrees of freedom in measuring the statistical significance of variable j to the new regression. We input the internal ratings as 9 dummy variables, one for each rating category except the last one (or we can use 10 dummy variables and eliminate the constant term from the logistic regression). The null hypothesis that the new variable has no explanatory power is rejected at some target probability level p, say 5%, then it is said that the new variable j adds to our ability to predict default. For more on logistic regression, see Hosmer and Lemeshow [2000].

We can do this analysis to answer the third question that we posed at the beginning of this chapter:

- Can we combine two or more approaches and get better results than using any one approach by itself?

Table 5.14 below shows how we use the ratio D, the likelihood ratio chi-squared test, to answer this question for the four hypothetical credit modeling techniques we have been testing in this chapter.

As we outlined above, there are a number of steps in asking whether a second model, added to a base model, adds explanatory power:

1. We fit a logistic regression to each of the four ratings modeling technologies. The top of the table above shows the results of doing that. We get the ROC ratios we discussed previously, and we get the 'D' statistic for each of the models, which is the D statistic compared to the base model using the constant only. In each regression, we get the 'log likelihood,' the natural log of the 'likelihood' that the model

Table 5.14 Comparison of Likelihood Ratios

	Internal Ratings	Agency Ratings	Model 1	Model 2
Number of Observations	30	30	30	30
Likelihood Ratio Chi-Squared	6.42	5.16	12.3	11.79
Significant for p =	17.01%	27.08%	0.05%	0.06%
Log likelihood	−15.117104	−15.743482	−12.175599	−12.429988
Wald ratios on main variable(s)	−1.55	−1.45	2.82	2.62
	−1.67	−1.18		
	−1.24	−1		
	0	0.33		
ROC Accuracy Ratio	0.7381	0.754	0.9048	0.8942

Base Model Before Adding Second Model

Log likelihood after adding	Internal Ratings	Agency Ratings	Model 1	Model 2
Internal Ratings	na	−13.644174	−8.385806	−7.2659047
Agency Ratings	−13.644174	na	−10.701914	−10.409279
Model 1	−8.385806	−10.701914	na	−12.03326
Model 2	−7.2659047	−10.409279	−12.03326	na
Degrees of Freedom	4	4	1	1

Likelihood Ratio Chi-Squared	Internal Ratings	Agency Ratings	Model 1	Model 2
Internal Ratings	na	4.198616	7.579586	10.3281666
Agency Ratings	2.94586	na	2.94737	4.041418
Model 1	13.462596	10.083136	na	0.793456
Model 2	15.7023986	10.668406	0.284678	na

Likelihood Ratio Chi-Squared P-Test	Internal Ratings	Agency Ratings	Model 1	Model 2
Internal Ratings	na	37.98%	0.59%	0.13%
Agency Ratings	56.69%	na	8.60%	4.44%
Model 1	0.92%	3.91%	na	37.31%
Model 2	0.34%	3.06%	59.37%	na

fits the data. This statistic is produced by all standard logistic regression software.

2. We then add a second model (internal ratings, agency ratings, model 1 or model 2) to the first model. In the bottom of the table, we show the log likelihood of the new combined models, the D statistic (likelihood ratio chi-squared), and the statistical significance (the 'p-test') of adding the second model. For example, the 'internal ratings' approach had a log likelihood of -15.117 by itself. When model 2 is added to the logistic regression, the combined model has a log likelihood of -7.266. This produces a D ratio of 15.702. This is statistically a significant increase in explanatory power at the 0.34% level, or put differently, it has statistical significance of 99.66%. Normally, a statistician would look for significance at the 5.00% or less (95% or more) so most analysts would conclude that adding model 2 to the internal model improves the ability to predict default very significantly.

In the table, we have shaded the model additions that improve explanatory power at the 5% level of statistical significance. We conclude:

* Model 1 and Model 2 both add explanatory power to the internal bank ratings approach;
* Model 1 and Model 2 also both add explanatory power to the rating agency ratings;
* Adding internal bank ratings to Model 1 improves its explanatory power;
* Adding both internal ratings and rating agency ratings to Model 2 adds its explanatory power.

We can rank the combined models using the ROC accuracy ratio, as we did above, or by the chi-squared test of significance versus the assumption that the combined model has no explanatory power. This produces the

Table 5.15 'P-Test' for the combination of credit models

Combination of 2 Credit Models:		p-Test
Model 2	Internal Ratings	0.05%
Model 1	Internal Ratings	0.13%
Model 1	Model 2	0.18%
Model 2	Rating Agency	0.73%
Model 1	Rating Agency	0.94%
Internal Ratings	Rating Agency	31.26%

'p-test' (not shown in Table 5.14) for the combined model, and statistical significance at the smallest level of probability denotes the best model. This test ranks the models from best to worst as follows.

The combination of Model 2 and internal ratings is statistically better than random chance even at the very high 0.05% statistical significance, meaning that we can reject the hypothesis that the model is no better than random chance with 99.95% confidence. The combination of Model 1 and internal ratings is almost as good, since it is statistically significant at the 0.13% level. Finally, Model 1 and Model 2 in combination round out the top three combinations, coming in at the 0.18% level of statistical significance.

In a similar way, we can now turn to each of our hypothetical questions to put this kind of analysis to use on a practical basis.

Does the Use of Model 2 Default Probabilities with Accounting Data Improve our Ability to Predict Default?

Just as we saw in the example above, we run the base regression 0, which has Model 2 default probabilities as the only input. We use the logistic regression formula to predict default with Model 2 default probabilities to get the base regression 0 and its likelihood. We then add accounting data one by one. Let the ratio of net income to assets be the first candidate variable. Logistic regression j then becomes the logistic regression with the Model 2 default probabilities and this accounting ratio as the only two inputs. We calculate the likelihood of this logistic regression and test the statistical significance of the improvement in our ability to explain default. If the improvement is significant, we have definitively answered this question. For examples of studies which have found that accounting data improves the explanatory variable of equity based default models, see Shumway [2001], and Chava and Jarrow [2001a, 2001b].

How do We Combine Rating Agency Ratings, Internal Ordinal Ratings, and a Default Probability Model to Produce Maximum Accuracy in Predicting Default?

We use all of them as explanatory variables in a logistic regression applied to a database of historical defaults. If any of the candidate variables is not statistically significant (i.e. does not add to the explanatory power of the other variables), those variables can be omitted. The output of the logistic regression is the default probability forecast by the multiple inputs (agency ratings, internal ordinal ratings, and a default probability model).

Does Market Data, When Combined with Various Credit Models, Improve Our Ability to Predict Default?

To test this proposition, the base regression 0 includes the various credit models as explanatory variables. We calculate the likelihood for the base regression 0. We then add the candidate market data as additional explanatory variables. We calculate the likelihood ratio test given above, and if the market variables add explanatory power at the desired level of statistical significance, then our conclusion to this question will be yes.

- Is it more accurate to use a combination of credit models for default prediction or to use just one?

We test this proposition by adding credit models one at a time as explanatory variables, and we keep those which add explanatory power by the likelihood ratio test above, exactly as we did with our four hypothetical ratings technologies above.

- How can we convert an ordinal credit rating to a default probability?

Van Deventer and Outram [2002] explain that we convert ordinal credit ratings to dummy variables (for example, variable 1 = 1 means the rating is AAA, 0 if not AAA; variable 2 = 1 means AA, 2 means not AA, etc.). The number of dummy variables should either be (a) one less than the number of ratings with the constant term in the logistic regression retained or (b) equal to the number of ratings with the constant term in the logistic regression omitted. The coefficients of the logistic regression produce estimates of the default probabilities associated with each rating for a given data base of defaults. More importantly, they also allow the analyst to determine the confidence intervals around that default estimate.

Wald Ratio

Another statistical test sometimes used with logistic regression is the Wald ratio, which is the logistic regression equivalent to the t-score often used in linear regression. Unfortunately the Wald ratio has been shown to be frequently inaccurate and most analysts recommend it be employed only in combination with the likelihood ratio test to determine the statistical significance of any given explanatory variable. See Hosmer and Lemeshow [2000] for more on this issue.

Using Market Data for Testing Credit Models

In addition to tests on historical databases of defaults, any diligent test of credit models will employ market data on companies of varying credit quality for testing. The universe of data available for this purpose is an order of magnitude greater than the amount of data on actual defaults. Moreover, the market data tests most closely replicate the usage of credit models in practical application and thus have the most significance. There are a number of different tests that are possible using market data, and we explain these tests in later chapters. The authors believe that all credit models should be subjected both to tests on historical default data bases, as we have done in this chapter, and tests on actual market data. We turn to that test in the next chapter.

References

Adams, K. and D. van Deventer, 1994, 'Fitting Yield Curves and Forward Rate Curves with Maximum Smoothness,' *Journal of Fixed Income*, June, 52–62.

Basel Committee on Banking Supervision, 2001, 'Consultative Document: The New Capital Accords,' monograph, Bank for International Settlements, Basel.

Black, F. and M. Scholes, 1973, 'The Pricing of Options and Corporate Liabilities,' *Journal of Political Economy*, 81, 399–418.

Chava, S. and R. Jarrow, 2001a, 'Bankruptcy Prediction with Industry Effects,' working paper, Cornell University and Kamakura Corporation.

Chava, S. and R. Jarrow, 2001b, 'A Comparison of Explicit versus Implicit Estimates of Default Probabilities,' working paper, Cornell University and Kamakura Corporation.

Delianedis, G. and R. Geske, 1998, 'Credit Risk and Risk Neutral Default Probabilities: Information About Rating Migrations and Defaults,' working paper, UCLA.

Duffie D. and K. Singleton, 1999, 'Modeling Term Structures of Defaultable Bonds.' *Review of Financial Studies*, vol. 12, no. 4: 197–226.

Eberhart, A. C., W.T. Moore and R.L. Roenfeldt, 1990, 'Security Pricing and Deviations from the Absolute Priority Rule in Bankruptcy Proceedings,' *Journal of Finance*, 4, 1457–1489.

Hosmer, D. W. and S. Lemeshow, 2000. *Applied Logistic Regression*, John Wiley & Sons.

Hull, J. and A. White, 1987, 'The Pricing of Options on Assets with Stochastic Volatility,' *Journal of Finance*, 2, 281–300.

Jarrow, R. 2001, 'Default Parameter Estimation Using Market Prices,' *Financial Analysts Journal*, September/October.

Janosi, T., R. Jarrow and Y. Yildirum, 2001a, 'Estimating Expected Losses and Liquidity Discounts Implicit in Debt Prices,' working paper, Cornell University.

Janosi, T., R. Jarrow and Y. Yildirum, 2001b, 'Estimating Default Probabilities Implicit in Equity Prices,' working paper, Cornell University.

Jarrow, R. and D. van Deventer, 1998, 'Integrating Interest Rate Risk and Credit Risk in Asset and Liability Management,' *Asset and Liability Management: The Synthesis of New Methodologies*, Risk Publications.

Jarrow, R. and D. van Deventer, 1999, 'Practical Usage of Credit Risk Models in Loan Portfolio and Counterparty Exposure Management,' *Credit Risk Models and Management*, Risk Publications.

Jarrow, R., D. van Deventer, and X. Wang, 2002, 'A Robust Test of Merton's Structural Model for Credit Risk,' working paper, Cornell University and Kamakura Corporation.

Jones, E., S. Mason and E. Rosenfeld, 1984, 'Contingent Claims Analysis of Corporate Capital Structures: An Empirical Investigation,' *Journal of Finance*, 39, 611–627.

Kealhofer, S. and M. Kurbat, 2001, 'The Default Prediction Power of the Merton Approach, Relative to Debt Ratings and Accounting Variables,' monograph, KMV Corporation, San Francisco, CA.

Merton, R.C., 1974, 'On the Pricing of Corporate Debt: The Risk Structure of Interest Rates,' *Journal of Finance*, 29, 449–470.

Shimko, D., H. Tejima and D. van Deventer, 1993, 'The Pricing of Risky Debt when Interest Rates are Stochastic,' *Journal of Fixed Income*, September, 58–66.

Sobehart, J., S. Keenan and R. Stein, 2000, 'Validation Methodologies for Default Risk Models,' *Credit*, May, 51–56.

Shumway, T., 2001, 'Forecasting Bankruptcy More Accurately: A Simple Hazard Model,' *Journal of Business*, forthcoming.

van Deventer, D. and K. Imai, 1996, *Financial Risk Analytics: A Term Structure Model Approach for Banking, Insurance, and Investment Management*, McGraw Hill.

Van Deventer, D. and X. Wang, 2002, 'Basel II and Lessons from Enron: The Consistency of the Merton Credit Model with Observable Credit Spreads and Equity Prices,' working paper, Kamakura Corporation.

Weiss, L.A., 1990, 'Bankruptcy Resolution: Direct Costs and Violations of Priority of Claims,' *Journal of Financial Economics*, 27, 286-5–314.

6

Tests of Credit Models using Historical Default Data

The New Basel Capital Accord states that 'A bank must demonstrate to its supervisor that the internal validation process enables it to assess the performance of internal rating and risk quantification systems consistently and meaningfully.'[1] In chapter 5, we reviewed a number of techniques for testing credit models that are consistent with the highest standards of statistical practice in areas such as medical science, where the prediction of the incidence of disease is analyzed in a manner similar to our analysis of credit risk. Now we turn to these techniques to analyze the relative performance of structural and reduced form credit models on a large data base of bankruptcies in the U.S. from 1963 to 1998, compiled by Chava and Jarrow [2001a, 2001b]. This kind of testing is necessary for many critical reasons:

- It is required by the Basel Accord;
- It is necessary for management to understand how much credit risk the institution is bearing, even though the models may not be perfect;
- It is necessary for management to understand how much measurement error there is in any credit risk modeling technology;
- It is essential for the Board of Directors to understand whether the institution's reserve for loan losses and capital is adequate for the risk being borne;
- It is critical for regulators in evaluating the safety and soundness of the institution.

---

[1] Section 302, p. 55, The New Basel Capital Accord, Basel Committee on Banking Supervision, May 31, 2001.

We now turn to the Chava Jarrow data base and model performance.

The Chava Jarrow Data Base

Chava and Jarrow, in their application of reduced form technology, compiled a bankruptcy data base that contains data on all listed companies in the United States from 1963 to 1998. The data base includes 1,461 bankruptcies[2] through the end of 1998, of which 826 were New York Stock Exchange-listed companies and the remainder was almost evenly split between the American Stock Exchange and NASDAQ. Of the bankrupt companies, the breakdown by industry was as follows:

Table 6.1 Company Bankruptcies – Breakdown by Industry

37%	manufacturing
14%	retail
12%	service industries
11%	finance, insurance and real estate
8%	transportation, communication and utilities
8%	mineral-related industries

The total number of firms covered over the 1963-1998 period was 17,460. As Figure 6.1 below shows, the number of firms covered varied over time.

The initial number of firms covered was slightly over 1,000 in 1963, growing to more than 8,000 by the end of 1998. The total number of observations in the data base, which is based on monthly data, is 1.9 million. This is one of the largest data bases ever analyzed for credit model performance.

The Chava-Jarrow data shows the wave of bankruptcies that troubled the U.S. market in the late 1980s and early 1990s.

The Basic Chava-Jarrow Model

Chava and Jarrow extend the work of Shumway [2001], who applied the hazard rate modeling technology we discussed in earlier chapters, to the

---

[2] At the time of this writing, the total number of bankruptcies by U.S. public companies has gone over 2,000.

Figure 6.1a   Composition of firms analyzed, 1963–1998

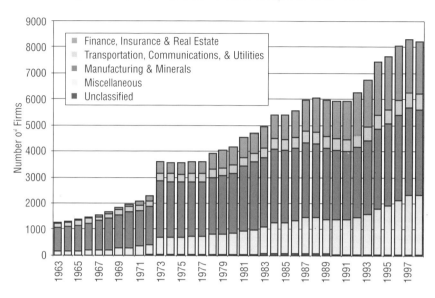

Figure 6.1b   Composition of U.S. bankruptcies, 1963–1998

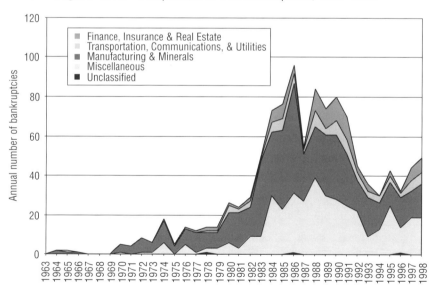

variables studied as potential predictors of bankruptcy by Edward Altman beginning in the 1960s. Chava and Jarrow show how logistic regression can be used to estimate a model of default that is consistent with the Jarrow [2001] reduced form model but which includes a more general set of inputs than the bond prices used to estimate parameters in the original Jarrow [2001] model or the credit derivatives prices used to estimate parameters in Jarrow and Yildiray [2002]. There are five variables which Chava and Jarrow used to predict default:

- Net income to total assets ratio;
- Total liabilities to total assets ratio;
- Relative size, the log of the ratio of total firm equity market value divided by total NYSE and AMEX equity value;
- Excess return, the monthly return on the firm minus the monthly value-weighted CRSP NYSE/Amex index return;
- Stock's volatility of the previous month's daily prices.

Note that the first two of these variables are accounting ratios and that the fourth and fifth variables are equity market-related. Note also that three of the variables are typically used as inputs, or are closely related to inputs, for the Merton and STV models:

- Total liabilities to total assets ratio, which is closely related to the amount of liabilities that is necessary as an input to the Merton model.
- Excess return, the monthly return on the firm minus the monthly value-weighted CRSP NYSE/Amex index return, which is closely related to the absolute level of the stock price, which is an input in the Merton model.
- Stock's volatility of previous month's daily prices, which is used to benchmark the volatility of company assets in the Merton model.

The Chava-Jarrow analysis allows us to address a number of issues and questions posed by credit risk researchers:

- Do accounting variables add explanatory power to equity prices?
- Is company size a determinant of bankruptcy that adds explanatory power above and beyond equity prices?

We now turn to the Chava Jarrow findings.

The Chava Jarrow Results

The Chava-Jarrow data base is the largest possible U.S. data base for the study of public company bankruptcies, since daily stock prices are not available in the U.S. for dates prior to 1963. Of the total 1.9 million observations, 1,403,898 were available for study. There were approximately 500,000 observations where one or more of the five explanatory variables were missing. After eliminating the missing data points, there were 979 defaults remaining in the Chava-Jarrow data base.

Are the Chava Jarrow Results Significantly Better than Random Chance?

The first question we addressed in the previous chapter is how to prove that a model is significantly better than random chance. For the Chava Jarrow model, the results show that we can say the Chava Jarrow results are significantly better than random chance with 99.99% confidence, far above the usual standard of 95%. The likelihood ratio test *(D)* which we discussed in the previous chapter, was 3932.35, with five (the number of explanatory variables) degrees of freedom on the sample of 1,403,898 observations.

Is Each of the Explanatory Variables Statistically Significant?

In the previous chapter, we discussed the Wald ratio, the equivalent of the t-score normally used in linear regression to measure the statistical significance of each variable. The Wald ratio is not as useful for this purpose in logistic regression, but it does give us a moderately useful indication that the variables we are using are important. Most statisticians would want to see a Wald ratio that is at least 2.00 in absolute value. All five of the Chava-Jarrow variables meet this test by a considerable margin, with the following Wald ratios:

- -14.12, Excess Return on Common Stock*;
- -8.90, Net Income/Total Assets;
- -14.27, Log (Relative Size);
- 18.06, Stock Price Volatility*;
- 29.08, Liabilities/Total Assets*.

The * denotes the three Chava-Jarrow input variables that are closely related to input variables for the Merton model. We will come back to the significance of these ratios after reviewing the ROC accuracy ratio for the Chava Jarrow model.

The ROC Curve Accuracy Ratio

The statement from the New Basel Accord at the beginning of this chapter confirms what we discussed in the previous chapter—a model should not be used by a sophisticated financial institution without a quantitative measure of model performance. A qualitative or graphical display of model performance, without the explicit publication of the quantitative or numerical measure of performance, doesn't meet the Basel test. Moreover, it doesn't meet the kind of test that should be applied by management and shareholders. Only a quantitative measure allows comparison across models by different researchers and different institutions.

In the previous chapter, we outlined the calculation of the ROC accuracy ratio in two ways: by making a pair-wise comparison of all defaulted and non-defaulted companies, and by measuring the area under the ROC curve. The two methods are identical. For the very large Chava-Jarrow data base, this requires the comparison of 979 defaulted companies multiplied by 1,402,919 observations on non-defaulting companies (out of a total of 1, 403, 898), equating to a total of 1,373,457,701 pairs of companies. This is a huge and comprehensive test of the basic Chava-Jarrow model. The results of this pair-wise comparison is a very impressive 92.74% accuracy ratio, as illustrated in Figure 6.2 below.

This is such an impressive performance that it makes sense to compare it both to the findings of other researchers and to the ROC accuracy ratios that would have prevailed if Chava and Jarrow had used a smaller set of explanatory variables. We turn to that analysis in the next section.

Comparing ROC Accuracy Ratios for Structural and Reduced Form Models

Perhaps the best work in the quantitative performance measurement of credit models has been done by a series of researchers formerly at Moody's Investors Service. Figure 6.3 compares their results with those of the Chava

Figure 6.2

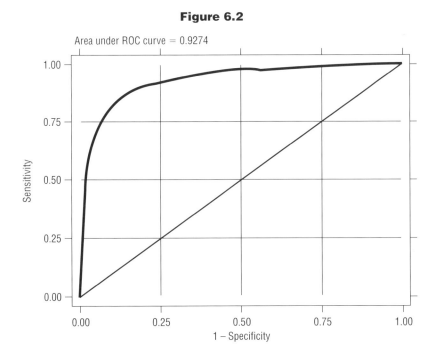

Figure 6.3   Ranking of credit models by ROC accuracy ratio

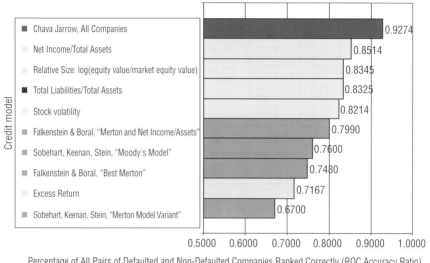

Percentage of All Pairs of Defaulted and Non-Defaulted Companies Ranked Correctly (ROC Accuracy Ratio)

Jarrow model's most basic version. The dark blue bar on the graph shows the 92.74% ROC accuracy ratio for the Chava Jarrow model. The light blue bars show the results for five other models, derived by taking each one of the Chava Jarrow input variables one at a time and fitting a logistic regression to form a 'one variable' credit model for each of them. This process allows us to better understand the sources of the Chava Jarrow model's explanatory power.

The first light blue bar is the ROC accuracy ratio for the credit model that uses only the net income/assets ratio as an input. This simple model has an ROC accuracy ratio of 85.14% on the Chava-Jarrow data base.

The second blue bar is the model that contains relative size as the only explanatory variable. Even this simple model has an ROC ratio of 83.45%. The total liabilities/total assets ratio produces an 83.25% ROC accuracy ratio when used on a stand-alone basis, and the stock volatility leads to an ROC accuracy ratio of 82.14% when used alone. The weakest of the Chava Jarrow variables, with an ROC accuracy ratio of 71.67%, was the excess return on common stock relative to all other equities.

The Moody's researchers provide "cumulative accuracy profiles" on a number of different credit models and data sets. While the data bases are not identical and therefore accuracy ratios can vary, there is a significant overlap between the Chava Jarrow data base and those used by the Moody's researchers. Statistics for the Chava Jarrow model are based on monthly observations, while the Moody's statistics are based on annual observations, which also lead to some differences in accuracy ratios. The ROC ratios we have presented in Chapters 5 and 6 are scaled from 50% for a model no better than random chance to 100% for a perfect model. The Moody's results, by contrast, are calculated slightly differently on a scale from 0 to 100%[1]. We have given the originally reported cumulative accuracy profile in what follows with the rescaled ROC accuracy ratios to be more consistent with Chapters 5 and 6 in parentheses thereafter. Falkenstein and Boral [Risk Professional, April 2001, or www.efalken.com/Mertonmodel.htm] reported that a combination of the Merton model and the net income to assets ratio produced a cumulative accuracy profile of 79.90% for their sample (an ROC accuracy ratio of 89.95% on a restated basis). Sobehart, Keenan, and Stein [Moody's Investors Services, "Validation methodologies for default risk models," and Credit Magazine, May 2000] found a 76%(±2%) cumulative accuracy profile for their sample (a ROC accuracy ratio of 88%(±1%) on a restated basis) for the "Moody's model" which combines the Merton model with a number of other financial ratios. Falkenstein and Boral found a 74.80% cumulative accuracy profile (an ROC accuracy ratio of about 87.4% on a restated basis) for their "best Merton" model, and Sobehart, Keenan and Stein report a 67%(±2%) cumulative accuracy profile (an ROC accuracy ratio of about 84%(±1%) on a restated basis) for a "Merton model variant."

By contrast, the explanatory power of the Chava Jarrow model is quite high. The 92.74% ROC accuracy ratio stems from the fact that four of the five input variables, even taken alone, produce ROC accuracy ratios above 80%. We can see the power of the Chava Jarrow inputs most clearly when we plot their values, year by year, for the companies that went bankrupt in each year and compare them to the values for the companies that did not go bankrupt in that time period, as illustrated by Figure 6.4.

The total liabilities/assets ratio was generally much higher for bankrupt companies than it was for non-bankrupt companies, although the data prior to 1972 is in need of closer examination.

Figure 6.5 shows that stock volatility was much higher for companies that went bankrupt, exactly as one would expect.

If we plot the relative size variable for bankrupt and non-bankrupt companies, we see another result that is consistent with our intuition— smaller companies are more likely to go bankrupt than larger companies (Figure 6.6).

When we plot the net income/assets ratio for bankrupt and non-bankrupt companies, we see clearly that, on average, bankrupt companies lose a lot

---

[1] The authors would like to thank Jorge Sobehart for making this distinction clear in a private communication.

Figure 6.4 Total liabilities/total assets for bankrupt and non-bankrupt companies suggest ignoring data prior to 1972

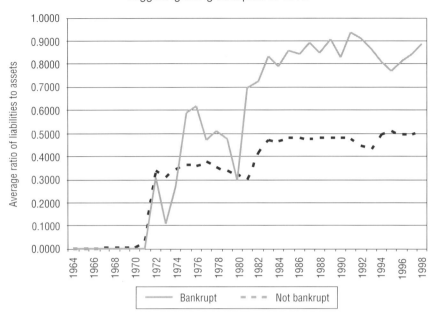

Figure 6.5 Bankrupt firms have higher stock price volatility

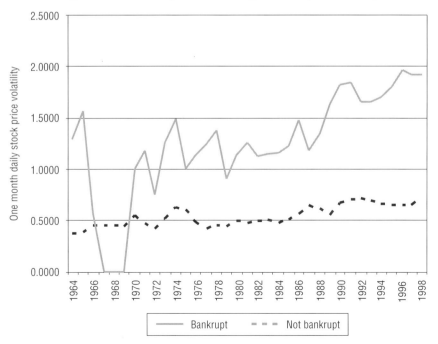

Figure 6.6   Bankrupt firms are smaller than firms that did not go bankrupt

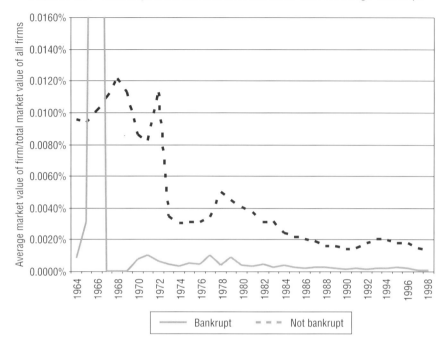

of money. Somewhat more surprisingly, we see that in recent years the average net income/assets ratio for non-bankrupt companies is also negative—but not as negative as it is for bankrupt companies (see Figure 6.7).

The final of the five variables is the relative return on the stock of bankrupt and non-bankrupt companies. The relative performance is lower for bankrupt companies, but it is also quite volatile. The data suggests that a closer examination of the pre-1972 data would be worthwhile (see Figure 6.8).

These graphs of the Chava Jarrow input variables are both consistent with the Chava Jarrow results and with the intuition of experienced lenders.

There is a subtle question that remains: why did Moody's research on the Merton model not show better results? We turn to that question in the next section.

Explaining the Performance of the Merton Model

Because the Chava Jarrow data base is not identical to the Moody's data base, we cannot rule out data differences as the source of some of the

Figure 6.7   Bankrupt firms lose much more money than healthy firms

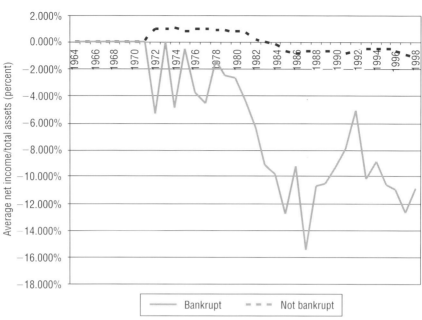

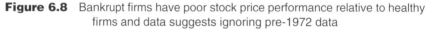

Figure 6.8   Bankrupt firms have poor stock price performance relative to healthy firms and data suggests ignoring pre-1972 data

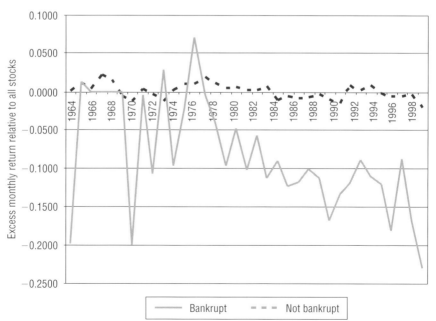

performance differential between the Chava Jarrow model and the models reviewed by Moody's, especially the Merton model. In fact, using small data sets on the most recent data, the Merton model's performance is better than reported by Moody's researchers and at times exceeds the reduced form model results.

As we showed in the cases of Long Term Credit Bank of Japan and Nippon Credit Bank, model performance is very dependent on the data selected. We place the most reliance on the full data set, and it is important to understand the larger performance differential between the Chava Jarrow model and the Merton model variants studied by Moody's. Chava and Jarrow found that two variables which are not related to the Merton model in any way had the highest ROC accuracy ratios on a stand-alone basis:

- Net income to total assets ratio;
- Relative size, ratio of total firm equity market value divided by total NYSE and AMEX equity value.

The other three Chava Jarrow variables are closely related to Merton model inputs. In short, the Merton model omits the two most important of the five Chava Jarrow variables over this data set—net income/assets and size. Net income/assets has been a key ratio in credit risk analysis for decades because of its close (but variable) links with cash flow, a critical consideration to a lender. Size is also one of the most common credit scoring variables used in credit risk analysis worldwide. Therefore it comes as no surprise that a model that omits these well-known variables can suffer from a performance perspective.

This is in part confirmed by both Moody's research groups, who find that models which pair the Merton model with other financial ratios result in improved performance. Falkenstein and Boral, for example, show that the Merton default probability with the net income/assets ratio has cumulative accuracy of 79.90% (restated as above, to 89.95% to be comparable to standard ROC accuracy ratio calculations), much better than the 74.80% CAP profile (restated to 87.4%) ROC accuracy ratio for the Merton model alone. We have in fact confirmed this finding by combining three inputs closely related with Merton with the two omitted variables and found superior performance on a data base of 1.4 million observations, spanning all public companies in the United States for the period 1963–1998.

Does Accounting Information Improve the Performance of Credit Models?

It is sometimes argued that equity markets are efficient and fully incorporate all available information, including accounting information. Therefore it is a violation of the no-arbitrage assumptions of financial theory for accounting information to improve default prediction. This comment is incorrect for a simple reason: equity prices fully incorporate all accounting information relevant to equity holders, who receive a large upside return in the event of corporate success and a large downside risk in the case of corporate failure. This is not the same information 'set' relevant to debt holders and default, because debt holders receive almost no upside from corporate success (at best, bonds are called early) and lots of downside from corporate failure. When we use equity market information to derive the probability of default, we lose some visibility on the factors most relevant to debt holders. Accounting variables help us regain the information disguised by the equity-related data. This is confirmed by the Chava Jarrow Wald statistics on the two key accounting variables in the model:

- -8.90, Net Income/Total Assets;
- 29.08, Liabilities/Total Assets.

The Wald statistics of 8.9 and 29.08 are well above the 2.00 level normally considered statistically significant, and again they are derived on a data base of 1.4 million observations. Similar results on other large data bases have been found by Shumway and the Moody's researchers cited above. There is no doubt about the importance of accounting ratios in the prediction of default for U.S. public companies for a sample of legitimate size.

The same cannot be said for private companies, where tax avoidance is a common reason for companies to understate net income, for example. This is an empirical question that the testing procedures detailed in this and the prior chapter can definitively resolve.

Statistical Significance of the Chava Jarrow Default Probabilities

The ROC accuracy ratio is the authors' preferred method for the testing of credit models on historical data, because the ratio efficiently uses every data point in the performance measurement process. Another important question, however, is whether or not the measured default probabilities on defaulting companies are different from those of non-defaulting companies by an amount that is statistically significant. This section addresses that question.

In the 1963–1998 Chava Jarrow data base, there were 979 defaults (of a total of 1,461) for which all five input variables were available. Figure 6.9 plots the 12 month moving average of the Chava Jarrow default probability (note that the figures below are *monthly* default probabilities, not annual) for companies which defaulted in each month versus the average for all non-defaulting companies for the 1982 to 1998 period.

Figure 6.9   12 month moving average Chava Jarrow default probability of defaulting companies vs non-defaulting companies, 1982–1998

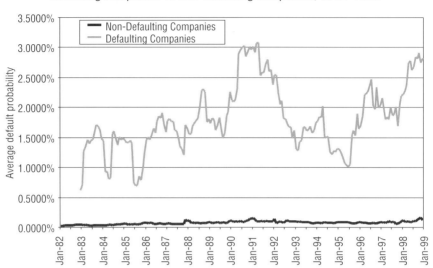

The monthly default probabilities are consistently higher for the defaulting companies than for the non-defaulting companies. A still more important question is whether this differential is statistically significant. Figure 6.10 shows the 12 month moving average of the number of standard deviations between the average monthly default probability on defaulting companies and the average monthly default probability on non-defaulting companies.

Figure 6.10   12 month moving average Chava Jarrow default probability for defaulting companies: Number of standard deviations from average default probability of all companies, 1982–1998

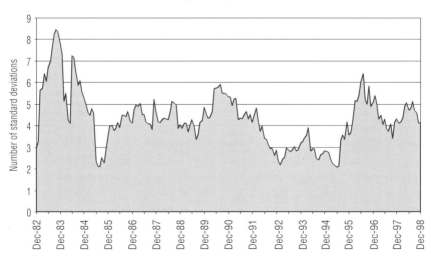

The number of standard deviations is consistently above 2.00 for the 1982–1998 time period. This is the kind of reassurance that Basel II requires of credit model users: proof not only that riskier companies have higher default probabilities but also proof that those differences are statistically significant.

Predictive Capability of the Chava Jarrow Default Probabilities

Another important question is the 'predictive capability' of credit models. This is a question that must be addressed with care, for the potential of misunderstanding is high. We want to answer this question: 'how early does a credit model 'predict' bankruptcy?'

In the case of both the Chava-Jarrow implementation of reduced form models and the Merton or STV models, we are using equity market data to predict the default of a debt instrument. Figure 6.11 below shows that the average one year probability of default for all of the 979 defaulting companies in the Chava Jarrow data base (data on the explanatory variables was not available for all of the 1461 companies which defaulted) rises steadily and sharply in the months approaching default.

The annualized default probability, on average over 979 defaults, was nearly 20% in the month of bankruptcy, which is the '0' point on the right-hand side of the horizontal scale. A more important question, again, is whether this average default probability is statistically different in a significant way from the average default probability of all companies. As Figure 6.12 below

Figure 6.11   One year default probability, basic Chava Jarrow Model, on all bankrupt companies 48 months prior to default

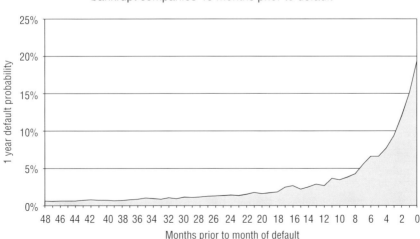

Months prior to month of default

Figure 6.12 Defaulting companies' estimated annual default probability:
Number of standard deviations from the average annual default probability of
all companies in the 48 months prior to bankruptcy

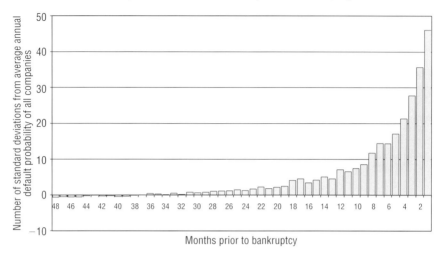

shows, the number of standard deviations from the average annual default
probability of all companies rises steadily as default approaches.

The number of standard deviations from the average is over 45 standard
deviations prior to default. If we examine Figure 6.13 shown below, we can
see that as early as 22 months prior to default the average defaulting company

Figure 6.13 Defaulting companies' estimated annual default probability:
Number of standard deviations from the average annual default probability of
all companies in the 48 months prior to bankruptcy

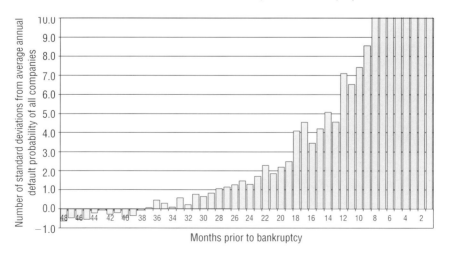

has an annual default probability more than two standard deviations away from the average annual default probability of all companies.

Graphs similar to this can be done for the Merton model and STV model.

Does this mean, as many lenders believe, that 'credit models help me make buy or sell decisions before debt market participants realize that credit quality is deteriorating?' While this view is held very seriously by many, the authors believe that the answer is firmly no. In the first place, the statistics presented above are not directly relevant to the information needed to answer the 'beat the market' question. A credit model 'beats the market' if it consistently provides a theoretical market value that is less than (and more accurate than) the market value in the market for companies whose credit quality is deteriorating and vice versa for a company whose credit quality is improving. This requires a full valuation framework, and as we mentioned in Chapter 5, that is one of the prime virtues of the reduced form modeling technology compared to the Merton or STV models.

If one believes that equity-based default models like Chava-Jarrow, Merton or STV help the user make arbitrage profits, then the user is implicitly saying that equity participants are smarter than debt market participants. Many amusing statistical tests of this proposition come to mind, none of which have been done (like comparing the college entrance examination results of fixed income managers versus equity managers).

The authors, in tests on millions of securities prices, have found no evidence that credit models provide arbitrage-free profits. Moreover, Robert Jarrow has found, in unpublished research, that default probabilities have the following statistical significance when ranked by input data used to benchmark the model:

- Highest statistical significance: Default models based on credit derivatives prices;
- Second highest statistical significance: Default models based on debt prices, like the Jarrow model;
- Third highest: Default models based on equity prices and accounting data, like the Chava Jarrow model;
- Fourth highest: Default probabilities based on equity data alone, like the Merton and STV models;
- Fifth highest: Default models based on accounting data alone.

What we *do* believe is this:

Quantitative credit models provide cheaper, faster and more accurate indices of credit quality than the traditional credit analysis practiced by most financial institutions.

This being said, the authors believe that market prices of both debt and equity, on average, fully reflect the credit quality of the issuer of that debt and equity. There is one more corollary, however, that is very important:

> *Sophisticated users of credit models will earn better risk-adjusted performance than unsophisticated users of credit models.*

An unsophisticated credit model user argues the following: 'My credit model (Chava-Jarrow, Merton or STV) shows the default probability on ABC company is going up, so I am going to sell the ABC bonds before the market realizes what is happening.'

A sophisticated credit model user makes a different statement: 'My credit model shows the default probability on ABC company is going up. If the market price doesn't reflect this deterioration, I will sell. If the market price has over-discounted this deterioration and is below its theoretical value, I will hold because the price is too low relative to the default probability.'

This is where the true value of a sophisticated credit model can be realized.

Credit Models versus the Rating Agencies

Proponents of credit models rarely show average performance like that shown above. Instead they argue models perform well because they 'beat' the rating agencies. This is 'proven' with anecdotal graphs of default probabilities for individual companies compared to the default probability implied by the company's debt rating.

The authors, as usual, have a different view of whether rating agency ratings or quantitative default probabilities are 'better.' We outlined this approach in Chapter 5. For a very large data set, we run a logistic regression and measure whether rating agency ratings add value to quantitative models and vice versa. In general, the authors have found that both have value. Graphs of individual companies show only one thing: that rating agencies adjust credit ratings less frequently than quantitative credit models are adjusted. The authors believe that ratings, on average, are just as good as quantitative models on the day a new rating is announced. Quality changes, however, as ratings 'grow old.' Again, we emphasize the virtues of models like the reduced form models, Merton model, and STV model in this statement from the prior section:

> *Quantitative credit models provide cheaper, faster and more accurate indices of credit quality than the traditional credit analysis practiced by most financial institutions.*

Macro Factors and the Chava Jarrow Model

In this chapter, we have reported impressive results for the Chava Jarrow implementation of reduced form models versus the published accuracy ratios for other models studied by Moody's Investors Service. The basic Chava Jarrow model reported here is not the best Chava Jarrow model, however, for reasons outlined in Chapter 4: macro economic factors drive default probabilities all over the world.

The Jarrow [2001] model incorporates these macro factors explicitly. In a similar way, we can incorporate macro factors in a Chava Jarrow logistic regression. Using the tests in Chapter 5, performance of the model improves and the statistical significance of the added variables can be confirmed in a scientific way. In the U.S. market for all public companies from 1963–1998, interest rates and the multi-year return on the Standard & Poor's 500 stock index have Wald ratios that are statistically significant:

Wald ratio for three month Treasury bill rates: 15.4
Multi-year return on the S&P 500: 7.7

In a 15-year study of 1 million small businesses in Japan that involved 15.7 million observations and more than 123,000 defaults, the authors also found very high statistical significance for exchange rates and the multi-year return on stock indices. As we saw in Chapter 5, macro factors drive default. This is provable on both an individual company name basis, as we did in Chapter 5, and on a country-wide basis using the Chava Jarrow approach. This is the way that the wave of defaults typical of the U.S. and other markets can be both understood and modeled accurately.

Model Performance: A Summary

The New Basel Capital Accord requires the testing of credit models. In Chapter 5, we outlined how to conduct those tests using established statistical procedures from medical statistics and electronics. We illustrated those tests on hypothetical data. In this chapter, we performed those same tests on a data set compiled by Chava and Jarrow that includes all public companies in the United States from 1963-1998. We found that even the most basic implementation of the reduced form models, that proposed by Chava and Jarrow, has excellent performance as measured by the ROC accuracy ratio. More importantly, we found that the net income/assets ratio and the size variable were the two most powerful Chava Jarrow inputs. This, along with a difference in data sets, provides a rational basis for understanding why the Chava Jarrow performance is so much higher than the performance of other models studied by Moody's Investors Service.

The most important conclusion of this chapter is that a multiple models approach is the only approach consistent with the pronouncements of the New Basel Capital Accords. For the large data sets which we have examined here, the reduced form models have ROC accuracy ratios that are higher than those found by other researchers on similar (but not identical) data sets. These conclusions can be reversed on smaller data sets, so there is some uncertainty as to which models are 'best' even when using all available data. Basel II requires that we perform these tests, understand the uncertainty that remains after using the best available credit models, and that we diversify the model risk by using multiple credit models on a fully informed basis.

We now turn to a different set of tests that rely on market data to test both model performance and the consistency of the models' assumptions with the observed movements of securities prices.

7

Market Data Tests of Credit Models: Lessons from Enron and Other Case Studies[1]

In Chapter 6, we presented the results of credit model tests on historical data bases of defaulted and non-defaulted companies. These tests are a critical part of the evaluation of credit model performance. Nonetheless, tests on market data are potentially much more enlightening because there is so much more data and because the tests can be focused explicitly on the objectives of the credit risk process. In the Chava Jarrow data base we discussed in Chapter 6, there were 1.9 million observations including 1, 461 defaults, but after allowing for missing data 1.4 million observations and 979 defaults were usable. More importantly, the historical tests don't directly address objectives of the credit risk process as we discussed in Chapter 1.

We can directly use market data to test the hedging capability of the credit models in which we have an interest. We can compare the theoretical pricing generated by the model to actual market prices as another test of the model's performance in practice. We can compare the model's stability to market data that has a close link in theory, to see if the model's results are reasonable. Finally, if the model's assumptions are so strong that they create testable implications, we can test those implications. We show how to do these kinds of tests in this Chapter.

The First Interstate Data Set

In many of the tests we do in this chapter, we will use data on the 'new issue spreads' of First Interstate Bancorp used by Jarrow and van Deventer [1998, 1999]. The data set contains weekly quotes on potential new issues

---

[1] This chapter is based on Jarrow and van Deventer [1998, 1999] and on a working paper prepared by Donald R. van Deventer and Xiaoming Wang [2001].

of various maturity non-call bonds of First Interstate Bancorp from January 3, 1986 to August 20, 1993. First Interstate Bancorp was ultimately acquired by Wells Fargo & Co. First Interstate collected this data for risk management purposes and to measure the internal profitability of key business units. First Interstate Bancorp, where one of the authors served as treasurer from 1984 to 1987, was one of the ten largest bank holding companies in the U.S. in the middle 1980s. In spite of the large number of bank failures at the time, First Interstate was an AA-rated issuer of debt and one of the most frequent issuers of debt in both the U.S. and the Euro markets. First Interstate was the world's first issuer of Euro medium-term notes and the first issuer of bank medium-term notes. It was also one of the most active early dealers in interest rate swaps and fixed income options, ranking at one time in the top 10 dealers in the U.S. As such, First Interstate represents exactly the type of institution for which the measurement of credit risk would be necessary and desirable because it was a derivatives counterparty of almost every financial institution trading derivatives world-wide. Its bonds were also in the portfolios of a wide array of institutional investors.

The data collection process was reported by Jarrow and van Deventer [1998]. In 1984, First Interstate's treasury department began polling leading investment banking firms regarding spreads to U.S. Treasury bonds for a new issue of $100 million of non-callable bonds at the 'on the run' maturities of 2, 3, 5, 7, and 10 years. The data series collected by First Interstate consists of quotations taken each Friday from six investment banks. The high and low estimates were eliminated and the remaining four quotes averaged. Because the spreads represent the 'on the run' maturities, there is no need to engage in yield curve smoothing to extract the 'on the run' spreads to Treasuries from odd dates, a practice often necessary when using secondary market quotes for corporate debt issues.

Jarrow and van Deventer [1998] reported that there was considerable economic pressure on the investment banks to provide accurate quotations, because a quoted spread that was too high ran the risk of causing the bond underwriting to be missed by the investment bank. Conversely, a quoted spread that was too low could lead to a 'prove it' request by First Interstate to underwrite the issue at the level. Finally, consistently inaccurate quotes relative to the mean spread of all the underwriters polled had an adverse impact on the relationship of the investment banking firm with First Interstate.

First Interstate provides a challenging test for any credit model, since its credit rating fell from AA to BBB+ in January 1990, to BBB in January 1991, but rose back to A− by January 1993. Furthermore, First Interstate's stock price also showed considerable variation over the sample period. The stock price varied from below $20 per share to almost $70 per share, as illustrated by Figure 7.1.

Figure 7.1 First Interstate Bancorp common stock price, 1986–1993

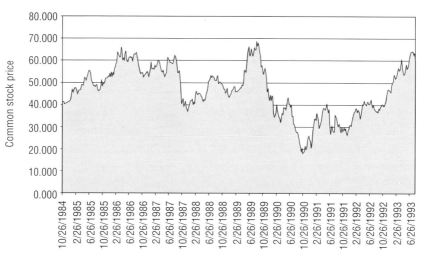

First Interstate credit spreads showed a high degree of variation over the sample period. During this period, First Interstate went through a failed attempt to acquire BankAmerica Corporation, was the subject of numerous merger rumors itself, and suffered from serious credit quality problems.

Figure 7.2 First Interstate Bancorp credit spreads, 1986–1993

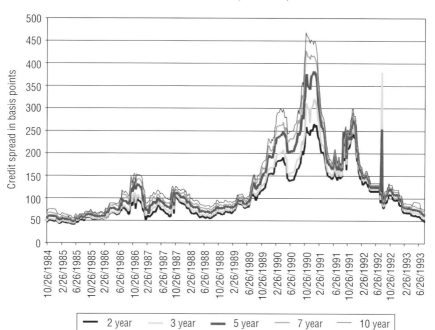

Only two weeks of data (2 out of 377 observations) were omitted as outliers in the tests that follow. On August 14, 1992, the First Interstate 2-year spread over Treasuries jumped from 90 basis points in the previous week to 350 basis points, and then back to 88 basis points on August 21. In contrast, over the same period, the stock price did not exhibit the same unusual movements— the three relevant values being $38.125 to $37.75 and then to $37.25. The week of August 14 was omitted from the data, and because much of the subsequent analysis concerns weekly changes in prices, the August 21 observation was necessarily omitted as well.

The entire First Interstate data set is reproduced as an appendix to this chapter.

Testing the Merton Model: Relating Credit Spread and Stock Price

One of the important differences between the Merton and STV structural models of risky debt and reduced form models is that both the Merton and STV models are models of both debt prices and equity prices. In both models, movements in the value of company assets drive changes in the value of risky debt and the value of the company's stock price. When the value of company assets rises, the Merton model postulates that the:

- stock price rises;
- debt price rises;
- credit spread falls.

When the value of company assets falls, the Merton model postulates that the:

- stock price falls;
- debt price falls;
- credit spread rises.

When the value of company assets does not change the:

- stock price is unchanged;
- debt price is unchanged;
- credit spread is unchanged.

Jarrow, van Deventer and Wang [2002] note that this movement is common to all single factor versions of the Merton model, regardless of the parameters used to benchmark the model. These prescriptions of the Merton model are testable—if they turn out to be true, it strengthens our confidence in the Merton model. If they turn out not to be true, we have to use the Merton model with caution.

The same tests cannot be done with respect to the reduced form models because they do not prescribe the same relationship between stock prices, debt prices, and credit spreads.

Step 1 in this analysis is to plot First Interstate's 2-year credit spread versus the stock price over the observation period. Figure 7.3 produces a downward sloping pattern that bends as the stock price increases, something that seems, at least at first glance, to be consistent with the Merton model of risky debt. Merton's risky debt model implies that the debt's value is negatively related to the stock price (all other things being equal—more precisely, assuming that all parameters assumed by Merton to be constant are in fact constant), and hence, the credit spread is non-linearly and negatively related to the stock price as well.

Figure 7.4 below shows the change in credit spread as a function of changes in stock prices for First Interstate Bancorp over the sample period. A regression on this relationship has the predicted downward slope, but a large number of data points fall in the upper right quadrant and lower left quadrant of the graph, which is inconsistent with the predictions of the Merton model.

If Merton's model is perfectly and completely valid, we would expect to see all of the data points clustered either in the upper left hand quadrant (lower stock prices and higher credit spreads) or lower right hand quadrant (higher stock prices and lower credit spreads). Casual observation indicates that this is not the case. Only 42% of the data points in the 375 weeks of First Interstate data are consistent with this relationship. More importantly, 58% of the data points are not.

Figure 7.3 Movements of First Interstate Bancorp
2 year credit spread as a function of stock price, 1986–1993

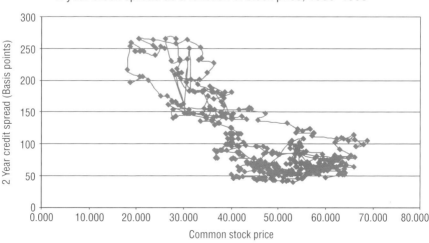

Figure 7.4 Change in First Interstate 2 year credit spread versus change in First Interstate common stock price, 1986–1993

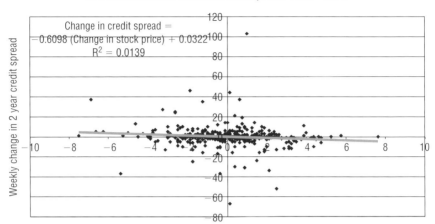

Weekly change in common stock price

We can measure the standard deviation of this estimate of Merton model consistency on the First Interstate data. For all five of the maturities studied, the consistency levels found are 23-25 standard deviations away from 100% consistency with the Merton model. Even more curiously, the consistency ratios found are 2.7 to 3.9 standard deviations below the 50% consistency level that a coin flip would have produced. This is the first clue that corporate capital structure and credit risk may be related in a more complex way than the Merton model postulates. We will come back to these issues frequently in this chapter.

Please note that these tests were not conducted on the reduced form models because they do not have the same implications for the relationship between stock price and credit spreads. They have no such implications.

Tests of Pricing Accuracy Using Reduced Form and Structural Models

At the beginning of this chapter, we listed one of the main objectives of the credit risk process:

> *How should this loan (bond, derivative) be priced to create shareholder value added for a strong institution? For my institution?*

A number of financial institutions have implemented this objective in the following sequence:

Table 7.1

Analysis of Changes in First Interstate Bancorp Credit Spreads and Stock Prices	SPREAD 2 Years	SPREAD 3 Years	SPREAD 5 Years	SPREAD 7 Years	SPREAD 10 Years	Total
Total Number of Data Points	427	427	427	427	427	2135
Data Points Consistent with Merton						
Opposite Move in Stock Price and Spreads	179	178	183	172	184	896
Stock Price and Credit Spreads Unchanged	3	3	1	2	2	11
Total Consistent	182	181	184	174	186	907
Percent Consistent With Merton Model	**42.6%**	**42.4%**	**43.1%**	**40.7%**	**43.6%**	**42.5%**
Standard Deviation	2.4%	2.4%	2.4%	2.4%	2.4%	1.1%
Standard Deviations from 100% Consistency	−23.9	−24.1	−23.7	−24.9	−23.5	−53.8
Standard Deviations from 50% Consistency	−3.1	−3.2	−2.9	−3.9	−2.7	−7.0

- They purchase default probability estimates for a large corporate universe;
- They build a capital allocation system around these default probabilities and allocate capital to each business unit;
- They estimate the cost of capital of the business unit;
- They combine the amount of capital, the cost of capital and the credit risk of an individual borrower to set target pricing for new transactions.

Many institutions that have completed this process have found that their pricing methodology is inconsistent with market prices. Therefore a very important test of reduced form models and structural models is to skip this process and measure pricing consistency with market prices directly. If the model is inconsistent with market prices in this direct test, performance will not be any more accurate after the longer and more expensive process described above is followed.

Please note that every pricing model can be 'extended' to exactly match market prices. This is extremely common, whether it is fitting the observable term structure of interest rates exactly or whether it is fitting the volatility 'smile' observed in the options markets.

What this means is that the lack of a good fit to market prices is not fatal—in fact it is common. Nonetheless, if there are two competing theories and one shows an excellent (but still imperfect) fit and the other shows a poor fit, most analysts would choose the better fitting model unless there is a very good reason to do otherwise. We now fit the reduced form and structural models to the First Interstate data set.

We used two parameter versions of both models in order to make a fair comparison. The Merton model parameters, as explained in Chapter 3, are the unobservable market value of company assets and the unobservable volatility of the unobservable value of company assets. Please note that we do not need the default probabilities from the Merton model to price risky debt. We can see in Chapter 3 that the value of company assets and the volatility of company assets are the only parameters we need. We chose these two parameters so that:

- the market value of company equity was exactly equal to the Black-Scholes call option on the underlying assets of the firm, as predicted by the Merton model;
- the observable two-year credit spread was as close as possible to the two-year zero-coupon spread predicted by the Merton model.

One of the challenges of using the Merton model of risky debt is extending its single period assumptions to handle the multiple payments on coupon-bearing debt, like the 20 payments we would observe on a 10-year First Interstate bond. We adjusted the amount of debt outstanding that the Merton model requires by compounding the amount of debt due by the average cost of First Interstate liabilities.

We used a two-parameter version of the Jarrow model in which there is a constant liquidity discount and a constant instantaneous expected loss intensity (default probability multiplied by one minus the recovery rate). We fit these parameters weekly by minimizing the sum of squared errors between the actual credit spread and the theoretical credit spread predicted by the Jarrow model.

The period covered by the pricing test was January 3, 1986 to October 20, 1993 using the weekly First Interstate data.

1. Performance for Pricing 2-Year Bonds

At first glance, both models seem to match the observable credit spreads for First Interstate 2-year bonds well, as illustrated in Figure 7.5.

A graph of the pricing errors (Figure 7.6), however, shows that the performance of the Jarrow model was more accurate than the Merton model even though the Merton model was parameterized to the 2-year credit spread.

Figure 7.5 Estimated vs actual First Interstate 2 year par coupons for Jarrow and Merton models, 1986–1993

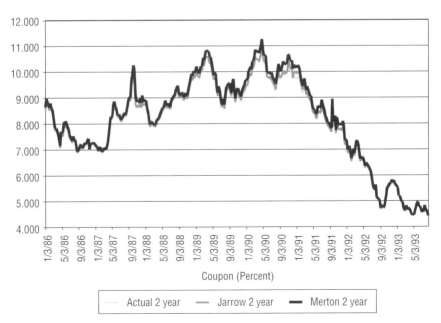

Figure 7.6 Jarrow error vs Merton error,
estimated First Interstate 2 year par coupon 1986–1993

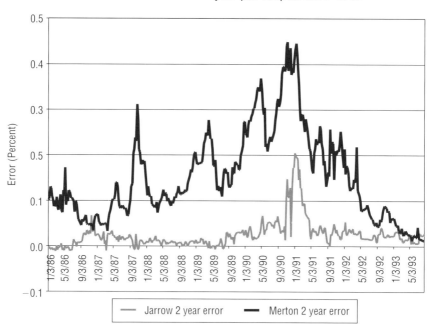

2. Performance for Pricing 3-Year Bonds

Pricing performance for the 3-year First Interstate credit spread showed a larger advantage for the Jarrow model than the Merton model (Figure 7.7).

The tendency of the Merton model to under price the long-term credit spreads is a phenomenon that becomes more important as maturities lengthen.

3. Performance for Pricing 5-Year Bonds

At five years, the advantage shown by the Jarrow model becomes quite large, with pricing errors reaching as much as 300 basis points for the Merton model about the time of First Interstate's greatest credit-related difficulties (Figure 7.8).

4. Performance for Pricing 7-Year Bonds

Merton model pricing widens still further at the 7-year maturity, exceeding 350 basis points (Figure 7.9).

Figure 7.7   Jarrow error vs Merton error,
estimated First Interstate 3 year par coupon 1986–1993

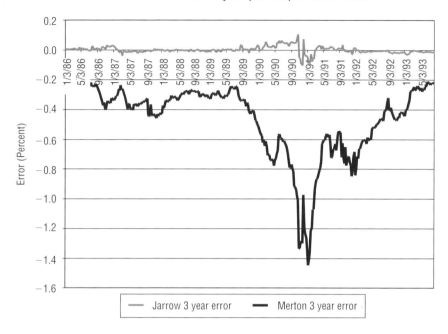

Figure 7.8   Jarrow error vs Merton error,
estimated First Interstate 5 year par coupon 1986–1993

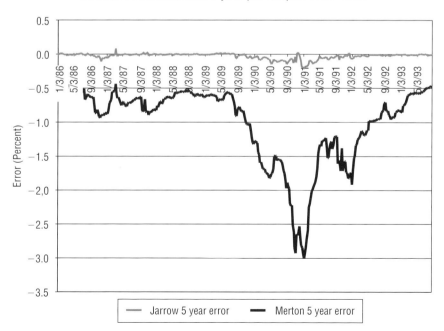

Figure 7.9   Jarrow error vs Merton error,
estimated First Interstate 7 year par coupon 1986–1993

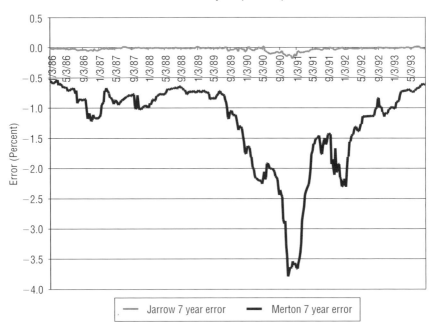

5. Performance for Pricing 10-Year Bonds

At 10 years, the Merton pricing error reaches more than 400 basis points at its largest point (Figure 7.10):

Summary of Merton and Jarrow Model Pricing Performance

The Jarrow model pricing performance was fairly consistent over the entire sample period, never exceeding 20 basis points error at any maturity, as shown in Figure 7.11.

The average Jarrow model pricing error, at about 3 basis points, was a small fraction of the Merton pricing error, where the longest maturity credit spreads were biased downwards to a considerable degree.

Figure 7.10 Jarrow error vs Merton error, estimated First Interstate 10 year par coupon 1986–1993

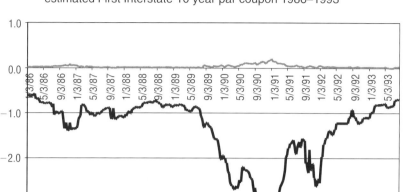

Figure 7.11 Error in estimating First Interstate Bancorp credit spreads from Jarrow Model, 1984–1993

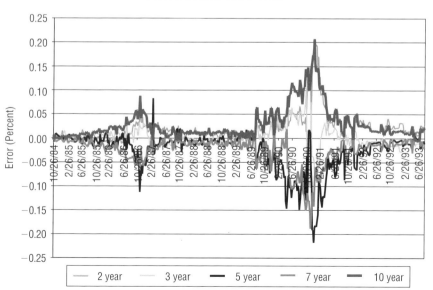

Average Error (Percent)		
Maturity	Jarrow Model	Merton Model
2 Years	0.025	0.155
3 Years	0.000	−0.468
5 Years	−0.031	−1.026
7 Years	−0.028	−1.280
10 Years	0.033	−1.452

This bias in the Merton model is not necessarily a problem. If there is no variation in the pricing bias at ten years, for example, we can simply add 1.45% to the Merton model pricing to match the market price. Therefore we next examine the volatility of pricing error.

The Merton model pricing errors showed considerabe volatility compared to the Jarrow models:

Average Error (Percent)		
Maturity	Jarrow Model	Merton Model
2 Years	0.033	0.100
3 Years	0.024	0.253
5 Years	0.042	0.579
7 Years	0.032	0.737
10 Years	0.036	0.846

The expected loss intensity[2] in the Jarrow model had a reassuringly high correlation with credit spread, as one would expect in an efficient market:

The Merton model default probability was less highly correlated with the credit spread, which is a source of concern if one believes that markets are reasonably efficient. This relatively low degree of correlation would be a positive only to those who believe that equity markets are more efficient than debt markets, a conclusion not supported by the Jarrow research findings on the statistical significance of default probabilities estimated from the debt and equity markets, which we discussed in Chapter 6.

We benchmarked the level of default probabilities in such a way that both models had the initial starting default probabilities that were equal. We then analyzed the correlation between default probabilities in each model and credit spreads. It is well known that credit spreads reflected more than

---

[2] The instantaneous default intensity times (1 minus the recovery rate)

Figure 7.12   Expected loss intensity in Jarrow Model versus 2 year credit spread, First Interstate Bancorp, 1984–1993

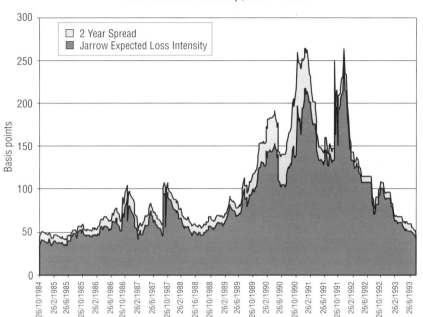

default probabilities and expected loss, particularly liquidity-related factors. Nonetheless, we know that expected loss is a large component of credit spreads and, all other things being equal, we would want to see a high degree of correlation. Over the First Interstate sample, the Jarrow model expected loss intensities have higher correlations with the credit spreads at all maturities than the Merton model default probabilities:

Correlation between credit spread and default probability	Jarrow Model	Merton Model
2 Years	0.982	0.765
3 Years	0.964	0.747
5 Years	0.924	0.691
7 Years	0.894	0.661
10 Years	0.875	0.635

Perhaps of greatest concern was the higher volatility of the Merton default probabilities compared to credit spreads.

Standard Deviation (Basis Points)
Jarrow Model   47.6
Merton Model   234.0

2 Year Spread   56.7
3 Year Spread   64.3
5 Year Spread   77.5
7 Year Spread   86.0
10 Year Spread   92.9

The Merton default probabilities were about five times more volatile than the expected loss intensities in the Jarrow model. This volatility would pose a challenge to bankers and others who intend to use Merton model default probabilities for performance measurement, which affects business strategy, shareholder value creation, and personal bonuses of senior management. This higher volatility is consistent with the research reported in Chapter 6 that debt and credit derivatives-based default probability estimates have higher statistical significance than default probability estimates benchmarked in equity prices.

Analyzing the Reasons for Pricing Performance Differential

There are a number of reasons why the Jarrow reduced form model was more effective in matching First Interstate credit spreads than the Merton model:

- The implicit assumptions about capital structure in the Jarrow model appear to be more realistic than those of the Merton model. The Jarrow model implicitly assumes that management is trying to maintain a relatively constant capital ratio (ratio of the market value of equity to market value of debt) and that market shocks from interest rates and the market index randomly push management away from its target default probability. The Merton model implicitly assumes that the dollar amount of debt outstanding does not change, which implies a volatile ratio of the market value of equity to the market value of debt.
- The Jarrow model is a full valuation framework for any contingent claim issued by a corporation with any capital structure, while the Merton model, in its purest form, is a suitable pricing model only for zero-coupon bonds for a corporation which has no other debt outstanding.

- The Merton model significantly understates the risk of long-term bond issues for companies with asset values that are highly volatile, because if the company does not go bankrupt in the near term it is likely to have a very high asset value, reducing the credit spread on company bonds to near zero. This is inconsistent with actual pricing on First Interstate bonds. Similarly, the Merton model implies a credit spread of near zero on very short-term liabilities, if the value of company assets is well above the amount of debt that needs to be repaid.

In the next section we turn to another objective of the credit risk process—hedging.

References

Derek H. Chen, Harry H. Huang, Rui Kan, Ashok Varikooty, and Henry N. Wang, 'Modelling and Managing Credit Risk,' *Asset & Liability Management: A Synthesis of New Methodologies*, RISK Publications, 1998.

Gregory Duffee, 'Estimating the Price of Default Risk,' *The Review of Financial Studies*, 12(1), 197–226, Spring 1999.

D. Heath, R. Jarrow and A. Morton, 'Bond Pricing and the Term Structure of Interest Rates: A New Methodology for Contingent Claim Valuation,' *Econometrica*, 60(1), 77–105, 1992.

R. Jarrow and S. Turnbull, 'Pricing Derivatives on Financial Securities Subject to Credit Risk,' *Journal of Finance* 50(1), 53–85, 1995.

R. Jarrow, D. Lando and S. Turnbull, 'A Markov Model for the Term Structure of Credit Risk Spreads,' *The Review of Financial Studies*, 10(2), 481–523, 1997.

R Jarrow and D. van Deventer, 'Integrating Interest Rate Risk and Credit Risk in ALM,' *Asset & Liability Management: A Synthesis of New Methodologies*, RISK Publications, 1998.

E.P. Jones, S. P. Mason, and E. Rosenfeld, 'Contingent Claims Analysis of Corporate Capital Structure: An Empirical Investigation,' *Journal of Finance* 39, 611–626, 1984.

F. A. Longstaff and E. S. Schwartz, 'A Simple Approach to Valuing Risky Fixed and Floating Rate Debt', *Journal of Finance* 50, 789–820, 1995.

R. C. Merton, 'An Intertemporal Capital Asset Pricing Model,' *Econometrica* 41, 867–887, September 1973.

R. C. Merton, 'On the Pricing of Corporate Debt: The Risk Structure of Interest Rates,' *Journal of Finance* 29, 449–470, 1974.

L. Nielsen, J. Saa-Requejo and P. Santa-Clara, 'Default Risk and Interest Rate Risk: The Term Structure of Default Spreads,' working paper, INSEAD, 1993.

D. Shimko, N. Tejima and van Deventer, 'The Pricing of Risky Debt when Interest Rates are Stochastic,' *Journal of Fixed Income*, 58–66, September 1993.

Tests of Hedging Accuracy

The authors believe that perhaps the most important test of credit models is based on this critical objective of the credit risk process:

How can I hedge the risk of my portfolio?

Even in an era of securitization, financial institutions cannot easily sell much of the portfolios of small business loans and consumer loans that they originate. Therefore a model that shows the best hedging performance has enormous appeal. We turn to an analysis of hedging performance in this chapter using the work of Jarrow and van Deventer [1998, 1999].

To compare the hedging performance of the Jarrow reduced form model and the Merton structural model, we again turn to the First Interstate data set.

For hedging purposes, the frequency of the data is important, as hedging theory is based on the notion of 'continuous' trading. Monthly observation intervals are too long to approximate 'continuous trading'. Weekly or daily price observations are best, so the First Interstate data set is attractive from that perspective.

Constructing the Hedge

The hedging test using the First Interstate data set was constructed as follows:

- At the start of the observation period, we simulate the purchase of a principal amount of $1 million of First Interstate 2-year zero-coupon bonds by using the 2-year credit spread from the data set and 2-year U.S. Treasury zero-coupon bond yields.
- Simultaneously, we construct the appropriate hedge with U.S. Treasury 2-year bonds, First Interstate common stock, or both. The exact hedge ratios (discussed below) differ for each of the models tested.
- After one week, the position is liquidated. The First Interstate bonds are 'sold' and all hedging positions closed out. The sale price of the First Interstate bonds and the U.S Treasury bonds accurately reflects the fact that they now have one year and 358 days to maturity. The yields used for pricing the First Interstate bonds, however, are the prevailing 2-year zero-coupon yields quoted at the end of the one-week holding period.
- The net profit or loss from this one-week strategy is calculated, stored, and then the process is repeated 375 times.

Since the net investment in the hedged portfolio is non-zero, if the model is correct, the hedged portfolio will be risk-free and therefore earn the weekly Treasury rate. We examined changes in the value of the hedged portfolio (profits or losses) over the week. For comparison purposes, this change should be nearly constant across time and approximately zero[3].

To avoid computing the return on the net investment, Jarrow and van Deventer [1998] computed the standard deviation of the hedged position's weekly profits. For all practical purposes, computing the standard deviation of the profits across time eliminates this expected (risk-free) profit on the net investment from the analysis. This is because the expected profit is approximately constant (and small) and therefore its value is incorporated into the computation of the standard deviation.

Thus, the 'best' credit model using this hedge is the one with the lowest standard deviation of weekly profit numbers over the sample period.

Implementing the Merton Model Hedge

To implement the hedge based on Merton's model, Jarrow and van Deventer [1998] discuss the need to estimate the strike price of the single zero-coupon bond issued by the firm, the value of the firm's assets, and the volatility of the firm's assets.

Estimating the strike price for the assumed zero-coupon bond liability structure is the most problematic of the three. This needs to be estimated from balance sheet data. Firstly, First Interstate's quarterly financial statements were used to measure the 'book value' of all of its liabilities[4]. Second, two years of interest expense, calculated by compounding the quarterly average cost of liabilities for two years, was added to this to account for the interest appreciation. The combined result is the estimate used.

The firm's asset values and the assets' volatility were estimated implicitly as in the previous section on pricing. The Merton model's parameters were calibrated weekly to fit the observable credit spread and stock price at the initiation of the trading position.

---

[3] To see this, as Jarrow and van Deventer observed, let I = the net investment. The theoretical change in the value of the hedged position is $Ir(1/52)$ where r is the weekly rate on a per year basis. This change is less than $(.07)(1/52) = .0013$ times the net investment. For a net investment of 500,000 dollars, this change is 673 dollars. Since the net investment is approximately constant across time, so will be this expected profit.

[4] Merton's model was treated more favorably than would be possible in practice. It was assumed that financial statements for a given quarter were instantly known to the trader on the last day of the quarter, but in reality there would be a lag of some weeks before detailed balance sheets were publicly available.

The Merton risky debt hedge consists of two securities, both stock and the U.S. Treasury note[5]. For the stock position, hedge ratios were calculated using the well-known 'deltas' from the Black Scholes model (see Jarrow and Turnbull [1996] for this calculation)[6]. The U.S. Treasury hedge implied by the model was calculated by computing 'rho,' the derivative of risky debt with respect to changes in the risk-free interest rate, and then neutralizing this derivative with a position in U.S. Treasury bonds.

Implementing the Jarrow Model Hedge

A closely related question to that posed in previous sections is how well the Jarrow model performs in the same hedging test applied to the Merton model. Jarrow and van Deventer [1999] assumed that the 'market index' M in the Jarrow model was the S&P 500 equity index, and the hedging instruments were 2-year Treasuries and S&P 500 futures contracts.

Comparing Model Hedging Performance

Jarrow and van Deventer [1999] found that the Jarrow model consistently had less hedging error than the Merton model, even though the parameters of the Jarrow model were held constant over the sample period and the Merton parameters were updated weekly. It is easiest to compare the two models if we graph the 13-week hedging error standard deviation for the Jarrow model as a percentage of the 13-week standard deviation for the Merton model. The results show that the Jarrow model rarely performed worse (i.e. at a level greater than 100% of Merton) than the Merton model over the 282 13-week sample periods.

A histogram in 10 percentile increments shows that largest decile of the 13 week sample periods was the decile for 50–60% of the Merton model hedging error. This means that the most frequent result reflected the Jarrow hedging error as being 40–50% less than the Merton hedging error.

Jarrow and van Deventer [1999] found that only 16 out of 282 13-week periods showed the Jarrow model with a greater hedging error than the Merton model. The average figure for the Jarrow model's hedging error standard deviation as a percent of the Merton model was 63.6%. The median ratio was 60.3%.

---

[5] Although the model implies an interest rate hedge is unnecessary, we use a simple Taylor series expansion to extend the model to include an interest rate hedge. The expansion is: $\Delta D = (\partial D/\partial E)\Delta E + (\partial D/\partial r)\Delta r$. To use the Black-Scholes deltas, note that $\partial D/\partial E = (\partial D/\partial V)/(\partial E/\partial V)$. The ratios in the last expression can be obtained using the Black-Scholes formula.

[6] See footnote 8.

Figure 7.13 13 week standard deviation for Jarrow Model as percent of Merton Model 13-week standard deviations

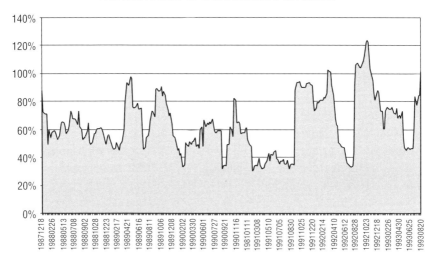

Figure 7.14 Histogram of Jarrow 13-week standard deviations as percent of Merton 13-week standard deviations

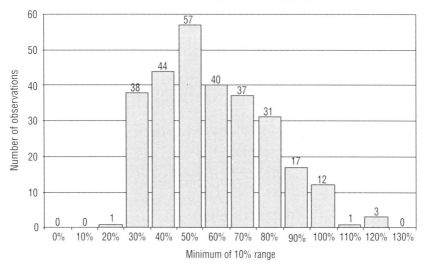

Therefore the Jarrow model, with the S&P500 as the macro factor driving default probabilities for First Interstate, provided a 40% reduction in hedging error compared to the Merton model on average. This is encouraging in a number of respects. It implies that macro-hedging of credit risk is a viable alternative to much more costly hedging on a micro-basis, issuer by issuer. It is also reassuring in the sense that the Merton hedge using common stock, even in a theoretical sense, is only executable for borrowers whose credit quality is relatively strong. If the borrower is near bankruptcy and the stock price is almost zero, there is not enough common stock in existence which can be shorted to hedge further declines in bond prices because the stock price has a floor at zero and the supply of common stock is finite in supply. The realistic alternative presented by the reduced form models avoids this problem.

Conclusions Regarding Relative Credit Model Hedging Performance

In order to better understand the reasons for the relative performance of the Jarrow model and the Merton model, Jarrow and van Deventer [1999] performed a regression analysis to better understand potential biases in hedge results.

An ordinary least squares regression was performed on the hedging errors for each of the models that sought to explain the hedging error as a function of three variables: the dollar change in the value of the U.S. Treasury zero-coupon bond, the change in the First Interstate stock price, and the change in value of an S&P500 futures contract.

Jarrow and van Deventer found the following results for the Jarrow model:

Regression of Jarrow Model Hedging Errors

Regression Statistics	
Multiple R	0.105326056
R Square	0.011093578
Adjusted R Square	0.000828114
Standard Error	1985.267218
Observations	293

	Coefficients	*Standard Error*	*t Stat*
Intercept	299.0779583	130.7137557	2.288037
Change in UST Zero	0.000591391	0.043013917	0.013749
Change in Stock Price	112.9782128	62.74794439	1.800509
Change in S&P500 Futures	−0.03206161	0.03801913	−0.8433

None of the explanatory variables have statistical significance, although the change in stock price is fairly close to statistical significance. The adjusted *R* Squared of the regression is zero to two significant digits. That means there was no significant bias in the Jarrow hedging results.

There is apparent bias in the Merton model results, however, as the figure below shows:

Regression of Merton Model Hedging Errors

Regression Statistics	
Multiple R	0.601433256
R Square	0.361721962
Adjusted R Square	0.355096238
Standard Error	2183.422085
Observations	293

	Coefficients	Standard Error	t Stat
Intercept	287.7734679	143.7606476	2.001754
Change in UST Zero	−0.04048238	0.047307252	−0.85573
Change in Stock Price	777.7323007	69.01098566	11.26969
Change in S&P500 Futures	0.004517238	0.041813922	0.108032

The results show a very significant coefficient on the First Interstate common stock variable, with a t-statistic of more than 11 and an adjusted R square of 0.355. On average, the Merton hedging error would have been reduced by approximately $500 in standard deviation if the number of shares used to hedge the position in risky debt was increased by 778 shares per week. As we saw earlier in this chapter, stock price and credit spread movements were contrary to that predicted by the Merton model in 58% of the weekly periods. If the Merton hedge ratios are optimized by a scale factor, Jarrow and van Deventer report that the hedge ratios prescribed by the model would be improved by multiplying times a constant equal to −0.21. That is, optimizing the hedge 'in sample', reverses the direction of the Merton model hedge. This is because 58% of the First Interstate data points moved in a direction opposite to that predicted by the Merton model.

Another potential problem in the Merton model hedge was the constant interest rate assumption, an assumption relaxed in the Shimko, Tejima and van Deventer [1993]. The regression results above, however, show no simple bias in the U.S. Treasury hedge ratio of the Merton model.

Jarrow and van Deventer discuss two other factors that are much more significant: the simplicity of the capital structure assumption implied by the

Merton model and liquidity factors. The capital structure problem is the more important one. The Merton model assumes that management determines a dollar amount of debt and then leaves that debt structure in place no matter what happens to the value of company assets. In terms of a specific example, consider a real estate investor who buys a building for $100 million and finances it with a fixed-rate term loan of $80 million. The Merton model assumes that the debt stays in place even if the value of the building goes to $200 million. In market value terms, this increase in asset values will reduce the credit spread to near zero and increase the market value of the loan to approximately $81 million or $82 million. The market value of equity, however, will skyrocket from approximately $25 million (depending on interest rates and the volatility of building prices) to approximately $120 million. This implies a very high degree of volatility in the capital structure and credit spread assumed by the Merton model.

According to Jarrow and van Deventer, most market participants (especially those who lend against buildings) have found it much more likely that the real estate investor would refinance the building with a loan of $160 million if the price of the building went to $200 million. Put simply, management acts dynamically in setting capital structure but the Merton model assumes management is static in this respect. The result of dynamic management action with respect to capital structure is a much greater stability in credit spreads, debt equity ratios and the probability of default than the Merton model implies. This is consistent with the clustering of debt/equity ratios within industries and the relative stability of capital structures over time for specific companies. The reduced form nature of the Jarrow model is consistent with this stability; the probability of default is shocked by interest rate and equity index (and other factor) movements, but on average management implicitly seeks to maintain a stable capital structure with relatively constant probability of default. When company asset values decline, management is not able to meet their objective of a stable capital structure but management takes the most effective action it can to slow the increase in the probability of default. In short, optimal capital ratios exist because it is expensive to deviate from them. It seems clear that the Jarrow model captures this fact more accurately than the Merton model based on this limited hedging experiment.

Liquidity factors also come into play. By liquidity, we mean a phenomenon with broader implications than merely the bid-offered spread in a given market. If we assume that debt and equity markets are linked but that risk aversion is different (something true almost by definition) between the two respective sets of investors, a change in risk aversion will impact the two markets differently. Assume both sets of investors become more risk averse simultaneously but the reaction in the debt markets is relatively more severe. The result will be, at any given level of equity prices, a higher level of credit spreads across the board than prevailed previously even if the probability of default has not changed. This is effectively what happened during the events surrounding Long Term Capital Management. The Merton model attributes all of this increase in credit spreads to an increase in the probability of default, while the Jarrow model can properly distinguish the change in conditions via its explicit incorporation of a liquidity factor.

Lessons from Enron and Others: Tests of the Consistency of Implications with Observable Market Behavior[7]

The Basel Committee on Banking Supervision [2001] states in its proposed new capital accord that:

> '*A bank must demonstrate to its supervisor that the internal validation process enables it to assess the performance of internal rating and risk quantification systems consistently and meaningfully.*'[8]

In Chapter 6, we used historical default data bases to test credit models. Even the tools in Chapter 6 have limited usefulness due to the scarcity of defaults and bankruptcies in major economies, leading researchers to draw conclusions from very small data sets. An example is Kealhofer and Kurbat [2001], who examine data sets with only 10–121 defaults. In this section we use a sample data base of 36,974 credit spreads on 64 bonds issued by eight major corporations to conduct a non-parametric test of the Merton [1974] model of risky debt. Specifically, we want to use these 36,974 observations to see whether or not the First Interstate finding (only 42% of data points are consistent with Merton) is unique to First Interstate or a more general finding that provides important guidance in credit modeling. As we saw earlier in this chapter, the lack of consistency with Merton assumptions in the First Interstate case resulted in a Merton hedge that was in the wrong direction from the optimal 'in sample' hedge of First Interstate debt with a position in First Interstate common stock.

Specifically, in this section we anticipate the results of a hedging performance test of the Merton model for other companies by first testing

---

[7] Xaioming Wang was responsible for the empirical work in this section.
[8] Section 302, page 55.

for *directional correctness*; if less than 50% of data points are consistent with the Merton model, then a hedge with any variation of a single factor Merton model will likely be incorrect in direction for market conditions within the sample period. Enron Corporation, which filed for voluntary protection under Chapter 11 on December 2, 2001, was one of the corporate names studied in this regard. We illustrate the testing for directional correctness in most depth with respect to Enron, which at the time of its bankruptcy petition was the largest corporate bankruptcy in U.S. history.

Note again that these tests are not relevant to reduced form models, because they do imply the same relationship between common stock and credit spreads that the single factor Merton model does.

Description of Credit Spread Data

Market convention for credit spread quotations is extremely simple. The yield to maturity on the nearest liquid U.S. Treasury security is subtracted from the yield to maturity on the bond in question. The difference is the market convention for the credit spread. There are many sources of error in this convention: a mismatch in maturity dates, a mismatch in payment dates, the implied use of the same discount rate at all maturities, etc. The virtue of this convention is that the calculation is independent of any particular credit model.

This study employs a more exact calculation designed to remedy these deficiencies while still remaining 'credit model independent.' Credit spreads were obtained by the following process:

a. The exact date of each payment on the risky bond is determined
b. The continuously compounded yield to maturity to the exact payment date in the U.S. Treasury market was calculated for each payment date.
c. The amount of payment due on the risky bond was determined for each payment date.
d. The credit spread was defined as the constant x which, when added to the zero-coupon Treasury yields for each payment date, causes the theoretical present value of cash flows to equal the observable sum of price plus accrued interest on the bonds.

The input data for the U.S. Treasury yield curve smoothing process is the constant maturity treasury series made available daily on statistical release

The authors wish to thank Ms Xaioming Wang, Kamakura Corporation and University of Hawaii, who was responsible for the empirical work in this section.

H15 by the Board of Governors of the Federal Reserve. The smoothing method is the maximum smoothness forward rate method of van Deventer and Imai [1996] and Adams and van Deventer [1994]. Van Deventer and Imai provide a mathematical proof that any other smoothing method produces forward rates that are less smooth than the maximum smoothness forward rate technique. Risky bond prices and bond descriptions were provided by Bridge Information Systems and Data Stream.

Enron Corporation Results

The objective of this section is to test the directional correctness of the Merton model of risky debt in the most straightforward manner possible. The Merton model has a large number of variations, but all single factor variations (where the single factor is the value of company assets) share a common dependence on the value of company assets as the sole random determinant of the value of risky debt as we have discussed throughout this book. See Bohn [1999] for a comprehensive survey of the variations in the Merton model. For each of the single factor variations in the Merton model, Jarrow, van Deventer and Wang [2002] show that the derivatives of risky debt with respect to the value of company assets and the derivative of company equity with respect to the value of company assets are both positive. Jarrow, van Deventer and Wang [2002] also show the derivative of the credit spread with respect to changes in the value of company assets is negative.

All other things being equal for instantaneous changes, the Merton model and its principal variants all lead us to expect that higher stock prices will be accompanied by lower credit spreads. If this is not the case, either other parameters (which Merton assumed to be constant) are changing, there are errors in the data, or the model is not applicable to the data set being tested. Most of the commercially available time series on Merton model default probabilities explicitly assume that interest rates are constant and that all other parameters of the model are constant during the month or within a financial accounting period, changing only when new data on company liabilities and shares outstanding become public.

The table below shows the results of a simple regression that seeks to explain the absolute level of the credit spread as a linear function of the stock price, as we did earlier in this chapter for First Interstate. The Merton model and its variants predict that, all other things being equal, a higher value of company assets will lead to higher stock prices and lower credit spreads, leading to a negative coefficient on the stock price if the credit spread is regressed on observable stock price data. The table below shows that this relationship did not prevail for any of the eight bond issues of Enron studied, covering a sample of 16,200 daily bond price observations. In no

Enron: Regression of Credit Spread on Stock Price

Issues	9.88% 293561AF3 due on 6/15/2003	9.65% 293561AH9 due on 5/15/2001	9.5% 293561AN6 due on 6/15/2001	9.13% 293561AQ9 due on 4/1/2003	7.63% 293561AR7 due on 9/10/2004	8.25% 293561AS5 due on 9/15/2012	6.75% 293561AT3 due on 7/1/2005	7% 293561AU0 due on 8/15/23
Adjusted R^2 on stock price Level data*	17.0%	14.0%	15.0%	24.0%	43.0%	59.0%	57.0%	0.3%
Coefficient B Level data	0.0078	0.0051	0.0057	0.0071	0.0093	0.0120	0.0110	0.0056
T-score of B Level data	21.7	19.1	20.0	27.1	40.0	54.9	50.7	1.9
Consistent with Merton?	No	No	No	No	No	No	No	No
Data Information Starting Date	1/2/93	1/2/92	2/6/92	12/4/91	8/31/92	9/22/92	6/18/93	8/19/93
Ending Date	3/12/01	3/12/01	3/12/01	3/12/01	3/12/01	3/12/01	3/12/01	4/14/97
Number of observations	2307	2286	2261	2305	2119	2104	1915	903

* Level data uses model: $CS_i = A + BE_i + \varepsilon$

CS is credit spread and E stands for equity/stock price.

case did the stock price explain more than 59% of movements in credit spread, although the single factor nature of the Merton model implies that movements in the value of company assets would be the sole random variable determining stock price and credit spread movements.

The coefficient B of the regression of credit spread on stock price was positive and very statistically significant for six of the eight bond issues studied and positive with marginal statistical significance for the other two bond issues. The graph below shows the reasons for these conclusions, graphing stock price versus the credit spread of the Enron 9.13% bonds due 1st April 2003.

Credit spreads declined and then rose over the sample period while stock price was primarily rising. The graph below plots credit spread as a function of stock price for the 8.25% Enron bonds due 15th September 2012, the bond issue that had the highest R^2 in credit spread movements when regressed on stock price.

Results were somewhat better when the first difference of credit spread was regressed on the first difference of stock price for each of the eight Enron issues. The table below shows that four of eight bond issues had credit spread movements that were directionally consistent with the basic Merton model (and any one factor version of it), and that two of these four had a coefficient that was statistically significant in the predicted direction.

Figure 7.15 Enron stock price versus credit spread on 9.13% bonds due 4/1/2003, December 1991 to April 2001

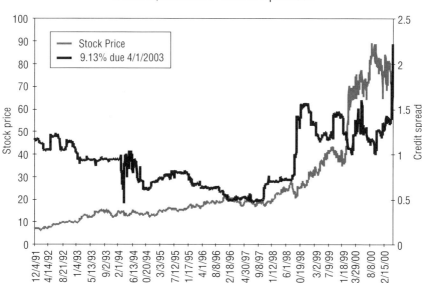

Figure 7.16   Enron credit spread on 8.25% bonds due 9/15/2012 as a function of stock price, December 1991 to April 2001

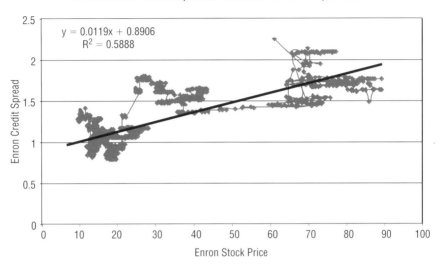

The next table classifies data points by whether the changes in stock price and credit spread over the daily time frame are consistent with the predictions of all one-factor Merton models. Consistent movement is any combination of stock price and credit spread where:

- Stock price rises and credit spread falls;
- Stock price falls and credit spread rises;
- Stock price and credit spread are both unchanged.

All other combinations of stock price and credit spread movements were classified as inconsistent with the one factor Merton model, as we did in the First Interstate case earlier in the chapter.

This table shows that none of the bonds had credit spread movements and stock price movements that were consistent with the Merton model as much as 50% of the time. Over all 16,200 data points, 46% were consistent with the Merton model. Results were 35-53 standard deviations from the 100% consistency that would be predicted by the joint hypothesis that the single factor Merton model is true and the data contains no errors. For all eight bond issues, the percentage of data points consistent with all single factor Merton models was less than 50% by a statistically significant number of standard deviations. The implications are that a trader with one day advance notice of Enron stock price movements who took the bond position indicated

Issues	9.88% 293561AF3 due on 6/15/2003	9.65% 293561AH9 due on 5/15/2001	9.5% 293561AN6 due on 6/15/2001	9.13% 293561AQ9 due on 4/1/2003	7.63% 293561AR7 due on 9/10/2004	8.25% 293561AS5 due on 9/15/2012	6.75% 293561AT3 due on 7/1/2005	7% 293561AU0 due on 8/15/23
Enron: Regression of Change in Credit Spread on Change in Stock Price								
Adjusted R² on stock price								
First difference data**	0.0%	0.0%	0.0%	0.6%	0.0%	0.4%	0.1%	−0.1%
Coefficient B								
First difference data	0.0036	0.0001	−0.0018	−0.0029	0.0014	−0.0020	−0.0010	0.0165
T-score of B								
First difference data	1.4	0.1	−0.9	−4.0	1.2	−3.1	−1.8	0.7
Consistent with Merton?	No	No	Yes	Yes	No	Yes	Yes	No
Data Information								
Starting Date	1/2/93	1/2/92	2/6/92	12/4/91	8/31/92	9/22/92	6/18/93	8/19/93
Ending Date	3/12/01	3/12/01	3/12/01	3/12/01	3/12/01	3/12/01	3/12/01	4/14/97
Number of observations	2307	2286	2261	2305	2119	2104	1915	903

** First Difference data uses model: Change in CS_i = A + B[Change in E_i] + ε
CS is credit spread and E stands for equity/stock price.

by the single-factor Merton models would have lost money 54% of the time. This is consistent with the First Interstate data, but it is still surprising. We now seek to find an explanation for this result.

Impact of Different Time Intervals on Results

Thoughtful analysts of the data in the previous section suggested that a longer time period than daily data might have led to results more favorable to the Merton model. The table below repeats this analysis for the four Enron bond issues with the longest price history over a common time period from February 6, 1992 to March 12, 2001 using daily data and time intervals of 30 business days and 90 business days. The consistency ratio does rise slightly, to about 55% when the period used is 90 business days. The table shows, however, that the joint hypothesis that the single factor versions of the Merton model are true and that the data contains no errors is still rejected for all time intervals by 35–52 standard deviations.

Analysis of Relative Correlation of Credit Spreads and Stock Price

The next table compares the correlation between stock price movements and credit spread movements for the four Enron bonds with the longest price series. Credit spreads for Enron have a correlation with equity prices of 36–51%, much lower than the 100% predicted by a single factor Merton model. The credit spreads show a high correlation with each other, however, with correlations ranging from 83–98%. While it is sometimes argued that secondary bond market price quotations are of low quality, this high degree of internal consistency is reassuring.

Correlation between Enron Stock Price and Credit Spreads
On Four Enron Debt Issues, 2/6/92 to 3/12/2001

Security	Stock Price	9.88% due 6/15/2003	9.65% due 5/15/2001	9.5% due 6/15/2001	9.13% due 4/1/2003
Stock Price	100.00%	48.73%	36.25%	41.52%	50.55%
9.88% due 6/15/2003		100.00%	83.21%	90.34%	98.16%
9.65% due 5/15/2001			100.00%	95.49%	83.99%
9.5% due 6/15/2001				100.00%	90.28%
9.13% due 4/1/2003					100.00%

Note: 11 outliers eliminated in 2263 data points from 2/6/92 to 3/12/2001.

Analysis of Relative Smoothness of Credit Spreads and Stock Price

Another criterion for reasonableness is the relative smoothness of the equity and credit spread time series. Adams and van Deventer [1994] note that the

Enron Corporation
Percentage of Observable Credit Spreads Consistent with Merton Model
December 1991 to April 2001

| Change over | Enron Bond Issue Used for Credit Spread Calculation | | | | |
	9.88% due 6/15/2003	9.65% due 5/15/2001	9.5% due 6/15/2001	9.13% due 4/1/2003	Total
Percentage of Data Points Consistent With Merton Model					
1 Business Day	45.4%	46.6%	46.4%	46.1%	46.1%
30 Business Days	53.0%	48.4%	49.7%	51.7%	50.7%
90 Business Days	61.5%	46.2%	54.8%	56.6%	54.8%
Standard Deviation of Merton Consistency Percentage					
1 Business Day	1.0%	1.0%	1.0%	1.0%	0.5%
30 Business Days	1.1%	1.1%	1.1%	1.1%	0.5%
90 Business Days	1.0%	1.1%	1.1%	1.1%	0.5%
Number of Standard Deviations from 50% Of Total Data					
1 Business Day	−4.4	−3.2	−3.4	−3.7	−7.4
30 Business Days	2.8	−1.5	−0.3	1.6	1.3
90 Business Days	11.1	−3.5	4.5	6.2	9.0
Number of Standard Deviations from 100% Of Total Data					
1 Business Day	−52.2	−50.9	−51.1	−51.4	−102.8
30 Business Days	−44.5	−48.8	−47.6	−45.7	−93.2
90 Business Days	−36.8	−50.3	−42.3	−40.8	−84.7

integral of the squared second derivative of a function is a common measure
of 'smoothness' in engineering, computer science, and recently finance, with
zero representing perfect smoothness.

$$Z = \int_0^T [f''(s)]^2 \, ds$$

Since we expect that credit spreads and equity prices are continuous, but
non-differentiable functions of stochastic variables, 'smoothness' may well
be less appropriate than volatility as a measure of noise. Nonetheless,
smoothness has an intuitive appeal. As a proxy index for smoothness, we
compute the sum of the squared second differences of the equity price and
the four credit spread series after normalizing the series so that the value for
all series on 6th February 1992 is 1. The next table reports the smoothness
statistics for each series; a smoothness of zero would indicate a series that
is perfectly smooth.

Enron Corporation Smoothness of Equity and Credit Spread Time Series February 1992 to March 2001		Enron Bond Issue Used for Credit Spread Calculation			
	Equity Price	9.88% due 6/15/2003	9.65% due 5/15/2001	9.5% due 6/15/2001	9.13% due 4/1/2003
Sum of squared second differences of normalized (2/6/1992 = 1) series	90.75	3.96	6.37	6.52	6.97

After elimination of outliers from the credit spread series (6, 2, 1, and 1
data points respectively) the smoothness statistics show that the credit spread
series are approximately 14 times more smooth than the equity series after
all have been indexed to an identical starting value.

Analysis of Impact of 'Noise' in the Data

If one source of 'noise' in a data series is the random jumping from bid to
offered to bid and back in the price quotation, one would expect that
problem to be most prevalent in the series that is least smooth. From 1992
to 2001 for Enron, that would lead one to suspect the equity price series in
that regard rather than the credit spread series. Alternatively, as suggested by
Jarrow [2001], there could be price bubbles, consistent with no arbitrage, in
equity prices but not in debt prices.

Note that if there is a persistent, non-random bias or error in reporting either equity prices or debt prices (and therefore credit spreads) the classification of data points with regard to consistency with the Merton model will be unaffected. Only random errors can affect that classification.

Analysis of Omitted Variables

Another potential source of error in measuring consistency with the Merton model is the implicit assumption that certain random variables are in fact constant. There are a number of variables for which omission might cause measurement errors:

- Random interest rates, by far the most significant omission in the single-factor variants of the Merton model;
- Asset volatility, which is usually assumed to be constant, could in fact be random as in the options pricing model of Hull and White [1987];
- Accounting data, which determines the 'strike price' of the option in the risky debt model, changes quarterly, or about once in every 66 observations in the Enron data set.

The table below shows what happens if random interest rates are incorporated in a linear regression that explains credit spreads as a linear function of stock prices and the 3-month Treasury bill rate for four Enron bond issues from 2/6/1992 to 3/12/2001. The interest rate is a highly significant contributor to explanatory power, but stock prices continue to have the wrong sign from that predicted by the Merton model (and its variant the Shimko, Tejima and van Deventer model), with t-scores of 35–49. This confirms that the omission of interest rates, by far the most significant random variable missing from the original Merton model of risky debt, was not the reason that a regression of credit spreads on stock prices reported earlier had the opposite sign than that predicted by the original Merton model.

Impact of Expected Return on the Consistency of the Merton Model with Observable Data

There is one other possible explanation for the low level of consistency of the observable data with the Merton model. That is the impact of the expected return on the drift in bond prices and equity prices, since the daily time interval used here is not in fact instantaneous as we have assumed above. The impact of expected return is explored in a separate paper by Jarrow, van Deventer and Wang [2002], who also find all single factor variants of the Merton model to be inconsistent with the data after this adjustment.

Enron Corporation
Credit Spread as Linear Function of Stock Price and 3-Month T-bill Rate
2/6/1992 to 3/12/2001

	9.88% due 6/15/2003	9.65% due 5/15/2001	9.5% due 6/15/2001	9.13% due 4/1/2003	
Consistent with Merton?	No	No	No	No
Coefficient					
Stock Price	0.0131	0.0101	0.0109	0.0122
3-Month T-bill Rate	−0.1974	−0.1955	−0.2040	−0.1866
T-Score					
Stock Price	35.1	40.2	40.5	49.3
3-Month T-bill Rate	−25.1	−37.0	−36.1	−36.0
Adjusted R^2	36.3%	46.4%	46.2%	53.1%
Standard Error (%)	0.305	0.205	0.219	0.201

Consistency of Single Factor Merton Model with Observed Credit Spreads and Equity Data for Other Corporations

We analyzed a number of other corporations for consistency with the Merton model. The corporations studied were suggested by credit experts at major international banks as those most likely to be most illustrative. We report those results in this section.

Bank One Corporation

The next table shows that not one of the fourteen bond issues of Bank One Corporation had a credit spread series that exceeded a 50% consistency with the Merton model. This sample includes 10,797 credit spread observations for Bank One. The joint hypothesis that the Merton model is true and that there are no errors in the data was rejected for all fourteen bond issue credit spread series by a minimum of 18 standard deviations. Six of the fourteen price series had percentages consistent with Merton that were statistically significantly less than the minimum 50% level that one would find in the face of large data errors.

Exxon

The table below reports similar totals for Exxon Corporation for a sample of three bond issues and a total of 690 daily price observations. Two of the three bond issues had credit spreads that were consistent with Merton less than 50% of the time, and the third issue had a 51% consistency ratio. The joint hypothesis that the Merton model is true and there are no errors in the

Bank One Corporation

Issues	10% 059438AB7 due on 8/15/2010	7.25% 059438AD3 due on 8/1/2002	8.74% 059438AE1 due on 9/15/2003	7% 059438AF8 due on 7/15/2005	7.75% 059438AG6 due on 7/15/2025	7.63% 059438AH4 due on 10/15/2026	7.8% 059438AJ0 due on 5/1/2007	9% 059438AK7 due on 4/29/2027	9.88% 059438AL5 due on 3/1/2019	6.6% 05943FAC9 due on 3/23/2001	7% 05943FAD7 due on 3/25/2002
Percent of data points consistent with Merton model	48%	46%	46%	47%	47%	48%	48%	49%	42%	43%	47%
Adjusted R^2 on Stock Price											
Level data*	0.5%	0.0%	0.1%	14.0%	18.0%	4.7%	-0.1%	-0.1%	62.0%	1.0%	-0.2%
First difference data**	0.1%	-0.1%	0.0%	0.1%	0.2%	0.2%	0.6%	1.2%	-0.2%	0.2%	-0.2%
Coefficient B											
Level data	-0.003	0.00064	0.0019	0.0083	0.009	0.0075	-0.0018	-0.0013	-0.047	0.061	0.00035
First difference data	-0.015	0.00057	-0.015	-0.0036	-0.0021	-0.0018	-0.017	-0.0037	0.0034	0.23	-0.01
T-score of B											
Level data	-3.05	0.62	1.88	12.2	14.21	5.48	-0.76	-0.67	-20.36	2.44	0.046
First difference data	-1.38	0.036	-0.82	-1.44	-1.7	-1.41	-1.99	-2.6	0.65	1.31	-0.21
Std. Dev. Of Merton Percent	1.2%	1.2%	1.2%	1.7%	1.7%	2.1%	2.3%	2.3%	3.2%	2.3%	2.3%
Standard Deviations from 50%	-1.7	-3.2	-3.4	-1.8	-1.8	-1.0	-0.9	-0.4	-2.5	-3.1	-1.3
Standard Deviations from 100%	-44.2	-43.8	-45.9	-31.9	-31.9	-25.0	-22.3	-21.8	-18.2	-25.3	-23.2
Date information											
Starting date	1/2/92	8/3/92	12/4/91	7/21/95	7/21/95	10/25/96	4/25/97	4/28/97	3/25/98	3/25/97	3/25/97
Ending date	3/18/99	3/18/99	3/18/99	3/18/99	3/18/99	3/18/99	3/18/99	3/18/99	3/18/99	3/18/99	3/18/99
Number of observations	1808	1633	1796	904	903	580	458	458	242	484	478

Issues	Exxon		
	6% 190157 due on 7/1/2005	6.15% 383210 due on 3/11/2003	6.13% 384907 due on 9/8/2008
Percent of data points consistent with Merton model	49%	46%	51%
Adjusted R^2 on stock price			
Level data*	4.5%	20.0%	13.0%
First difference data**	−0.3%	−0.3%	0.0%
Coefficient B			
Level data	0.0069	0.0150	0.0090
First difference data	0.0064	−0.0018	0.0058
T-score of B			
Level data	3.4	7.7	5.9
First difference data	0.5	−0.4	1.1
Std. Dev. Of Merton Percent	3.3%	3.3%	3.3%
Standard Deviations from 50%	0.3	1.2	−0.3
Standard Deviations from 100%	15.4	16.4	14.8
Data Information			
Starting Date	4/18/95	4/18/95	4/18/95
Ending Date	9/28/99	9/28/99	9/28/99
Number of observations	230	230	230

data is rejected by a minimum of 14 standard deviations for all three credit spread series.

Lucent Technologies

The following table reports results for seven bond issues of Lucent Technologies with 4,434 observable bond prices and credit spreads. Two issues had less than 50% of credit spread movements inconsistent with Merton, two were at the 50% level, and three were slightly over the 50% level. In no case was the percentage consistent with Merton statistically different from 50%, but the joint hypothesis that the Merton model is true and there are no data errors is rejected by all bond series by at least 12 standard deviations.

Merrill Lynch

The table below describes results from 1,112 weekly data points on 12 bond issues by Merrill Lynch. Only four of the 12 bond issues have a consistency ratio versus the Merton model of less than 50%, but in none of the 12 cases is the consistency ratio different from 50% in a statistically significant fashion.

	Lucent Technology						
Issues	6.9% 549463AA5 due on 7/5/2001	7.25% 549463AB3 due on 7/15/2006	6.5% 549463AC1 due on 1/15/2028	5.5% 549463AD9 due on 11/15/2008	6.45% 549463AE7 due on 3/15/2029	8.0% 54946EAC7 due on 5/18/2015	7.7% 54946EAD5 due on 5/19/2010
Percent of data points consistent with Merton model	50%	48%	51%	48%	50%	54%	53%
Adjusted R^2 on stock price							
Level data*	0.0%	0.8%	22.0%	20.0%	77.0%	46.0%	34.0%
First difference data**	−0.1%	−0.1%	0.9%	0.4%	0.1%	−0.3%	−0.4%
Coefficient B							
Level data	0.0008	−0.0038	−0.0160	−0.0410	−0.0290	−0.0440	0.5500
First difference data	0.0012	0.0021	−0.0037	−0.0460	−0.0023	−0.0056	0.0590
T-score of B							
Level data	0.7	−3.1	−14.6	−11.9	−39.6	−12.7	10.1
First difference data	0.1	0.3	−2.8	−1.7	−1.2	0.0	0.5
Std. Dev. Of Merton Percent	1.5%	1.5%	1.8%	2.1%	2.3%	3.6%	3.6%
Standard Deviations from 50%	0.0	−1.3	0.6	−0.9	0.0	1.1	0.8
Standard Deviations from 100%	−33.5	−34.9	−27.1	−24.5	−21.9	−12.7	−13.0
Data Information							
Stating Date	7/22/96	7/22/96	1/9/98	11/24/98	3/18/99	5/18/00	5/15/00
Ending Date	2/23/01	2/23/01	2/23/01	2/23/01	2/23/01	2/23/01	2/23/01
Number of observations	1123	1123	766	557	482	190	193

Merrill Lynch

Issues	6% 600687 due on 11/15/2004	6.88% 600689 due on 11/15/2018	6% 602080 due on 7/15/2005	6.5% 602081 due on 7/15/2018	6% 604189 due on 2/12/2003	6.38% 604646 due on 4/3/2008	5.75% 605295 due on 12/1/2003	6% 640884 due on 2/17/2009	7.25% 816021 due on 5/2/2002	7% 817342 due on 6/25/2004	6.5% 838204 due on 8/21/2001	6.75% 838875 due on 9/24/2004
Percent of data points consistent with Merton model	48%	52%	59%	59%	57%	54%	44%	44%	54%	53%	45%	52%
Adjusted R^2 on stock price												
Level data*	9.9%	6.5%	65.0%	43.0%	59.0%	71.0%	8.8%	−0.3%	0.6%	−0.8%	20.0%	28.0%
First difference data**	1.3%	0.6%	−17.0%	13.0%	16.0%	13.0%	7.6%	7.8%	5.8%	−0.9%	−1.1%	2.0%
Coefficient B												
Level data	−0.0140	−0.0100	−0.0310	−0.0260	−0.0350	−0.0340	−0.0190	0.0089	−0.0056	−0.0013	−0.0270	−0.0300
First difference data	−0.0051	−0.0051	−0.0150	−0.0140	−0.0140	−0.0130	0.0230	0.0380	−0.0079	−0.0002	−0.0056	−0.0070
T-score of B												
Level data	−2.4	−2.0	−10.9	−7.0	−10.9	−13.8	−2.3	0.9	−1.3	−0.2	−5.2	−6.4
First difference data	−1.3	−1.1	−3.7	−3.1	−4.0	−3.6	2.1	1.9	−2.9	−0.1	−1.5	−1.8
Std. Dev. Of Merton Percent	7.5%	7.5%	6.2%	6.2%	5.4%	5.6%	7.6%	8.8%	4.5%	4.8%	4.8%	4.9%
Standard Deviations from 50%	−0.3	0.3	1.5	1.5	1.3	0.7	−0.8	−0.7	0.9	0.6	−1.0	0.4
Standard Deviations from 100%	−6.9	−6.4	−6.6	−6.6	−8.0	−8.2	−7.4	−6.4	−10.3	−9.8	−11.4	−9.8
Date information												
Starting date	11/24/98	11/24/98	7/14/98	7/14/98	2/17/98	3/24/98	12/1/98	2/16/99	4/29/97	6/24/97	9/2/97	9/30/97
Ending date	9/28/99	9/28/99	9/28/99	9/28/99	9/28/99	9/28/99	9/28/99	9/28/99	9/28/99	9/28/99	9/28/99	9/28/99
Number of observations	45	45	64	64	85	80	44	33	126	110	108	104

The joint hypothesis that the Merton model is true and that there are no errors in the data is rejected for all issues by at least six standard deviations.

Whirlpool

The next table reports on 2,943 credit spreads on five issues by Whirlpool during a period in the early 1990s. None of the five bond issues have a credit spread series that exceeds 50% consistency with Merton. The joint hypothesis that the Merton model is true and the data has no errors can be rejected for all five bond issues by at least 20 standard deviations.

Xerox

399 observable credit spreads on seven bond issues are studied for Xerox in the table below. Four of the seven issues have Merton consistency ratios at or above 50%, but the difference from 50% is statistically significant for only one of the bond issues. The joint hypothesis that the Merton model is true and the data contains no errors is rejected by more than four standard deviations for all seven bond issues.

Whirlpool					
Issues	9.02% 96332HAS8 due on 3/15/2001	9.1% 96332HAR0 due on 3/15/2004	9.14% 96332HAQ2 due on 3/15/2006	9.0% 963320AG1 due on 3/1/2003	9.1% 963320AE6 due on 2/1/2008
Percent of data points consistent with Merton model	48%	46%	44%	46%	46%
Adjusted R^2 on stock price					
Level data*	26.0%	15.2%	1.7%	10.0%	13.0%
First difference data**	0.7%	0.0%	−0.2%	−0.1%	−0.8%
Coefficient B					
Level data	0.0120	0.0037	0.0009	0.0028	−0.0050
First difference data	0.0030	0.0011	0.0004	0.0006	0.0004
T-score of B					
Level data	11.9	8.6	2.8	9.4	−12.1
First difference data	2.0	0.9	0.3	0.4	0.5
Std. Dev. Of Merton Percent	2.5%	2.5%	2.5%	1.8%	1.6%
Standard Deviations from 50%	−0.8	−1.6	−2.4	−2.2	−2.5
Standard Deviations from 100%	−20.9	−21.8	−22.7	−30.0	−33.5
Data Information					
Starting Date	5/17/93	5/17/93	5/17/93	12/5/91	3/4/91
Data Ending Date	12/29/94	12/29/94	12/29/94	12/29/94	12/29/94
Number of Observations	406	406	406	767	958

Issues	Xerox						
	0.57% 984121AY9 due on 4/12/2018	5.5% 984121AW3 due on 11/15/2036	6.6% 98412JAZ7 due on 3/15/2011	5.91% 98412JBN3 due on 4/1/2037	5.77% 98412JBT0 due on 11/5/2001	5.19% 98412JBU7 due on 11/4/2038	5.25% 98412JBW3 due on 12/15/2003
Percent of data points consistent with Merton model	68%	51%	56%	41%	49%	50%	43%
Adjusted R^2 on stock price							
Level data*	64.0%	42.0%	46.0%	49.0%	13.0%	−1.3%	18.0%
First difference data**	43.0%	−0.8%	−2.4%	−2.0%	−0.2%	2.6%	0.0%
Coefficient B							
Level data	−0.2300	0.1500	−0.0670	−0.1300	0.0320	0.0029	0.1000
First difference data	−0.1800	−0.0290	0.0012	−0.0079	−0.0160	−0.0170	−0.0700
T-score of B							
Level data	−8.2	7.0	−6.0	−6.3	3.5	0.2	3.5
First difference data	−6.0	−0.7	0.0	0.0	−0.9	−1.7	−1.0
Std. Dev. Of Merton Percent	6.8%	6.1%	7.8%	7.7%	5.9%	5.9%	6.9%
Standard Deviations from 50%	2.6	0.2	0.8	−1.2	−0.2	0.0	−1.0
Standard Deviations from 100%	−4.7	−8.0	−5.7	−7.7	−8.7	−8.5	−8.2
Data Information							
Stating Date	12/17/1999	11/18/1999	12/28/1999	12/28/1999	11/9/1999	11/10/1999	12/13/1999
Ending Date	2/25/2000	2/25/2000	2/25/2000	2/25/2000	2/25/2000	2/25/2000	2/25/2000
Number of observations	48	68	42	42	74	73	52

Implications of Market Data Testing for Credit Modeling

In this chapter, we have used a number of tests based on market data to measure the merits of reduced form and structural models. The first set of tests were explicitly based on key objectives of the credit risk process—pricing and hedging. Another test was a 'common sense' test, measuring the correlation and volatility of theoretical default probabilities with the real world credit spreads that we expect reflect changes in default probabilities in a reasonably direct way. In general, reduced form models performed better than a single factor Merton model, the Merton variation in widest commercial application.

Another set of tests applies only to Merton models, because only the Merton model postulates a direct one-factor relationship between stock prices, debt prices, and credit spreads. This test confirms the findings of Jarrow and van Deventer [1998] that in general less than half of the observable changes in credit spread and stock price are consistent with a single factor version of the Merton model of risky debt, using a sample of 36,974 observable data points for 64 bonds of 8 issuers. On average, only 46% of Enron's 16,200 observable credit spreads moved in a manner consistent with the Merton model over the 1991-2001 period. The joint hypothesis that the Merton model is true and the data has no errors is rejected for all bond issues by all bond issuers studied by at least six standard deviations.

This chapter shows how market data can be used to address the concern by the Basel Committee on Banking Supervision that credit models have been too informally tested by major financial institutions. In this chapter, we found that if a major bank had relied on a single factor version of the Merton model over the 36,974 observed credit spreads for eight issuers of the 64 bond issues used in this study, the bank would have used estimated default probabilities that moved in the opposite direction of observable credit spreads 53% of the time. This has important implications for credit modeling and the Basel capital accord that we discuss in Chapter 9.

Jarrow, van Deventer and Wang [2002] suggest a number of assumptions of the Merton model that may have contributed to the inconsistency with market data that we have observed in this chapter:

(a) the assets of the company in the Merton model do not trade (in their entirety), causing the no arbitrage argument used to derive the Merton model to fail—equity could not then be argued to be a Black-Scholes option on the assets of the firm because those assets are not traded in an efficient market;

(b) the liability structure in practice is both more complex than assumed by the Merton model and is dynamic, not constant as assumed by Merton, and;

(c) in the event of default, the absolute priority is not adhered to strictly by the bankruptcy courts.

These issues with the Merton model certainly don't mean that it is not useful. Moreover, they don't even imply that the model ranks second to reduced form models, necessarily. What the findings of this chapter show us is that the testing requirements of the New Capital Accord are appropriate and help financial institutions better understand the quality of the credit modeling that they are doing to drive shareholder value and to assure the safety and soundness of their institutions.

We now turn to one more type of testing that we can do in the credit modeling process.

Appendix: First Interstate Bancorp Stock Price and Credit Spreads

Row	Date	Stock Price	SPREAD 2 year	SPREAD 3 year	SPREAD 5 year	SPREAD 7 year	SPREAD 10 year
1	10/26/1984	40.625	45	47	53	59	67
2	11/2/1984	41.125	48	52	60	66	73
3	11/9/1984	41.250	48	52	59	66	74
4	11/16/1984	40.250	51	54	60	68	75
5	1/4/1985	41.625	47	51	59	65	74
6	1/11/1985	42.500	49	54	60	65	71
7	1/25/1985	47.000	46	47	53	59	64
8	2/1/1985	45.500	43	44	52	57	63
9	2/15/1985	47.500	43	47	51	55	62
10	3/1/1985	47.500	47	50	55	61	66
11	3/8/1985	46.250	47	50	55	61	66
12	3/15/1985	44.875	46	48	53	59	65
13	3/22/1985	46.250	45	48	53	58	63
14	3/29/1985	46.500	45	48	53	58	63
16	4/12/1985	46.750	44	47	53	58	63
17	4/19/1985	48.875	44	48	53	58	63
18	4/26/1985	49.000	43	45	50	53	56
19	5/3/1985	48.625	45	47	53	56	61
20	5/10/1985	49.500	43	46	52	56	61
21	5/17/1985	52.250	42	45	51	55	60
22	5/24/1985	51.875	41	44	48	52	57
23	5/31/1985	51.000	41	44	47	50	56
24	6/7/1985	52.250	42	44	48	51	56
25	6/14/1985	53.250	40	43	47	52	56
26	6/21/1985	54.875	45	48	54	58	62
27	6/28/1985	55.375	47	50	55	60	64
28	7/5/1985	55.250	45	50	55	58	62
29	7/12/1985	54.125	45	49	53	55	59
30	7/19/1985	51.250	47	50	53	57	59

31	7/26/1985	50.250	50	53	56	60	63
32	8/2/1985	49.250	52	53	58	62	64
33	8/9/1985	48.500	53	55	59	62	63
34	8/16/1985	48.625	53	56	58	63	64
35	8/23/1985	48.000	53	56	58	63	64
36	8/30/1985	48.750	53	55	57	61	63
37	9/6/1985	49.000	48	52	56	59	63
38	9/13/1985	47.000	55	57	61	66	69
39	9/20/1985	46.250	56	58	62	65	70
41	10/4/1985	46.625	57	59	65	67	69
42	10/11/1985	48.500	57	59	65	67	69
43	10/18/1985	51.250	55	57	62	67	69
44	10/25/1985	48.250	60	61	65	70	71
45	11/1/1985	49.625	56	57	64	70	74
46	11/8/1985	49.375	54	55	62	67	70
47	11/15/1985	50.000	53	55	61	66	68
48	11/22/1985	51.750	52	54	61	65	68
49	11/29/1985	52.000	51	53	60	64	66
50	12/6/1985	51.875	54	57	60	66	69
51	12/13/1985	52.375	53	55	60	65	67
52	12/20/1985	52.875	52	53	59	62	65
53	12/27/1985	52.625	53	54	59	63	66
54	1/3/1986	54.125	52	53	59	63	66
55	1/10/1986	52.500	51	53	58	64	66
56	1/17/1986	54.750	53	54	59	66	68
57	1/24/1986	52.625	55	56	60	68	69
58	1/31/1986	54.250	53	55	59	66	68
59	2/7/1986	53.500	55	56	60	66	69
60	2/14/1986	56.250	54	55	61	65	67
61	2/21/1986	56.875	53	54	59	64	66
62	2/28/1986	58.500	52	52	59	63	64
63	3/7/1986	59.000	57	60	68	74	77
64	3/14/1986	63.750	56	57	67	72	76
65	3/21/1986	63.000	56	58	66	72	75
67	4/4/1986	61.500	64	67	73	79	83
68	4/11/1986	61.625	65	69	78	84	89
69	4/18/1986	66.000	64	65	76	84	88
70	4/25/1986	64.500	67	69	78	84	89
71	5/2/1986	60.000	67	69	75	82	88
72	5/9/1986	61.000	67	69	79	85	89
73	5/16/1986	59.750	67	69	77	85	89
74	5/23/1986	63.125	66	68	76	85	88
75	5/30/1986	64.250	65	68	75	85	88
76	6/6/1986	60.375	63	66	73	82	86
77	6/13/1986	59.375	62	64	73	82	88
78	6/20/1986	59.500	64	67	73	83	88
79	6/27/1986	61.125	63	66	72	82	88
81	7/11/1986	61.750	72	78	87	95	100
82	7/18/1986	61.125	70	75	81	90	93
83	7/25/1986	61.375	76	81	98	112	118
84	8/1/1986	59.500	76	79	95	108	114
85	8/8/1986	62.125	78	84	94	108	113
86	8/15/1986	62.875	78	84	92	106	111
87	8/22/1986	62.625	74	80	94	108	115

88	9/5/1986	63.500	71	77	91	104	111
89	9/12/1986	61.250	69	75	89	102	109
90	9/19/1986	59.375	63	71	86	97	104
91	9/26/1986	57.250	63	73	86	98	105
92	10/10/1986	54.000	90	99	122	138	148
93	10/17/1986	54.375	85	95	118	132	140
94	10/24/1986	54.500	82	91	113	126	133
95	10/31/1986	54.375	96	106	124	139	149
96	11/7/1986	52.500	99	110	130	144	154
97	11/14/1986	53.125	105	112	136	146	154
98	11/21/1986	53.500	75	88	118	128	133
99	11/28/1986	53.875	96	106	131	140	154
100	12/5/1986	54.500	97	106	129	141	150
101	12/12/1986	55.000	95	106	131	142	151
102	12/19/1986	54.250	93	101	126	142	152
103	12/26/1986	52.500	93	101	126	142	151
104	1/9/1987	56.000	88	97	122	135	147
105	1/16/1987	59.375	84	93	116	130	142
106	1/23/1987	56.250	71	80	98	110	124
107	1/30/1987	56.125	70	78	94	106	119
108	2/6/1987	56.500	68	76	91	104	115
109	2/13/1987	56.000	51	60	71	80	88
110	2/20/1987	57.750	54	64	74	83	89
111	2/27/1987	57.000	58	63	73	78	88
112	3/6/1987	57.375	61	68	75	83	91
113	3/13/1987	58.250	59	67	64	84	93
114	3/20/1987	59.625	57	66	78	87	95
115	3/27/1987	59.750	60	70	85	95	105
116	4/3/1987	59.500	61	71	83	94	104
117	4/10/1987	57.500	63	73	84	95	104
119	4/24/1987	55.000	70	81	93	104	113
120	5/1/1987	54.750	68	77	88	98	108
121	5/8/1987	55.750	68	77	88	98	107
122	5/15/1987	53.875	71	80	89	100	111
123	5/22/1987	52.625	76	85	94	104	115
124	5/29/1987	53.625	83	90	99	109	118
125	6/5/1987	54.375	84	92	100	106	115
126	6/12/1987	58.125	81	87	96	105	114
127	6/19/1987	61.500	78	86	94	101	108
128	6/26/1987	60.375	73	80	92	99	111
130	7/10/1987	59.000	74	83	91	97	109
131	7/24/1987	58.750	69	76	85	92	103
132	7/31/1987	58.500	69	76	85	92	102
133	8/7/1987	58.750	65	73	81	89	99
134	8/14/1987	60.750	65	73	81	89	99
135	8/21/1987	62.250	64	72	80	88	98
136	8/28/1987	61.750	63	71	81	90	96
137	9/4/1987	60.250	58	67	78	89	97
138	9/11/1987	57.500	59	67	77	86	96
139	9/18/1987	54.500	58	65	76	87	96
140	9/25/1987	54.625	102	105	110	114	120
141	10/2/1987	55.375	107	110	113	120	127
142	10/9/1987	52.500	102	105	109	117	124
143	10/16/1987	47.125	65	74	83	91	100

144	10/23/1987	40.250	102	105	110	114	120
145	10/30/1987	41.500	107	110	113	120	127
146	11/6/1987	42.750	102	105	109	117	124
147	11/13/1987	39.250	98	102	113	117	123
148	11/20/1987	40.000	96	101	108	113	118
149	11/27/1987	41.625	95	100	107	112	118
150	12/4/1987	39.125	90	95	105	111	119
151	12/11/1987	37.875	90	94	103	109	116
152	12/18/1987	37.000	88	93	101	110	118
154	1/8/1988	41.250	87	93	103	112	120
155	1/15/1988	41.750	84	89	98	105	113
156	1/22/1988	41.875	86	92	101	108	117
157	1/29/1988	42.500	80	87	96	104	111
158	2/5/1988	40.000	76	82	90	98	106
159	2/12/1988	41.000	76	81	89	97	104
160	2/19/1988	40.500	77	83	93	100	109
161	2/26/1988	44.875	77	83	93	100	109
162	3/4/1988	46.250	70	77	85	91	99
163	3/11/1988	45.000	67	75	84	91	99
164	3/18/1988	44.500	65	71	81	88	98
165	3/25/1988	45.250	66	72	80	87	95
167	4/8/1988	44.750	64	70	78	86	93
168	4/22/1988	43.500	68	72	80	88	96
169	5/6/1988	41.500	63	69	79	86	94
170	5/13/1988	42.250	61	67	77	84	93
171	5/20/1988	41.875	58	64	73	80	89
172	5/27/1988	42.875	56	61	68	77	85
173	6/3/1988	45.000	58	63	71	79	85
174	6/10/1988	46.000	60	64	71	78	84
175	6/17/1988	48.000	59	64	71	78	85
176	6/24/1988	50.625	58	63	70	78	84
177	7/1/1988	51.000	57	62	70	76	83
178	7/8/1988	51.875	56	61	69	77	81
179	7/15/1988	53.125	55	60	68	75	82
180	7/22/1988	52.375	58	63	70	76	83
181	7/29/1988	53.000	58	64	70	76	84
182	8/5/1988	52.750	57	62	70	77	84
183	8/12/1988	52.250	55	59	68	76	83
184	8/19/1988	51.125	54	59	66	73	79
185	8/26/1988	51.000	56	61	67	74	80
186	9/2/1988	51.000	56	61	68	74	81
187	9/9/1988	52.875	59	64	71	77	83
188	9/16/1988	53.125	58	63	70	77	83
189	9/23/1988	49.375	62	66	74	81	88
190	9/30/1988	50.250	61	65	74	81	87
191	10/7/1988	50.250	63	67	75	83	90
192	10/14/1988	49.750	67	73	80	89	96
193	10/21/1988	49.500	67	73	80	88	95
194	10/28/1988	49.000	67	72	79	86	93
195	11/4/1988	48.000	65	69	75	83	89
196	11/11/1988	47.125	67	72	79	86	92
197	11/18/1988	47.000	64	69	77	85	90
198	11/25/1988	45.250	63	69	77	84	91
199	12/2/1988	45.875	64	70	77	83	90

200	12/9/1988	47.625	63	69	76	84	90
201	12/16/1988	44.750	66	72	79	86	92
202	12/23/1988	43.500	70	75	82	87	96
203	12/30/1988	43.375	70	75	82	86	95
204	1/6/1989	44.375	69	75	81	85	94
205	1/13/1989	44.875	69	73	80	83	92
206	1/20/1989	46.375	68	72	79	86	91
207	1/27/1989	46.750	68	72	80	87	92
208	2/3/1989	47.250	70	74	81	87	93
209	2/10/1989	48.125	66	72	79	85	91
210	2/17/1989	48.125	66	72	77	83	91
211	2/24/1989	45.875	67	73	78	85	90
212	3/3/1989	46.000	72	75	82	88	93
213	3/10/1989	45.875	71	75	81	88	93
214	3/17/1989	46.375	73	78	82	88	93
216	3/31/1989	46.875	83	86	88	93	98
217	4/7/1989	47.750	92	93	98	105	108
218	4/14/1989	47.625	87	91	95	102	104
219	4/21/1989	48.875	88	90	95	103	108
220	4/28/1989	48.750	87	90	94	101	107
221	5/5/1989	49.750	85	88	94	101	107
222	5/12/1989	55.500	86	89	96	104	109
223	5/19/1989	55.375	85	88	95	102	109
224	5/26/1989	54.750	84	86	90	98	104
225	6/2/1989	57.750	78	81	87	96	101
226	6/9/1989	63.000	78	81	88	97	101
227	6/16/1989	64.875	78	81	86	92	99
228	6/23/1989	66.250	79	83	87	93	100
229	6/30/1989	62.000	82	86	91	98	103
230	7/7/1989	63.125	79	85	91	98	103
231	7/14/1989	65.375	82	86	93	101	105
232	7/21/1989	63.000	91	93	98	105	111
233	7/28/1989	62.000	101	104	111	118	127
234	8/4/1989	63.750	107	111	117	123	132
235	8/11/1989	65.875	113	118	126	134	143
236	8/18/1989	64.750	104	111	134	146	151
237	8/25/1989	64.875	104	111	135	148	153
238	9/1/1989	68.750	105	111	127	138	144
239	9/8/1989	66.500	95	104	120	133	141
240	9/15/1989	68.000	98	107	120	133	141
241	9/22/1989	66.250	106	113	127	142	149
242	9/29/1989	63.375	109	117	129	142	151
243	10/6/1989	62.250	108	116	131	143	153
244	10/13/1989	57.250	112	118	130	143	154
245	10/20/1989	57.625	117	128	139	151	165
246	11/3/1989	53.750	117	128	150	170	179
247	11/10/1989	55.250	120	131	154	164	181
248	11/17/1989	56.625	122	133	156	167	183
249	11/24/1989	54.250	122	133	156	167	183
250	12/1/1989	52.000	132	143	160	173	186
251	12/8/1989	45.750	137	148	171	186	199
252	12/15/1989	47.500	147	159	187	199	216
253	12/22/1989	43.750	153	164	195	217	232
254	12/29/1989	41.875	153	164	195	217	232

255	1/5/1990	44.375	155	168	193	209	225
256	1/12/1990	41.750	154	167	190	204	222
257	1/19/1990	44.000	156	169	192	206	231
258	1/26/1990	43.500	153	166	189	205	227
259	2/2/1990	36.000	154	168	199	217	235
260	2/9/1990	34.500	155	169	202	217	235
261	2/16/1990	35.250	174	187	222	240	258
262	2/23/1990	36.250	170	180	220	241	261
263	3/2/1990	40.125	181	194	233	258	284
264	3/9/1990	37.250	182	198	235	260	289
265	3/16/1990	35.875	182	198	235	260	291
266	3/23/1990	34.250	184	199	236	262	291
267	3/30/1990	34.000	183	200	239	262	298
268	4/6/1990	32.000	183	200	239	262	298
270	4/20/1990	36.000	187	202	243	263	291
271	4/27/1990	35.625	191	208	248	269	298
272	5/4/1990	38.750	181	201	246	259	291
273	5/11/1990	38.375	177	197	240	248	278
274	5/18/1990	38.625	172	188	236	258	280
275	5/25/1990	37.875	177	191	233	257	281
276	6/1/1990	40.000	143	156	201	225	243
277	6/8/1990	42.375	143	156	201	225	243
278	6/15/1990	43.250	138	155	200	228	246
279	6/22/1990	40.250	138	154	205	232	249
280	6/29/1990	40.375	140	157	204	232	249
281	7/6/1990	39.000	140	157	204	232	249
282	7/13/1990	40.000	140	157	204	232	250
283	7/20/1990	34.750	141	158	203	232	251
284	7/27/1990	34.875	140	158	205	235	255
285	8/3/1990	31.250	147	164	212	242	263
286	8/10/1990	31.125	153	172	219	244	265
287	8/17/1990	29.375	159	179	223	248	269
288	8/24/1990	28.250	166	186	235	263	285
289	8/31/1990	27.500	165	187	246	274	297
290	9/7/1990	27.625	167	186	239	266	287
291	9/14/1990	26.500	174	193	246	275	301
292	9/21/1990	25.125	176	195	248	278	310
293	9/28/1990	22.500	200	223	279	321	351
294	10/5/1990	21.250	205	228	285	329	358
295	10/12/1990	18.750	196	218	276	320	348
296	10/19/1990	20.625	205	233	313	365	401
297	10/26/1990	18.125	216	241	325	384	423
298	11/2/1990	18.750	253	303	364	428	468
299	11/9/1990	18.875	259	311	376	425	462
300	11/16/1990	21.375	246	299	348	415	458
301	11/23/1990	19.875	246	299	348	415	458
302	11/30/1990	20.625	246	301	348	415	452
303	12/7/1990	23.875	239	267	341	408	444
304	12/14/1990	25.250	253	301	364	420	453
305	12/21/1990	25.875	250	302	374	415	450
306	12/28/1990	24.125	250	302	374	415	450
307	1/4/1991	23.500	255	309	379	417	442
308	1/11/1991	20.500	265	321	382	416	449
309	1/18/1991	23.500	264	320	380	412	449

310	1/25/1991	28.250	258	313	374	406	442
311	2/1/1991	30.625	263	306	368	401	430
312	2/8/1991	33.500	251	299	353	385	414
313	2/15/1991	33.750	235	273	311	342	364
314	2/22/1991	33.125	232	268	303	329	349
315	3/1/1991	36.250	227	252	291	316	330
316	3/8/1991	35.000	211	234	273	290	304
317	3/15/1991	33.375	201	223	264	280	292
318	3/22/1991	29.375	202	220	257	272	285
320	4/5/1991	31.625	201	216	253	267	277
321	4/12/1991	33.000	194	209	242	256	266
322	4/19/1991	36.250	182	198	226	239	252
323	4/26/1991	37.875	166	174	199	210	220
324	5/3/1991	38.500	160	168	188	203	214
325	5/10/1991	38.000	149	159	177	187	197
326	5/17/1991	37.750	149	159	179	188	196
327	5/24/1991	39.000	148	156	172	179	186
328	5/31/1991	40.500	147	155	173	179	187
329	6/7/1991	38.375	145	153	170	177	183
330	6/14/1991	36.500	142	149	165	173	179
331	6/21/1991	38.000	143	149	164	171	177
332	6/28/1991	31.375	148	155	175	184	190
333	7/5/1991	26.750	161	170	193	201	207
334	7/12/1991	28.875	161	171	194	203	209
335	7/19/1991	30.750	148	157	178	187	193
336	7/26/1991	28.375	143	152	166	174	183
337	8/2/1991	27.750	140	148	163	171	178
338	8/9/1991	27.750	154	164	179	185	192
339	8/16/1991	35.375	154	164	179	185	192
340	8/23/1991	34.875	143	149	163	169	173
341	8/30/1991	33.875	147	151	163	168	177
342	9/6/1991	32.125	147	151	163	168	177
343	9/13/1991	30.125	147	151	163	168	177
344	9/20/1991	31.125	250	250	250	250	250
345	9/27/1991	31.250	183	190	216	222	233
346	10/4/1991	28.625	208	218	232	242	254
347	10/11/1991	27.500	215	225	243	255	261
348	10/18/1991	30.000	163	175	188	197	200
349	10/25/1991	28.125	209	220	238	247	253
350	11/1/1991	28.625	210	220	234	244	252
351	11/8/1991	29.625	211	221	230	237	241
352	11/15/1991	28.500	217	225	233	239	243
353	11/22/1991	29.250	230	240	255	265	275
354	11/29/1991	27.375	230	240	255	265	275
355	12/6/1991	26.125	265	275	280	290	300
356	12/13/1991	28.250	265	275	280	290	300
357	12/20/1991	29.125	234	244	265	274	283
358	12/27/1991	30.625	234	244	265	274	283
359	1/3/1992	30.875	234	244	265	274	283
360	1/10/1992	30.500	197	210	228	236	243
361	1/17/1992	32.375	182	190	202	210	216
362	1/24/1992	34.000	182	190	202	210	216
363	1/31/1992	35.500	158	166	176	180	185
364	2/7/1992	36.625	153	163	173	179	184

365	2/14/1992	37.000	143	153	161	167	172
366	2/21/1992	38.250	143	151	160	166	170
367	2/28/1992	38.375	143	151	160	166	170
368	3/6/1992	36.625	130	139	148	153	156
369	3/13/1992	37.625	132	139	144	150	152
370	3/20/1992	37.375	132	139	145	150	152
371	3/27/1992	36.125	138	145	150	155	157
372	4/3/1992	33.625	135	142	151	157	161
373	4/10/1992	35.875	135	142	151	157	161
375	4/24/1992	40.250	125	133	141	144	148
376	5/1/1992	39.875	125	133	141	144	148
377	5/8/1992	41.875	115	120	125	130	133
378	5/15/1992	40.500	115	120	125	130	133
379	5/22/1992	40.250	115	120	125	130	133
380	5/29/1992	39.750	115	120	125	130	133
381	6/5/1992	41.250	115	120	125	130	133
382	6/12/1992	41.375	115	120	125	130	133
383	6/19/1992	40.250	115	120	125	130	133
384	6/26/1992	40.375	115	120	125	130	133
386	7/10/1992	42.125	115	120	125	130	133
387	7/17/1992	39.875	115	120	125	130	133
388	7/24/1992	39.000	115	120	125	130	133
389	7/31/1992	39.875	115	120	125	130	133
390	8/7/1992	38.125	90	97	107	114	117
391	8/14/1992	37.750	350	380	254	113	118
392	8/21/1992	37.250	88	95	103	110	115
393	8/28/1992	36.875	78	82	89	93	99
394	9/4/1992	37.125	78	82	89	93	99
395	9/11/1992	36.625	90	98	105	110	116
396	9/18/1992	38.250	90	98	105	110	116
397	9/25/1992	37.750	90	98	105	110	116
398	10/2/1992	39.000	99	109	116	121	125
399	10/9/1992	39.250	99	109	116	121	125
400	10/16/1992	40.125	109	117	125	131	134
401	10/23/1992	40.250	107	114	119	124	130
402	10/30/1992	39.375	107	114	119	124	130
403	11/6/1992	39.375	107	114	119	124	130
404	11/13/1992	40.375	107	114	119	124	130
405	11/20/1992	41.250	97	105	109	116	120
406	11/27/1992	43.125	97	105	109	116	120
407	12/4/1992	45.250	95	102	107	114	119
408	12/11/1992	46.875	96	103	108	114	119
409	12/18/1992	47.000	96	103	108	114	119
412	1/8/1993	45.625	96	103	108	114	119
413	1/15/1993	48.750	84	93	96	102	106
414	1/22/1993	50.000	84	93	96	102	106
415	1/29/1993	50.375	84	93	96	102	106
416	2/5/1993	53.625	84	93	96	102	106
417	2/12/1993	53.250	73	81	86	90	95
418	2/19/1993	51.875	68	73	79	83	88
419	2/26/1993	52.500	68	73	79	83	88
420	3/5/1993	53.750	69	75	80	84	90
421	3/12/1993	55.750	68	72	78	83	88
422	3/19/1993	56.625	67	71	77	83	88

423	3/26/1993	55.625	67	72	78	82	88
424	4/2/1993	56.125	67	72	78	82	88
426	4/16/1993	60.750	67	72	78	82	88
427	4/23/1993	56.750	67	72	78	82	88
428	4/30/1993	55.000	61	68	75	80	84
429	5/7/1993	53.750	63	70	75	83	85
430	5/14/1993	54.000	63	68	75	82	91
431	5/21/1993	56.000	60	68	75	84	92
432	5/28/1993	58.375	63	69	75	82	93
433	6/4/1993	56.250	62	69	75	82	93
434	6/11/1993	57.000	60	66	73	79	91
435	6/18/1993	58.250	60	66	73	79	91
436	6/25/1993	60.750	60	66	73	79	91
437	7/2/1993	62.500	60	66	73	79	91
438	7/9/1993	63.875	60	66	72	79	90
439	7/16/1993	63.750	55	62	69	74	78
440	7/23/1993	64.250	55	62	69	74	78
441	7/30/1993	63.875	52	59	65	70	76
442	8/6/1993	62.750	52	59	65	72	76
443	8/13/1993	63.500	52	59	64	71	75
444	8/20/1993	59.875	47	55	62	70	75

References

Adams, K. and D. van Deventer, 1994, 'Fitting Yield Curves and Forward Rate Curves with Maximum Smoothness,' *Journal of Fixed Income*, June, 52–62.

Basel Committee on Banking Supervision, 2001, 'Consultative Document: The New Capital Accords,' monograph, Bank for International Settlements, Basel.

Black, F. and M. Scholes, 1973, 'The Pricing of Options and Corporate Liabilities,' *Journal of Political Economy*, 81, 399–418.

Delianedis, G. and R. Geske, 1998, 'Credit Risk and Risk Neutral Default Probabilities: Information About Rating Migrations and Defaults,' working paper, UCLA.

Eberhart, A. C., W.T. Moore and R.L. Roenfeldt, 1990, 'Security Pricing and Deviations from the Absolute Priority Rule in Bankruptcy Proceedings,' *Journal of Finance*, 4, 1457–1489.

Hull, J. and A. White, 1987, 'The Pricing of Options on Assets with Stochastic Volatility,' *Journal of Finance*, 2, 281–300.

Jarrow, R. 2001, 'Default Parameter Estimation Using Market Prices,' *Financial Analysts Journal*, September/October.

Janosi, T., R. Jarrow and Y. Yildirum, 2001a, 'Estimating Expected Losses and Liquidity Discounts Implicit in Debt Prices,' working paper, Cornell University.

Janosi, T., R. Jarrow and Y. Yildirum, 2001b, 'Estimating Default Probabilities Implicit in Equity Prices,' working paper, Cornell University.

Jarrow, R. and D. van Deventer, 1998, 'Integrating Interest Rate Risk and Credit Risk in Asset and Liability Management,' *Asset and Liability Management: The Synthesis of New Methodologies*, Risk Publications.

Jarrow, R. and D. van Deventer, 1999, 'Practical Usage of Credit Risk Models in Loan Portfolio and Counterparty Exposure Management,' *Credit Risk Models and Management*, Risk Publications.

Jarrow, R., D. van Deventer, and X. Wang, 2002, 'A Robust Test of Merton's Structural

Model for Credit Risk,' working paper, Cornell University and Kamakura Corporation.

Jones, E., S. Mason and E. Rosenfeld, 1984, 'Contingent Claims Analysis of Corporate Capital Structures: An Empirical Investigation,' *Journal of Finance*, 39, 611–627.

Kealhofer, S. and M. Kurbat, 2001, 'The Default Prediction Power of the Merton Approach, Relative to Debt Ratings and Accounting Variables,' monograph, KMV Corporation, San Francisco, CA.

Merton, R.C., 1974, 'On the Pricing of Corporate Debt: The Risk Structure of Interest Rates,' *Journal of Finance*, 29, 449–470.

Shimko, D., H. Tejima and D. van Deventer, 1993, 'The Pricing of Risky Debt when Interest Rates are Stochastic,' *Journal of Fixed Income*, September, 58–66.

Sobehart, J., S. Keenan and R. Stein, 2000, 'Validation Methodologies for Default Risk Models,' *Credit*, May, 51–56.

van Deventer, D. and K. Imai, 1996, *Financial Risk Analytics: A Term Structure Model Approach for Banking, Insurance, and Investment Management*, McGraw Hill.

Weiss, L.A., 1990, 'Bankruptcy Resolution: Direct Costs and Violations of Priority of Claims,' *Journal of Financial Economics*, 27, 286-5–314.

Out of Sample Testing of Credit Models

In Chapters 5 and 6, we outlined a number of ways in which historical default data can be used to measure the performance of credit models as required under the New Basel Capital Accord. In Chapter 7, we extended credit model testing to a series of tests using market data—pricing tests, hedging tests, and tests of model implications. In this chapter, we complete the array of tests with a discussion of 'out of sample testing.'

'Out of Sample' testing refers to a two-stage test of credit models:

1. We choose a set of historical data as the sample to estimate credit model parameters.
2. We use the parameters estimated on historical performance and measure how well the model works on newer data, outside of the data sample ('out of sample').

Out of sample testing can be very important if the historical data is small and the model has been heavily 'massaged' to fit the historical data set. Given any historical data set, there is no limit to the performance that can be achieved if any arbitrary mathematical formula is allowed in the modeling process. For example, in Chapter 4 we examined the credit spreads of the Korean Development Bank during the Asian crisis. If we allow any explanatory variables and any mathematical formulas to be used, we can improve the explanation of KDB credit spread movements considerably over what we reported in Chapter 4, where the value of the Korean won was the dominant explanatory variable. The reason is that the German DAX equity index has an even higher correlation with the credit spreads of the Korean Development Bank than the Korean won does (an 89% correlation during the sample period). Using this knowledge 'improves' the model, and the coefficient of the DAX in the credit spread relationship is statistically significant. Nonetheless, it is nonsense to use this variable as an explanatory variable because the link between German equities and the Korean Development Bank's credit spreads has near-zero economic content. The correlation is strictly coincidental.

In this example, we don't need a fancy test to know that our model is nonsensical, but in other cases this lack of plausibility is not obvious. The best way to detect an 'over-specified' or 'over-engineered' model with no real economics content is to combine 'out of sample' testing with the market tests in Chapter 7.

We illustrate this process with data from Chava and Jarrow [2002].[1]

The Chava and Jarrow Test

We studied the bankruptcy data base of Chava and Jarrow extensively in Chapter 6. The data base consists of more than 1.4 million monthly observations on 17,460 companies from 1963 to 1998, of which 1,461 defaulted. How can out of sample testing be employed to test the Chava Jarrow logistic regression reduced form model that we introduced in Chapter 3?

Chava and Jarrow wanted to test the performance of three different logistic models that are consistent with reduced form modeling technology:

- A private firm model, which uses accounting ratios and industry information but no market data as explanatory variables;
- A public firm model, which uses all of the variables in the private firm model plus the excess return variable, the size variable, and the volatility variable that we studied in Chapter 6;
- An 'efficient markets' version of the public firm model, which uses only excess return, size and volatility.

The objective is to answer the following questions with an 'out of sample' test:

- Do accounting ratios improve our ability to forecast default?
- When estimating default, do the market variables (excess return, size, and volatility) contain all accounting information relevant to debt holders, making the market variables the only necessary inputs in default prediction?

Of course, these questions are effectively equivalent.

---

[1] Sudheer Chava and Robert A. Jarrow, 'A Comparison of Explicit versus Implicit Estimates of Default Probabilities,' Cornell University, 2002.

Chava and Jarrow do the following to implement this test:

- They fit the logistic regression to each of the three models for the period 1963–1990 for all listed companies in the United States for which data was available.
- Month by month for the 1991–1998 period, Chava and Jarrow rank the firm into deciles of risk based on their estimated bankruptcy probabilities. The riskiest firms are in the first decile, and the least risky firms are in the 10th decile.
- Chava and Jarrow count the firms monthly in each decile which file for bankruptcy.

If the model is no better than random chance, only 10% of the bankruptcies will fall in the first decile. We can test this null hypothesis using the chi-squared tests that we discussed in Chapter 5. We now turn to the Chava Jarrow results.

Results of the Chava Jarrow Out of Sample Tests

Chava and Jarrow report the following results on forecasting accuracy for the 349 bankruptcies that occurred between 1991 and 1998:

Percentage of Bankruptcies in the First Decile, the Riskiest Decile

Public Firm Model	81.38%
Public Firm Model 'Efficient Markets' Version	75.93%
Private Firm Model	65.33%

Clearly, the addition of accounting ratios and industry variables added explanatory power to the model, because the 'public firm model' which includes all of these variables and the market variables (excess return, size, and volatility) predicted a higher percentage of bankruptcies (81.38%) than the 'efficient markets' version of the model which relied only on the market variables.

Similarly, both versions of the model which used market variables, outperformed the 'private firm' version of the model which did not use the market variables as explanatory variables.

This 'out of sample' test confirms the 'in sample' findings of Chapter 6—accounting variables improve the prediction of default when using equity market variables as input. We can interpret this result using another test from Chapters 5 and 6, and that is the task to which we now turn.

Interpreting the Chava Jarrow Results as an ROC Curve

In Chapter 5, we studied the receiver operating characteristics (ROC) curve and the ROC accuracy ratio as a powerful measure of model performance on a historical default data base. The ROC curve can also be used for out of sample tests.

In Chapter 5, we discussed the process of drawing the ROC curve. We start by picking a 'cut-off' for 'predicting' default. For that cut-off, we calculate the x and y coordinates that will give us one point on the ROC curve:

- The percentage of the defaulting companies we have correctly classified (the 'y' data point);
- The percentage of non-defaulting companies that we have incorrectly classified.

We plot this point on the curve. We then change the cut-off and repeat the process continuously until we have drawn the entire curve.

The Chava and Jarrow out of sample test can be interpreted as the drawing of one 'dot' on the out of sample ROC curve for these three models. The 'cut-off' for predicting bankruptcy that we have chosen is the 90th percentile of estimated default probabilities. Each firm over the 90th percentile (i.e. in the 'first decile'), we predict to default. Figure 8.1 shows the Chava Jarrow results:

Figure 8.1   ROC curve for Chava Jarrow model 10 years out of sample

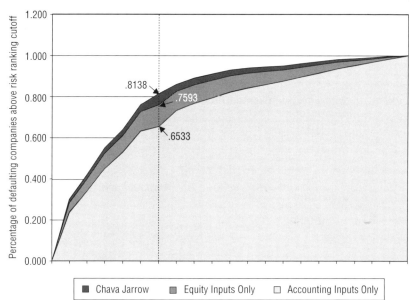

At that cut-off level, the Chava Jarrow public firm model correctly predicts 81.38% of the defaulting companies. The 'efficient markets' version of the model, which uses equity market variables only, correctly classifies 75.93% of the defaults. The private firm model, which uses accounting variables only, correctly classifies 65.33% of the model. We don't know from the Chava Jarrow paper what percentage of the non-defaulting companies were mis-classified by the three models, so, for convenience we have plotted them all on the same vertical line. The public firm model covers more of the area of the graph and has the highest ROC accuracy ratio out of sample in this hypothetical example.[2] We draw the full curve by changing the cutoff we are using, from the 90th percentile to the following sequence: 100th percentile, 99th percentile, 98th percentile, etc. and continue down to the 1st percentile. By plotting the percentage of defaults correctly predicted and the percentage of non-defaults that were mis-classified, we can draw the entire ROC curve for all three models. As explained in Chapter 5, once we have the entire curve, the ROC accuracy ratio is the area under the curve and we can quantitatively rank the models by their out of sample performance. We know from Chapter 5 that a model no better than random chance would have an accuracy ratio of 50%, while a perfect model would have an accuracy ratio of 100%.

Out of Sample Testing: In Summary

Out of sample testing is a very useful way of making sure that a model isn't over-specified or over-engineered, and it will detect a model that has been built on accidental correlations from the sample period. The tests of Chapters 5 and 6 can be used directly on out of sample test results, with little or no modification except for the interpretation of the results. These tests are very much in the spirit of the New Capital Accords of the Basel Committee on Banking Supervision, to which we now turn.

---

[2] The example is hypothetical because we have plotted only one point on the curve. We would need to plot all the points using actual instead of hypothetical data to know this for sure.

9

Implications of the Tests for the Basel Accords and Management of Financial Institutions

As we mentioned in Chapter 1, the primary focus of this book is using modern credit technology to drive shareholder value. In that chapter, we said: 'Surprisingly, because of the sophistication of the Basel Committee's recent work, there is less contradiction between shareholder value-added maximization and regulatory requirements than there has been in the past, when quantitative regulations were so perverse that arbitrage was not only profitable but just.' The Basel pronouncements have a number of positive aspects, particularly in the measurement of credit risk. The authors' favorite quotation from the Basel Committee on Banking Supervision is as follows:

> 'A bank must demonstrate to its supervisor that the internal validation process enables it to assess the performance of internal rating and risk quantification systems consistently and meaningfully.'[1]

Credit modeling and performance measurement, thanks to the Basel Committee, is emerging from an era of 'semi-religious' and philosophical arguments about model performance and entering into an era where scientific techniques well established in medical statistics can used to clearly establish the attributes of a model. We illustrated these procedures in Chapters 5–8. In this chapter, we turn to the implications of the first eight chapters for the Basel Committee's objectives. In the remainder of this book, we examine alternatives to the Basel approach that the authors believe more

---

[1] Section 302, p. 55, The New Basel Capital Accord, Basel Committee on Banking Supervision, May 31, 2001.

directly link credit risk not only to shareholder value creation but also to safety and soundness of financial institutions, the Basel Committee's primary concern.

Safety and Soundness: Achieving Regulatory Objectives

In looking at the implications of new credit modeling technology for the New Capital Accords, it is important to note the objectives of banking regulation. In an American context, the staff of the Board of Governors of the Federal Reserve System summarized those objectives this way:

> *'One of the primary responsibilities of bank regulatory agencies is to minimize the financial loss to the Bank Insurance Fund that results from the failure of insured depository institutions.'*[2]

In an international financial institutions context, this can be restated as follows:

> *'One of the primary responsibilities of financial institutions' regulatory agencies is to minimize the financial loss to taxpayers that results from the failure of financial institutions while maintaining the fairness of competition among different types of financial institutions around the world.'*

With this in mind, we can now turn to a practical regulatory implementation. There are three steps in protecting taxpayers from the costs of the failure of a key financial institution:

1. Measuring risk of financial institutions using publicly available data;
2. Measuring risk of financial institutions using internal portfolio data;
3. Imposing measures to reduce excessive risk to levels consistent with long-term safety and soundness of the financial institution.

After a brief review of these three steps in light of what we have learned in Chapters 1 to 8, we can turn to an examination of the New Capital Accords and their implications.

---

[2] Rebel A. Cole, Barbara Cornyn, and Jeffery W. Gunther, 'FIMS: A New Monitoring System for Banking Institutions,' *Federal Reserve Bulletin*, January 1995, pp. 1–15.

Measuring Risk of Financial Institutions Using Publicly Available Data

A primary tactical concern of financial regulators is to focus their limited resources for examinations and remedial action on the institutions that are in the most danger of failure. There are three techniques that we have extensively discussed that can be applied by regulators today for this purpose:

1. Monitor reduced form model default probabilities for publicly traded financial institutions;
2. Monitor Merton model default probabilities for publicly traded financial institutions;
3. Monitor STV model default probabilities for publicly traded financial institutions.

We believe that regulators world-wide should be doing this. The majority of financial institutions world-wide, however, are not listed on stock exchanges. The need for careful regulatory scrutiny is just as great, however, if not greater, with respect to these institutions. Many regulatory agencies use standard regulatory reports and their history, in combination with a record of financial institutions failures, to develop a Chava-Jarrow type hazard model to predict the default probability of all financial institutions based on the latest available regulatory reports. In many countries, this data is public information. Jarrow and Duffie[3] recently presented a paper showing excellent performance for reduced form models in predicting bank default and in setting the proper levels of bank deposit insurance.

Perhaps the best study of default prediction using public information is the Financial Institutions Monitoring System implemented by the Federal Reserve in 1993 and mentioned in earlier chapters.[4] The FIMS system provides two 'surveillance scores' based on two different models. The first is the FIMS rating, which is an assessment of the bank's current financial condition. The second is the FIMS risk rank, which is a longer-term assessment of the expected future condition of the bank. The FIMS risk rank is the probability that the bank will fail in the next two years. Both measures use the logistic regression technology also used by Chava and Jarrow in Chapters 6 and 8.

---

[3] Robert A. Jarrow and Darrell Duffie, presentation on the use of reduced form credit models to determine the proper level of bank deposit insurance premiums, at a conference sponsored by the Federal Deposit Insurance Corporation of the United States, September 13, 2002.
[4] Rebel A. Cole, Barbara Cornyn, and Jeffery W. Gunther, 'FIMS: A New Monitoring System for Banking Institutions,' Federal Reserve Bulletin, January 1995, pp. 1–15.

The variables found by the Federal Reserve to be the best predictors of bank failure in the next two years, from the entire universe of data collected on quarterly reports of bank condition, are the following:

- Loans past due 30-89 days/Assets;
- Loans past due 90 or more days/Assets;
- Nonaccrual loans/Assets;
- Foreclosed real estate/Assets;
- Tangible capital/Assets;
- Net income/Assets;
- Reserves/Assets;
- Investment Securities/Assets;
- Large CDs/Assets.

Note that net income/assets is a Chava Jarrow model variable, and tangible capital/assets is closely related to the Chava Jarrow model variable liabilities/assets. The Federal Reserve reported excellent accuracy of the FIMS risk rank using a close relative of the ROC curve to report results. Note that the capital ratio, tangible capital/assets, is just one of nine input variables that the Federal Reserve found to be relevant to predicting bank failure in the U.S. The FIMS study was done on a sample with 27,083 observations on banks, of which 262 banks failed.

We believe that all regulators should be using this close relative of Chava Jarrow technology to predict bank failure.

Measuring Risk of Financial Institutions Using Internal Portfolio Data

The three credit models and the Chava-Jarrow variation used by the Federal Reserve FIMS system all use publicly available or regulatory information that represents fairly aggregated accounting data. A much better approach for estimating the probability of the failure of a financial institution is a detailed and highly accurate simulation of the performance of all of the assets and all of the liabilities owned by the institution. This is the current best practice in risk management at financial institutions world-wide[5], although it is a development largely overlooked by the Basel Committee on Banking Supervision.

With detailed portfolio data and advanced credit model default probability estimates for every corporate and retail counterparty, a detailed and highly accurate multi-period simulation can be done to measure the

---

[5] The National Australia Bank, for example, reports processing more than one million transactions daily in its risk management software according to a recent 2001 press release.

probability of default of the financial institution at many future points in time. We discuss how this is done in detail in later chapters.

Supervisory agencies have the authority to collect this data and to conduct their own simulations or to require that financial institutions do this simulation and review the results with regulators. This is one of the alternatives the Basel Committee on Banking Supervision had at its disposal in contemplating the provisions of the New Capital Accord.

Imposing Measures to Reduce Excessive Risk

In the two previous sections, we discussed the many ways covered in this book for rating the risk of a financial institution using both public information and internal bank portfolio information. Some of these techniques are already practiced by the Federal Reserve Board and they are being studied seriously for more aggressive implementation by the FDIC. What actions can regulators take if the risk of a financial institution, by any of these measures, appears excessive and that excess risk is confirmed by an on-site inspection by regulatory agencies?

There are a number of actions regulators can and do take, depending on the urgency of the situation:

- Replacement of some or all members of senior management;
- Forced disposal of liquid assets to restore liquidity;
- Forced disposal of marketable high-risk assets to reduce aggregate risk;
- Borrowing from the lender of last resort to restore liquidity;
- Increase in accounting reserves for potential loses (this is a signaling device that flags a problem but doesn't solve it);
- Mandatory increase in true equity capital;
- Nationalization or regulatory seizure of the institution.

The credit modeling technology in the first eight chapters of this book helps concentrate the managerial resources of financial institutions regulators on those institutions who will most likely be the recipients of these emergency regulatory measures. The advanced simulation and capital allocation technology discussed in later chapters adds depth and accuracy to the credit modeling process. We now look at the methodologies proposed by the Basel Committee on Banking Supervision.

The New Basel Capital Accord

In examining the approach taken by the Basel Committee on Banking Supervision, the first challenge is to answer the question 'which approach?'

In this chapter, we will focus on three main documents by the Basel Committee on Banking Supervision:

- The New Basel Capital Accord, May 31, 2001;
- The Internal Ratings-Based Approach, January 2001;
- The Standardized Approach to Credit Risk, January 2001.

These documents, which total hundreds of pages, go into great detail on the precise calculations specified by the Basel Committee on Banking Supervision. We refer readers who want precise instruction in these calculations to seek them out on the web site of the Bank for International Settlements. We also recommend the following documents:

- Credit Risk Modeling: Current Practices and Implications;
- Range of Practice in Banks' Internal Ratings Systems;
- Principals for Management of Credit Risk.

These documents have been compiled very thoughtfully by well-meaning international regulators with the cooperation of thousands of bankers around the world. The documents themselves, however, have provoked huge volumes of critical comments and controversy even among regulators. Some regulatory bodies in the U.S. believe that the Basel Accords are unworkable and that the U.S. should withdraw from the Basel process.[6] The applicability of the Basel Accords is also subject to tremendous uncertainty, with the more concerned regulators in the U.S. hoping to restrict its application to no more than the 50 largest banks. Regulators in other countries seem, on average, much more determined to carry the Basel pronouncements far deeper in the ranks of the financial institutions hierarchy. In the remainder of this section, we outline what the Basel Accord proposes and compare that with what some of the alternatives could have been, based on the first eight chapters in this book.

The New Basel Capital Accord: A Noble Attempt

The New Basel Capital Accord has as its objective a combination of 'early warning' triggers, such as the FIMS system and built-in remedial action, forcing risky institutions to take corrective action to maintain the Basel risk index at an acceptable level. The Basel Committee repeatedly states in its documents that its seeks two improvements over the 1988 Basel capital ratios—additional risk sensitivity and incentive compatibility. This

---

[6] Off-the-record presentation by a U.S. banking regulator who wishes to remain anonymous, September 2002.

effectively means that banks are encouraged to increase the quality of their risk management systems and processes and also to take the corrective action we just mentioned.[7] The Basel documents repeatedly state that '...the Committee realizes that a balance between simplicity and accuracy needs to be struck.'[8] This desire for simplicity has, in effect, constrained both the form of the proposed accords and the mathematics eligible for use in the calculations. The result is a string of mathematical calculations, none of which is complex, that in total is more complicated and less accurate than a more straightforward adoption of the credit modeling technology we have discussed in the last eight chapters. We will summarize the principal steps in the Basel Committee's thinking in the following section.

The Risk Index Must be a Single Number

The Basel Committee, influenced by the 1988 capital rules and the history of capital regulation in the United States, has concluded that there must be a single index of risk for each institution, and all classes of institutions must essentially produce the same index, although they are allowed modest flexibility in how they make the calculation.

The Risk Index is Not a Default Probability

The Basel Committee could have chosen any of the following single numbers as its risk index, all of which we have covered to some extent in earlier chapters:

- Merton model default probability for the institution derived from current equity prices;
- STV model default probability for the institution derived from equity prices and interest rates;
- Chava Jarrow default probability for the institution derived from equity prices and accounting data;
- Jarrow default probability derived from the bank's debt prices;
- Jarrow default probability derived from credit derivatives on the bank, if available;
- FIMS-type logistic regression model based on regulatory reporting data, with parameters specified by regulators;

---

[7] Section 1, page 1, The Internal Ratings-Based Approach, Basel Committee on Banking Supervision, January 2001.
[8] Section 3, page 1, The Standardized Approach to Credit Risk, Basel Committee on Banking Supervision, January 2001.

- Simulated default probability using internal financial institution's portfolio data.

Frankly, any of these choices would be more logical, more intuitive, cheaper to implement, and easier to understand than the calculation specified by the Committee. The Committee said; 'The main deficiencies identified by the Committee in using credit risk models as a basis for minimum regulatory capital requirements were the quality of the data and ability of banks and supervisors to validate model outputs.' As we have seen in the earlier chapters, there are no data quality problems. Chava and Jarrow were able to compile default probabilities for all public companies in the U.S. on a monthly basis going back 39 years. Similarly, chapters 5 and 6 specify exactly how model outputs can be tested and validated. Clearly, this is an issue that the Federal Reserve formally disagrees with the Basel Committee, as the FIMS system has been used since 1993 and is formally mandated by the U.S. Congress. With the passage of time, we are sure the Basel Committee will reverse this position, as it is indefensible.

The Risk Index Must be a Ratio of Capital to Assets

The New Basel Capital Accord concludes that the risk index must be a ratio of 'capital' to 'assets.' The definition of capital and assets is specified by the Basel Committee and national regulators, not by an accounting standards body. We know from the FIMS study that the Basel Committee is sacrificing accuracy by leaving out the eight variables that the Federal Reserve Board found to be statistically significant predictors of default (outlined earlier in this chapter).

As we mentioned previously, the Federal Reserve found that tangible capital (an accounting definition) divided by assets was a statistically significant predictor of default and this is related to the Basel ratio. By leaving out the other eight variables, all of which are standard elements in bank regulatory reports in most countries, the Basel Committee has sacrificed a huge degree of financial institutions default predictability.

Why did the Basel Committee choose to leave out eight significant variables that are combined into one risk index by the logistic regression formula used in FIMS and the Chava Jarrow model? There can only be one reason. In the logistic regression formula, one has to do the following calculation:

$$P_t^i = \frac{1}{[1 + \exp(-\alpha_t - \beta' X_{it})]} \tag{6}$$

The exponential function is a standard calculation in common spreadsheet software. The variables in the vector X are the bank ratios like those in the FIMS study. The constant alpha and the coefficients beta would be supplied by national regulators. Therefore all banks would have had to use FIMS or Chava Jarrow technology to substitute the values of their ratios into this formula. Elsewhere the Committee argues that the normal distribution function is in spreadsheet software and therefore is an appropriate formula for use in the New Basel Capital Accords[9]. Therefore it is a mystery why the Federal Reserve's FIMS study was not adopted instead of the hundreds of pages of Basel pronouncements. A replica of the FIMS study, done for each major country subject to Basel, adapted for special national characteristics, would have been far less expensive to regulators than the current Basel process.

The Risk Index Should Use 'Risk-adjusted Assets' Which Adjust for the Riskiness of the 'Actual' Assets Held

The Basel Committee could have achieved the higher risk sensitivity it sought by implying the institution's risk from market securities prices or by an exact modeling process that uses a default probability for every counterparty, the macro risk drivers for those counterparties as we outlined in Chapter 4, and the exact transaction level data which describes the institutions' transaction with that counterparty. Instead, the Committee has chosen a rough method of approximation that only faintly resembles conventional wisdom and is weakly unrelated to best practice.

There are two different calculation alternatives for risk-adjusted assets:

- The Internal Ratings-Based Approach;
- The Standardized Approach to Credit Risk.

We focus here on the internal ratings-based approach. The standardized approach replaces multiples of five and 10% for the risk-weights in accordance with a set of arbitrary schedules that approximate the calculations one would have derived using the internal ratings-based approach.

Risk-adjusted assets are calculated in two broad classes, retail assets and all other assets.[10]

---

[9] Basel Committee on Banking Supervision, The Internal Ratings-based Approach, January 2001.
[10] The differences for sovereigns and project finance, as opposed to traditional corporate business, are relatively minor.

Risk-adjusted Assets and Risk-weights are Derived Ignoring Correlations with Other Assets and Liabilities

The Basel Committee specifies that the risk-adjusted asset amount for each corporate transaction be determined for that asset on a stand-alone basis, ignoring correlations with other borrowers and transactions.[11] The risk-adjusted asset calculation is a function of:

- Probability of default;
- Loss given default;
- Exposure at default (normally principal outstanding, but more complex than this for an undrawn line of credit);
- Time to maturity.

Banks may provide their own estimates of default probability under the New Basel Capital Accord, subject to certain conditions, the principal one being that '...banks using the advanced approach will be required to demonstrate to their supervisors the appropriateness of these estimates'[12]. Our discussions of credit models in Chapters 3 to 8 represent the best practice in credit modeling and far exceed the Basel requirements. Chapters 5 and 6 provide the methodology for demonstrating to supervisors that the default probability estimates are appropriate. Much of the Basel documents are concerned with how to move from an ordinal credit rating to a default probability estimate. Chapter 5 in this volume shows exactly how this should be done. The Basel documents, by contrast, simply say that one should use the average[13] default experience for that ratings grade. In this book, we have shown how logistic regression and macro factors can be combined with historical default experience to give 'scenario specific' default probabilities that reflect the current economic conditions much more accurately than using a simple historical average.

Risk-Weights are Determined on the Assumption that Corporate Exposures Have a Three Year Maturity

In relation to corporate exposures, the Basel Committee says, without justification, that 'the average maturity of all exposures will be assumed to be three years.'[14] The corporate risk-weight is calculated according to the following formula:

---

[11] An ad hoc adjustment is made after the fact for a 'granularity adjustment.' See page 91, The Internal Ratings-Based Approach, for the details.

[12] Section 58, page 13, The Internal Ratings-Based Approach.

[13] Section 67, page 15, The Internal Ratings-Based Approach.

Corporate Risk Weight *RW*

$$= \text{Minimum} \left[\frac{BRW_c(PD) \times LGD}{50}, 12.50 \times LGD \right]$$

BRW_c is the benchmark risk-weight for corporations, which we define below. *PD* is the probability of default and is a driver of the benchmark corporate risk-weight. *LGD* is the loss given default on the transaction.[15] As the probability of default increases, the risk-weight increases above 100% of par value. The Committee gives a maturity adjustment formula that is an approximation, instead of a more exact calculation.

Benchmark Corporate Risk-Weights are Calculated Assuming a 99.5% Probability of Solvency for the Institution and That There Is a 20% Correlation Between All Borrowers

The Basel Committee makes a number of important assumptions in setting the benchmark corporate risk-weight. We list them briefly here:

- The benchmark risk weight for a probability of default of 70 basis points and a loss given default of 50% should be 100% of principal. The benchmark risk-weight formula is scaled so that this is true.
- All corporate borrowers are assumed to have a correlation of 20% with the value of the assets of all companies, the beta in our discussion of the Merton model.
- The Merton model is assumed to be true.
- The average borrower is assumed to have a loss given default of 50% and the maturity is assumed to be three years.

The Basel Committee implies that the formula is an approximation of the capital that would be needed after a monte carlo simulation of loans to a portfolio of borrowers with the following characteristics:

- There are *N* identical borrowers. The Committee does not reveal *N*;
- All borrowers have 3-year loans;
- All loans are consistent with the Merton model (single payment zero coupon loans);
- The number of simulations is not specified;
- The initial probabilities of default are not specified.
- The simulation is done on a single period, not multi-period basis, and the length of that single period is three years.

---

[14] Section 155, page 32, The Internal Ratings-Based Approach.
[15] Section 156, page 32, ibid.

The Basel Committee makes no apologies for this set of assumptions or the high degree of approximation used in deriving the benchmark risk-weight formula.

Why did the Basel Committee not simply specify either that:

- Banks do their own simulation on proper risk-weights using the credit model they feel is the best (for example, the Merton model, the STV model, or a reduced form model) assuming all borrowers are identical OR;
- Banks do their own simulation on proper risk-weights using the actual portfolio they own, the actual default probabilities on their actual counterparties, and the actual correlation they believe exists between the macro factors driving the default probability for that counterparty?

On the latter point, the Committee commented, 'The Committee observed a tendency on the part of some banks to adjust [probability of default] or expected loss estimates subjectively based on internal macro-economic forecasts. There is no reason for the Committee to believe that such adjustments are in any way inconsistent with sound or best-practice risk measurement and economic capital allocation. Nevertheless, a significant and largely subjective component to [probability of default] estimates will pose difficult challenges for the internal validation of these estimates.'[16]

We have shown for both Japan and the U.S. that corporate defaults are strongly driven by macro factors, and that the coefficients for these impacts can be derived in a manner consistent with the highest standard of statistical practice, as represented by the FIMS study or the Chava Jarrow research. Internal validation, using these procedures, is routine, well-understood, and easily verified by supervisors. By way of contrast, if there are big influences of macro factors on risk, as we saw in Chapter 4, how can one justify ignoring these impacts?

The Basel 'Granularity Adjustment'

Any lender knows that diversification is the key to credit risk management and at the very heart of best practice. The Basel Committee on Banking Supervision ignores this principal almost completely. The Committee makes a 'granularity adjustment' for diversification or the lack thereof, that is based on an arbitrary portfolio that is completely homogeneous, but which has a varying number of borrowers as measured by the Herfindahl index of

---

[16] Section 298, page 61, The Internal Ratings-Based Approach.

concentration used in studies of industrial concentration and monopolistic competition.[17]

A precise methodology for this is a direct simulation of portfolio results based on what the financial institution actually owns. To do anything else is to obscure the truth. Direct monte carlo simulation of portfolio results in common spreadsheet software costs less than $500 and is much more accurate and much simpler than the ad hoc approximation outlined by the Basel Committee.

Back to Basics: Better Than Basel

A perusal of the 102-page Consultative Document, 'The Internal Ratings-Based Approach' raises the same question over and over—why are we doing this? The objective should be to measure the safety and soundness of the institution accurately and in a straightforward manner.

To do this correctly, we need to insure the following:

Probability of Default

- We should be using the best estimates available for all borrowers, corporate, retail and others.
- The Basel proposal allows this for corporate borrowers subject to conditions, but it implies that banks are not able to do this at the retail level. On the contrary, every major bank in the U.S. is using retail credit scoring for retail default probability estimation, borrower by borrower. Moreover, this is common practice to an increasing degree in many, many other countries around the world.

Freedom to Choose the Best Modeling Technology

- We should be able to model the financial institution's safety and soundness using multiple credit models (Merton, STV, or reduced form), emphasizing the model which has the best performance on data most relevant to our institution.
- The Basel proposal implies some freedom of model choice in the default probability section of The Internal Ratings-Based Approach, but the calculation of benchmark corporate risk-weights is 'hard-wired' into a close relative of the Merton model. The credit model performance measurement we have done in Chapters 5 to 7 indicates

---

[17] Chapter 8, The Internal Ratings-Based Approach.

that more flexibility is warranted to achieve best performance and best practice.

Loss Given Default

- Best practice should allow the financial institution the flexibility to choose between historical experience, or loss given default implied by (a) market prices of the debt instrument and/or (b) market prices of collateral or guarantees.
- Basel imposes arbitrary adjustments that are both more complex and less accurate than any of these alternatives.

Exposure at Default

- The utilization of loan commitments is a topic we address in later chapters. There is a powerful modeling technology and a range of techniques that can realistically address usage as a function of credit quality.
- Basel imposes arbitrary adjustments with the same problems as those for loss given default

Macro Risk Factors and Forward-Looking Correlation

- The true credit risk and default probability of a financial institution has to be measured with an accurate simulation of its real portfolio using the best estimates of the default probabilities of its counterparties, taking into account which macro factors drive correlation among defaults. This is the only way to deal with Japan in the 1990s and the Asian crisis, which we examined in detail in Chapter 4.
- The Basel approach grossly understates this risk by understating the impact of correlations.

The Most Important Point

The Basel ratios of adjusted capital to adjusted assets represent[18] only one of the nine variables the Federal Reserve FIMS study found best predict default:

- Loans past due 30-89 days/Assets;
- Loans past due 90 or more days/Assets;

---

[18] This ratio is most closely related to the tangible capital/assets ratio used by the Federal Reserve Board in FIMS.

- Nonaccrual loans/Assets;
- Foreclosed real estate/Assets;
- Tangible capital/Assets;
- Net income/Assets;
- Reserves/Assets;
- Investment Securities/Assets;
- Large CDs/Assets.

With the Basel ratio as specified, supervisory agencies will not be able to predict safety and soundness as well as the FIMS study does, because eight statistically significant variables are omitted.

Even more importantly, all of the market-based credit models (Merton, STV, and reduced form) will provide better estimates of financial institutions risk than the Basel capital ratios. The emphasis of the Basel Committee on credit model testing was a large step forward, but more complete usage of the credit technology detailed in chapters 1 to 8 is justified because of the very promising performance of the models outlined in Chapters 6 and 7. Chapter 10 discusses the usage of credit models that goes far beyond the Basel requirements.

10

Measuring Safety and Soundness and Capital Allocation Using the Merton and Reduced Form Models

In Chapter 9, we examined the prescriptions of the Internal Ratings-Based Approach of the Basel Committee on Banking Supervision. A number of conclusions were reached in that chapter:

- The capital ratios proposed omit eight significant inputs found to have statistical significance in predicting bank default by the Board of Governors of the Federal Reserve System in the United States, therefore the Basel capital ratios are at best weak predictors of which banks will default.
- The Committee does not reveal the derivation of the formula used to derive the benchmark corporate risk—weights that are the key to the capital ratios they propose.
- To the extent that the origins of the formula are discussed, the formula seems to be rooted in the 1974 Merton model. This makes it impossible for proponents of newer credit models, such as the 1993 STV model or 2001 reduced form models, to calculate capital necessary or undertake capital allocation on a consistent basis using the BIS prescriptions.
- The Basel proposal calculates capital ratios in a way that does not allow banks to measure correlations among their own borrowers and explicitly incorporate them in measuring capital allocation and capital adequacy.

We take a different approach in this chapter, measuring capital allocation and capital adequacy in a manner that is both more practical and more consistent with the theory of credit risk that the user may select.

Using the Shimko-Tejima-van Deventer Credit Model for Capital Allocation and Capital Adequacy Calculations[1]

Bankers and regulators are faced with the problem of determining what level of capital is adequate given an institution's risk level. The same problem is relevant in all financial institutions, although the banking industry has devoted perhaps the most effort to this topic. Financial institutions' management also faces the challenge of identifying which units within the organization, all with differing degrees of risk, produce the greatest return on risk-adjusted capital. Measures of capital adequacy and risk-adjusted return on capital were once simple rules of thumb that provided roughly correct information, and the approach outlined by the Basel Committee on Banking Supervision in Chapter 9 is a further step in this direction. Advances in financial theory and technology over the last decade, however, have produced a much more sophisticated and accurate measure for capital adequacy and risk-adjusted return on capital than that proposed by the Basel Committee on Banking Supervision. These approaches can be applied for either reduced form or structural models of credit risk like those outlined in Chapter 3. In this section, we focus on the Shimko-Tejima-van Deventer model for credit risk.

Starting in the early 1980s, U.S. bank regulators have imposed an absolute minimum acceptable numerical capital adequacy ratio. In the U.S. in the early 1970s, however, there was no such arbitrary hurdle. Both bankers and regulators believed that the capital adequacy problem was too difficult to capture in a single calculation. This was because research in finance had not advanced to the stage where the optimal capital structure problem could be answered.

Just as significantly, bankers and regulators felt that too many non-qualified variables such as management quality and loan portfolio quality were critical to the capital adequacy problem, which consequently could not be summarized in one number. When pressed by the need for internal profit allocation, management tended to direct the same amount of capital to each unit and keep the earnings target for each activity the same.

The numbers used in these allocations were equally simple—the right level of capital (measured by the ratio of assets to equity) was always an even multiple of 1%, and the required return was always an even multiple of 5%. The Basel proposal in Chapter 9 is another variation on the theme—

---

[1] This section is adapted from Donald R. van Deventer, 'Overcoming Inadequacy,' Balance Sheet Magazine, Summer, 1993.

why, for example, did the Basel Committee conclude that banks should have capital sufficient to insure only a 99.5% probability of solvency? In part, the reason must have been that 99.5% is a round number. Surely, however, modern technology gives us a better basis for setting this critical hurdle rate.

By the early 1980s, regulators and bankers reacted to the more risky economic environment and resulting industry troubles with a more complex but much less arbitrary approach. Capital adequacy in the U.S. was judged according to a primary capital ratio, which seemed to have the major purpose of generating revenue for investment bankers. Billions of dollars of debt, defined to be 'capital' by regulators, were issued in response to an arbitrary definition of capital that few bankers took seriously. A similar type of regulatory arbitrage is explicitly acknowledged by investment bankers in response to the 1988 Basel capital accord and subsequent proposals.[2]

There was progress on the interest rate risk front, however, as duration calculations and mark-to-market concepts showed the link between interest rate risk and shareholder value. At leading banks, the risk-adjusted return on capital concept gained in popularity. Risk, measured by the standard deviation of a banking activity's cash flow, was calculated using historical data.

The maximum allowable risk of bankruptcy was selected by management (the equivalent of the 99.5% solvency target set by the Basel Committee), and normal distribution probability tables were used to calculate the minimum level of capital that kept the risk of bankruptcy at or below this level.

In the late 1980s and early 1990s, capital adequacy and capital allocation management made one small step forward. The step forward was the abolition of the primary capital concept in the U.S. The impact of the New Basel Capital Accord remains to be seen. When viewed as a political exercise designed to equalize regulation of banks across national boundaries, perhaps the BIS capital ratio system has been a modest success. However, as a useful guide to management action and the creation of shareholder value, the ratios have a number of problems which we outlined in Chapter 9.

The virtue of early efforts to measure the risk-adjusted return on capital was the focus on total volatility in balance sheet values from all sources. In spite of the complexities and potential confusion that the Basel Accords and the Internal-Ratings Based Approach have engendered, it is important not to lose sight of this key risk concept, even if management actually manages total risk by manipulating one component (like interest rate risk and credit risk) at a time.

---

[2] This regulatory arbitrage was explicitly acknowledged by an investment banker from one of the largest firms in the United States at the *Risk* Magazine Asset and Liability Management Conference, New York, September 2002.

In Chapter 3, we explained how Merton (1973, 1974) made it clear that the equity in any firm is an option on the value of the firm's underlying assets— a useful base for calculating capital adequacy and internal capital allocation. Shimko, Tejima, and van Deventer (1993) expanded Merton's approach to allow for interest rate risk as well as basic asset volatility (credit risk), as we explained in Chapter 3. The STV approach allows for an arbitrary degree of correlation between interest rate fluctuations and total business risk that is integrated and analytically consistent. This correlation is ignored in the Basel prescriptions in Chapter 9, because the Merton model used as a base for the benchmark corporate risk-weights assumes interest rates are constant, so there is no correlation between asset values and interest rates by definition. A large amount of corporate credit spread information, such as that which we outlined in Chapter 4 and other chapters, shows that credit spreads are driven by interest rates. For that reason, we concentrate on capital allocation using the STV model in this section, rather than the Merton model.

In what follows, we will adopt the STV assumptions that we discussed in Chapter 3. We use the model to evaluate the credit risk of the bank and each of its business units in exactly the same way we used the model to measure corporate credit risk in Chapter 3. We assume that the bank (or any of the individual assets or business units on the bank's balance sheet) has an asset value of V. Like the Black-Scholes option model, we suppose that the rate of return on this asset has a volatility σ_v, and that the value of the asset is assumed to have a lognormal distribution—this is an approximation, but an extremely useful one. N is the cumulative normal distribution function.

We also assume that interest rates vary according to the model of the term structure of interest rates model proposed by Vasicek (1977). This model was extended to fit the yield curve exactly by Hull and White, and it is a special case of the Heath Jarrow and Morton Model. The Vasicek model supposes that all interest rates move in response to one random factor, the short-term risk-free interest rate, and that the short-term interest rate tends to revert to a long-term mean value and has a constant volatility. Interest rates and asset returns are assumed to have a correlation coefficient ρ that will normally be negative. We assume this risky asset V is financed with risky debt with a face value of B and no coupon payments—that is, it is zero-coupon debt. We denote the market value of this debt F. For any given level of asset risk and interest rate volatility, the value of F is:

$$F = V - VN(h_1) + BP(\tau)N(h_2)$$

where:

$$h_1 = \frac{\ln\left(\dfrac{V}{P(\tau)B}\right) + \dfrac{1}{2}T}{\sqrt{T}}$$

$$h_2 = h_1 - \sqrt{T}$$

$$T = \tau\left(\sigma_v^2 + \frac{\sigma_r^2}{k^2} + \frac{2\rho\sigma_v\sigma_r}{k}\right) + (e^{-kr} + 1)*\left(\frac{2\sigma_r^2}{k^3} + \frac{2\rho\sigma_r\sigma_v}{k^2}\right)$$

$$- \frac{\sigma_r^2}{2k^3}(e^{-2kr} - 1)$$

P is the price of a risk-free zero coupon bond, as given by the Vasicek model:

$$P(\tau) = \exp\left[\frac{1 - e^{-k\tau}}{k}(R(\infty) - r) - \tau R(\infty) - \frac{\sigma_r^2}{4k^3}(1 - e^{-k\tau})^2\right]$$

$$R(\infty) = \gamma + \frac{\sigma_r}{k}\lambda - \frac{1}{2}\frac{\sigma_r^2}{k^2}$$

r = short-term interest rate
τ = years to maturity
λ = market price of risk in the interest rate market
σ_v = volatility of asset returns
σ_r = volatility of r
ρ = correlation between r and asset returns
k = the speed of mean reversion in r
γ = the long run mean value for r.

How do we use this model for capital allocation? The following explains.

Step 1: Set the probability of solvency that management desires (the equivalent of the Basel Committee's 99.5%).

One choice is to solve for F such that the continuously compounded return on the debt used to finance the risky asset is the bank's *marginal cost of funds*. This sets the default probability or survival probability of the business unit to be the same as that for the bank as a whole, with the same adjustment for liquidity and other factors that impact the bank's credit spreads and therefore its marginal cost of funds. Of course, any other survival probability can be chosen as well, including the Basel recommendation of 99.5%. The equity necessary to support a given asset class with the same marginal cost as the bank is $V - F$, the value of the asset minus the value of debt used to finance it. The capital level consistent with a given continuously compounded return on the risky debt is $(V - F)/V$. Capital ratios are evaluated for a number of different parameter values in Figure 10.1.

Step 2: Assign Capital to Each Asset or Business Unit as a Function if Its Asset Risk, Interest Rate Risk and Correlation between Them

If we take this approach, we can simply list capital adequacy ratios as a function of asset volatility and correlation with interest rates in a simple table, a much, much more intuitive and theoretically correct approach than the Basel Committee has taken. Table 10.1 below gives a representative example.

Table 10.1 Value of capital ratios for varying levels of asset volatility, interest rate volatility and correlation

Correlation (ρ)	Asset volatility (σ_V)	Interest rate volatility (%)			
		0.05	**0.10**	**0.15**	**0.20**
−1.00	0.05	1.81	1.08	2.22	3.89
−1.00	0.10	7.90	4.75	2.93	2.55
−1.00	0.15	15.14	11.03	7.66	5.29
−1.00	0.20	22.61	18.03	13.87	10.36
−0.50	0.05	3.51	4.00	5.31	7.08
−0.50	0.10	9.79	8.65	8.42	8.85
−0.50	0.15	17.03	14.99	13.62	12.89
−0.50	0.20	24.44	21.87	19.77	18.19
0.00	0.05	4.92	6.24	7.95	9.79
0.00	0.10	11.48	11.74	12.44	13.39
0.00	0.15	18.65	18.32	18.22	18.42
0.00	0.20	26.16	25.21	24.53	24.12
0.05	0.05	6.15	8.24	10.12	12.02
0.50	0.10	13.02	14.37	15.77	17.15
0.50	0.15	20.40	21.23	22.08	22.95
0.50	0.20	27.76	28.17	28.58	29.01
1.00	0.05	7.26	9.79	12.06	13.82
1.00	0.10	14.45	16.71	18.67	20.40
1.00	0.15	21.91	23.83	25.45	26.84
1.00	0.20	29.28	30.85	32.13	33.20

Assumptions: $r = 0.04$; $k = 0.3$, $\lambda = -0.05$; $\gamma = 0.07$; $V = 120$; $\tau = 1$

Using these formulas, bankers and regulators can determine the amount of capital that should be allocated to different activities (with varying degrees of credit risk, interest rate risk, and the correlation between the two), such that all activities have the same risk of bankruptcy—and the same expected return on capital for each activity; we can also determine the amount of capital necessary at a given bank for a given degree of credit risk, interest rate risk and correlation between these two risks.

Important Note on Probability of Default and Loss Given Default

In the capital allocation example above, note that we didn't use the probability of default or the loss given default in allocating capital. *We don't need to*, because the probability of default and the loss given default are both implied by the STV model and the value of asset volatility, interest rate volatility, and correlation that we have derived for the business unit or individual asset. The probability of default and loss given default can be mapped directly back and forth to the value of company assets—whether one is using the Merton model or the STV model. Figure 10.1 above could have easily been designed in terms of default probabilities and loss given default, with no loss of accuracy and no loss of practicality. The Basel provisions ignore this precise mapping, especially when calculating the benchmark corporate risk-weights as a function of the probability of default. The theory should give us the benchmark corporate risk-weight and in the example above, it does.

A Practical Example

As an example, assume that First National Bank is engaged in five different activities that have varying degrees of credit risk and correlation between credit risk and interest rate risk. The five activities can be classified by the volatility of the return on each and the correlation of that return with the level of interest rates. Table 10.2 below illustrates this.. Assuming the bank

Table 10.2

Asset risk and correlation with interest rates		
	Asset Return Volatility (σ_r)	Correlation with the level of interest rates (ρ)
Fixed-rate home construction loan	0.20	−0.50
30-year Treasury Bonds	0.10	−1.00
3-month Treasury Bills	0.05	−1.00
30-year fixed rate mortgage loan	0.15	−0.50
Floating-rate loan to foreign corporation	0.10	0.00

has a one-year horizon, how much capital should be allocated internally to each of these activities if the bank's cost of one-year money is 5% and the rate on one-year Treasury Bills is 4%? We assume that the underlying volatility of very short-term interest rates is 0.10, that all assets of the bank were generated today, and that book values and market values are therefore the same.

How much capital should be allocated to each of these activities for the probability of bankruptcy in any one of these five activities to be the same as the bank's overall probability of default?

We go through the following steps:

1. Solve for the amount of debt F we can lend to each business unit given the asset return volatility and the correlation of that asset return with interest rates such that the continuous yield on the debt with a one year maturity has the same return as the marginal cost of bank debt, 5%.
2. Capital is then allocated so that the amount of capital plus the amount of debt equals the value of the asset. The asset value is V, the amount of debt is F, and the amount of capital is $V - F$.

Taking the appropriate values from Table 10.2, we find the following levels of capital in Table 10.3 below. These capital allocations take full account of the dual risk inherent in each activity—the risk of interest rate fluctuations, asset value risk from all sources, and the correlation of these risks. Since the volatility of asset returns is completely general, it has equal validity whether the risk consists of foreign exchange risk, stock market risk, or more traditional credit risk.

Table 10.3

Capital allocation to each activity	Capital as % of asset market value
Fixed-rate home construction loan	21.87
30-year Treasury Bonds	4.75
3-month Treasury Bills	1.08
30-year fixed rate mortgage loan	14.99
Floating-rate loan to foreign corporation	11.74

By allocating a fair level of capital with an explicit rationale to each activity, management can compare returns for each business. These activities could be thought of as individual banks. Regulators can set a minimum probability of default and work backwards, given asset volatility and interest rate volatility, to find the level of capital for any bank consistent with that level of risk.

How are the proper inputs determined for this calculation? There are two different approaches:

- The first is to use historical data to derive appropriate volatilities for the future time period that the bank sets as its time horizon;
- The second is to derive the implied values of risk parameters from the market prices for each asset class and related assets, like the treasury yield curve.

In general, the second approach has become the standard for the options industry because of its demonstrated superiority as a forecaster of true volatility.

But how is the asset volatility determined on a construction loan? One common technique is to find a listed, publicly traded security with risk that is as similar as possible to the asset under consideration and use that series of asset prices to derive risk parameters. A more difficult approach is to construct a historical series of past returns on actual construction loans.

The easiest and usually best approach takes advantage of the 'no free lunch' axiom. If a loan is priced at prime plus 6% in the market, it must be prime plus 6% for a reason. What is the level of asset volatility on that class of loan that would make the bank indifferent between making the loan and buying three-month Treasury Bills? There is an easy, inexpensive, and reasonably accurate method of forecasting the correct asset volatility.

What does this type of analysis imply for financial institutions, bank regulators, and the Basel Committee on Banking Supervision? The implications are considerable:

- Every asset class can have its own risk-adjusted capital level, calculated on a consistent and logical basis.
- The required capital for a bank overall can be calculated in the same way. The level of bank capital for a given level of default risk will be less than the sum of capital allocated to each asset class, because of the portfolio effect, that will cause individual risks to offset each other.
- The required level of capital can be set to a level consistent with the default probabilities built into the assumptions for a deposit insurance fund.
- The risk measure is completely general and can be used to treat interest rate risk, credit risk, foreign exchange risk, and stock market risk on a wholly integrated basis.

- The liquidity risk, or probability of default, for a given bank is a by-product of the calculation and can be used as a numerical index in place of arbitrary capital ratios previously imposed by regulators.

This methodology is completely consistent with the objectives of the Internal Ratings-Based Approach outlined in Chapter 9 but with a number of significant differences:

- It is explicitly based on a modern random interest rates framework, rather than the constant interest rates framework implied by the Basel Committee's quiet incorporation of the 1974 Merton technology.
- It uses a more advanced form of the Merton model, the STV model, than the Basel Committee. The STV model is much more consistent with the link between interest rates and credit spreads that we found in Chapter 4.
- It is much simpler and more transparent
- It is easier and much less expensive for financial institutions to apply because of its simplicity, accuracy, and greater realism.

Most importantly, however, this approach is still not as accurate a predictor of bank default as the FIMS system employed by the Federal Reserve Board, because the same eight variables omitted by the Basel Committee's proposal are also omitted from this approach.

Another Approach to Risk-Adjusted Performance Measurement

The Basel Committee's fascination with capital ratios has two roots in the history of the financial services industry. The first is that capital ratios were the first form of quantitative risk limits imposed by bankers, starting in the 1980s in the U.S.. The second is the popularity of capital allocation to business units by banks as a way of assessing which assets are 'good' (and therefore should be done in greater volume) and which assets are 'bad' and therefore should be de-emphasized. This desire by banks to measure shareholder value and to improve asset selection is consistent with the objectives of the credit risk process that we outlined in Chapter 1.

As highlighted by the limitations of the Basel approach, a successful implementation of the risk-adjusted performance measurement concept has to be done carefully to insure that the potential shareholder benefits are in fact realized. This section summarizes the key facts and key concepts that the authors believe are the hallmark of world-class risk-adjusted performance measurement.

Keys to Success in Risk-Adjusted Performance Measurement

The key success factors in implementing risk-adjusted performance measurement all revolve around the creation of shareholder value. A risk-adjusted performance measurement system with these characteristics will create the most shareholder value in the long-term:

- Performance measurement, when used as a guide for resource allocation, should focus on expected performance relative to risk, not past performance;
- Performance measurement should emphasize relative, not absolute, performance compared to a benchmark with the same risk and very low transactions costs. Benchmarks are easily determined for all major lines of business in banking, insurance, and investment management;
- Performance measurement focuses on market values of assets and liabilities, not financial accounting values, at the senior manager level and chief executive level
- Market-based performance measurement is automatically reconciled to financial accounting statements, just like a 'Sources and Uses of Funds' statement reconciles to cash balances;
- Financial accounting-based performance measures that are consistent with the market value approach are used to measure the performance of branches, since they are large in number, small in size, and run by managers who best understand the financial accounting approach.
- Capital allocation and risk-adjusted return on that capital are done on a market basis.
- Capital should be allocated to line units so that the cost of funds to each line unit has the same risk as the bank as a whole;
- The capital allocated to line units should be set equal to the total market value of the bank as a whole at least once a year, to emphasize the links to shareholder value;
- Regulatory capital, including the Basel proposals, is not used as the basis for allocation of capital, since regulatory capital has a strong financial accounting basis and consists of arbitrary securities defined as 'capital' but which can still trigger default (such as subordinated debt);
- Macro risk factors that can affect returns are properly taken into account, and risk management policies and procedures of the bank insure that these risks remain within prudent limits.

We discuss each of these factors in turn, but only after a review of the Bankers Trust RAROC system and other typical capital allocation formulas, with their pros and cons. Finally, we discuss what we see as the best practice approach to rational performance measurement and capital allocation.

The Bankers Trust RAROC Methodology

Even in the 1980s, more than 90% of Bankers Trust's assets were in traded securities with a readily observable market value. For that reason, it made sense for Bankers Trust to adopt a risk management system that is based on market values, not financial accounting values. 'Risk' in the Bankers Trust system was measured as the standard deviation of changes in the market value, not the net income, of each asset and liability. 'Return' was the total return (interest income plus capital gains) over an accounting period, not just interest income. Capital was allocated to each line unit so that the probability of bankruptcy for that line unit, assuming that historical asset value volatility continues, will exactly equal a target probability of default. Bankers Trust has arbitrarily set this target default level to 1%.[3] This level is no more accurate than the Basel Committee's 99.5% target—all it shows is the same preference for round numbers that the Basel Committee has. Risk-adjusted return on capital for a given accounting period at Bankers Trust was measured by the total return on the unit's assets divided by the risk-adjusted capital allocated to that unit.

The Bankers' Trust system is simple and is easy to apply, but only because this bank is such a unique institution in that:

- almost all assets are traded assets;
- the Bank has no retail banking activities to speak of;
- the Bank has very little corporate lending activity on the balance sheet.

The implication of the use of this approach to RAROC is that more capital should be allocated to high RAROC activities and less capital to low RAROC activities. The only problem with this implication is that it destroys shareholder value. An example using three possible business activities in Thai baht, yen and Deutsche Marks illustrates the point. These examples are put forth on the basis of a very simple premise:

---

[3] This is a much higher default probability than the observed default probability for Bankers Trust implied from debt prices for Bankers Trust. This summary of the Bankers Trust methodology is based on conversations with P. Daniel Borge, a 20 year veteran of Bankers Trust who was heavily involved in the implementation of the concept while reporting to Eugene Shanks, later President of the Bank. Dr. Borge is not responsible for any of the errors the authors may have made in summarizing his description of the Bankers Trust system.

If a capital allocation method is not correct at the transaction level, it can never be correct at the portfolio level either, because the portfolio is the sum of the transactions in it.

Problems with the Bankers Trust Approach to RAROC

The problems with the Bankers Trust approach to RAROC illustrate a number of problems with the concept of capital allocation generally. The same critiques can be made in regard to using the Basel prescriptions for capital allocation as well. Assume that the bank has three areas of its foreign exchange dealing business and the bank decides to use RAROC to decide how much capital should be allocated to long positions in yen versus the U.S. dollar, long positions in the Thai baht versus the U.S. dollar, and long positions in the Deutsche mark versus the U.S. dollar. We assume the amount being considered in each case is a notional amount of US$ 100.

The first observation we make is that the *historical standard deviations of the returns from these three strategies are not stable*, even given the inherent averaging properties of the 36-month standard deviations of monthly returns that we used as the Bankers Trust-style measure of risk (Figure 10.1):

Figure 10.1   3 year moving standard deviation of one month returns from a long position versus U.S. dollars

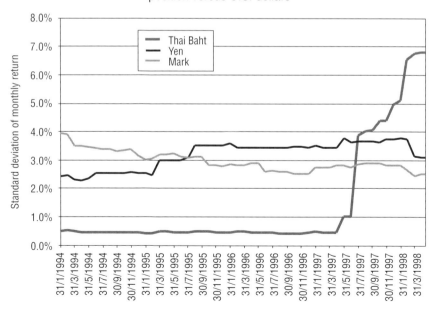

The required capital is not stable either, using a 1% probability of bankruptcy as the trigger for capital levels, as shown in Figure 10.2.

A more important and definitely fatal flaw in this approach is that past superior risk-adjusted return on capital has no apparent relation with future risk-adjusted capital. This is just a common-sense implication of the 'no free lunch' rule of finance, as the graph of the RAROC on a long position in the Thai baht shows (Figure 10.3):

This disappointing conclusion is made even more starkly when one plots risk-adjusted return versus risk-adjusted return the prior month, this time for the Deutsche Mark (Figure 10.4).

The strong desire by financial institutions to use a RAROC-like framework to 'pick winners' among financial businesses is offset by the fact that past market returns do not predict future market returns, even with the risk-adjustment proposed on a market value basis by Bankers Trust. We turn next to another alternative adopted by many banks.

Modified Financial Accounting-Based RAROC Approach

In part because of the volatility of market returns but more because of a lack of market prices, bankers have often allocated capital based on the risk of the business as measured by financial accounting measures such as net income (or, as we discuss below, shareholder value-added).

Figure 10.2 Risk-adjusted capital required for $100 notional long position versus U.S. dollars based on 3 year standard deviation of monthly returns and 1% probability of default

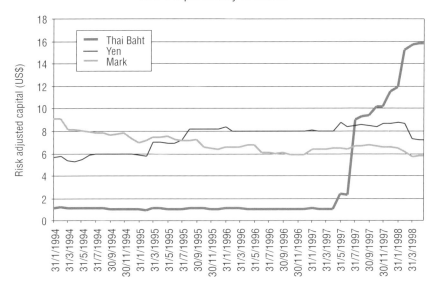

Figure 10.3 Annualized risk-adjusted return on capital for US$100 national long position in Thai Baht

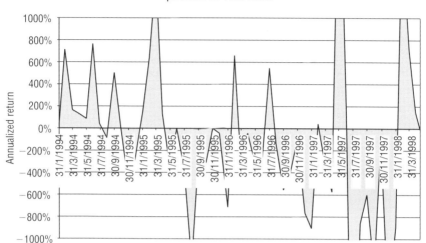

Figure 10.4 RAROC on long position in DM vs U.S. dollars as a function of prior month's RAROC

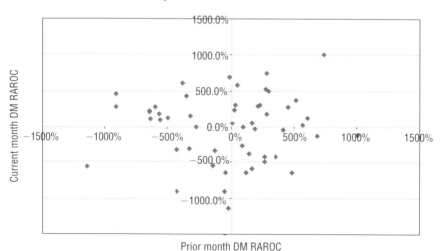

The Financial Accounting-Based RAROC approach has a number of benefits as well:

- It is easy to understand;
- It is easy to implement;
- It makes intuitive sense if one places high value on financial accounting information.

Its liabilities as a technique are even more striking:

- Like the Bankers Trust RAROC approach it has no predictive power and therefore cannot be an effective method for resource allocation;
- The method tends to over-reward high-risk lending areas during good times;
- High-risk lending tends to suffer massive losses by this measure during bad times.

Consider the example of Daiei, Ltd., a major Japanese retailer, over the 1994–1999 period.

A Case Study: Daiei, Ltd.

Daiei is one of the leading Japanese retailers whose fortunes have been fairly typical of the retailing industry in Japan since the mid-1990s. Assume that the bank effectively made a 1994 loan to Daiei by buying the company's 5.15% yen bonds due February 21, 2003. In addition, assume that the amount of the loan is 1000 yen and that the bank had 'match funded' the loan and fixed a 2% profit margin on the credit. Using actual data, Table 10.4 illustrates how the actual profitability of the credit would look

Table 10.4

Date	Interest Income	Interest Expense	Financial Accounting Profit
February 1994	25.75 yen	15.75 yen	10 yen
August 1994	25.75 yen	15.75 yen	10 yen
February 1995	25.75 yen	15.75 yen	10 yen
August 1995	25.75 yen	15.75 yen	10 yen
February 1996	25.75 yen	15.75 yen	10 yen
August 1996	25.75 yen	15.75 yen	10 yen
February 1997	25.75 yen	15.75 yen	10 yen
August 1997	25.75 yen	15.75 yen	10 yen
February 1998	25.75 yen	15.75 yen	10 yen
August 1998	25.75 yen	15.75 yen	10 yen
February 1999	25.75 yen	15.75 yen	10 yen
August 1999	25.75 yen	15.75 yen	10 yen

Standard Deviation of Financial Accounting Profit: 0 yen

Like the Bankers Trust RAROC approach, many institutions take the standard deviation of financial accounting income and allocate capital such that the maximum probability of bankruptcy from this line of business would be, say, 1%. The financial accounting-based RAROC would be the actual net income divided by this risk-adjusted capital. Unfortunately, this methodology is nonsensical for Daiei, especially when one considers the implication of a blind application of the RAROC technology.

- Daiei has made all interest payments on the 5.15% yen bonds due February 21, 2003;
- Net income from the Daiei business has a standard deviation of zero;
- Risk-adjusted capital for Daiei, then, is zero since this measure of business risk is zero;
- RAROC using this measure for Daiei is infinite, and the implication is that this is a great business and more capital should be allocated to it.

The reality of the Daiei situation from 1994 to 1999 is much different. As Figure 10.5 shows, Daiei bonds have plunged in value from almost 115% of par value to only 86% of par value in a very short time, a loss of 29% of par value. Financial accounting measures have completely missed a significant decline in market value and a significant increase in risk.

If, instead of the financial accounting approach, we had taken a market-value based Bankers Trust-type approach to RAROC, the 90 business day standard deviation of the Daiei bond price would have shown very substantial variation over time, as shown below in Figure 10.6:

The amount of capital that would have been allocated to Daiei by the Bankers Trust measure was also extremely volatile, ranging from less than 1% of principal to more than 13% of principal during the four-year period under study.

Figure 10.5   Price of Daiei 5.15% yen bonds due February 21, 2003

Figure 10.6   Daiei 5.15% yen bonds due February 21, 2003
90 business day standard deviation of price

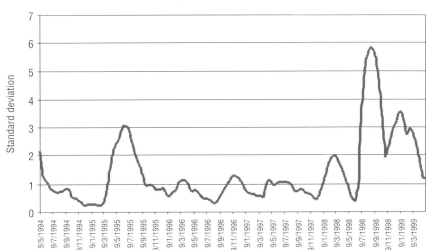

Figure 10.7   Risk-adjusted capital required for Daiei 5.15% yen bonds due
2/21/2003 with 1% probability of bankruptcy (or lending unit) in 90 days

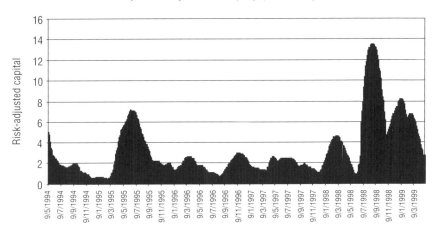

This example again leads to the conclusion that the simplest methods of
capital allocation and performance measurement lead to results that are
extremely difficult to use as a guide to practical action.

Shareholder Value-Added

A third approach that has gained popularity recently is a performance
measurement technique that focuses on shareholder value-added. The

technique, which attempts to measure the incremental returns earned above and beyond shareholder requirements, essentially works as follows:

- Financial accounting income for a business unit is determined;
- All non-cash items in financial accounting income, such as depreciation and loan loss provisions, are added back to financial accounting income;
- Recurring cash capital investment is subtracted;
- The result is 'free cash flow';
- The minimum shareholder return is then calculated, often using techniques like the 1965 Capital Asset Pricing model;
- Minimum shareholder cash returns are calculated by multiplying the minimum shareholder return times (sometimes) accounting capital or the actual market value of equity;
- The excess of free cash flow over minimum shareholder cash returns is shareholder value-added in dollar terms. It can be converted to a percentage by dividing by accounting capital.

This approach has an extensive appeal for a number of reasons:

- Risk is measured by the actual risk of the firm's common stock, not financial accounting figures;
- Shareholder expectations for minimum acceptable performance have an appeal as a relative performance measure;
- The adjustments to net income to calculate free-cash flow make sense;
- The methodology is easy to implement.

Unfortunately, the concerns of this approach are similar to the concerns with the other two methods discussed previously:

- The financial accounting return, free cash flow, understates risk, as the Daiei case shows;
- The financial accounting return is not a predictor of future performance, as we saw in the case of the three currencies measured earlier;
- The calculation of minimum shareholder returns is too simple for practical use: shareholder expectations for returns in the short-term government securities investment business are much less than shareholder expectations for returns in the long-term fixed-rate mortgage business and much less than shareholder expectations for returns in venture capital investments;
- There are large errors in the expected return on all stocks, a key parameter in setting minimum returns on capital, as reported by Fama and French [2002].

Looking at the Basel Internal Ratings-Based Approach as a Capital Allocation Approach

With this historical survey of financial institutions capital allocation techniques in mind, how does the Basel Internal Ratings Based Approach compare?

It has a number of virtues:

- The use of a market-based Daiei default probability to drive capital allocation, rather than the historical volatility of net income from a Daiei loan, is without doubt a step forward even given the other concerns with the Basel approach;
- The benchmark corporate risk-weight of the Basel approach is at least linked to a survival probability (99.5%) that is in a plausible range, although its derivation is a black box.

To apply the Basel approach in practice, however, creates a number of other difficulties for financial institutions:

- The Basel risk-weighted assets are based on accounting values, not market values—they therefore omit the deterioration in asset values that we saw in the Daiei example;
- The Basel proposals do not consider how 'return' should be calculated or what 'hurdle' rate for that return should be set.

As we saw above, future returns are not correlated with past returns, and accounting returns are very misleading when compared with market returns.

We now turn to an alternative approach that addresses these issues.

A New Approach to Measuring Safety and Soundness and Capital Allocation: Risk-Adjusted Performance Advantage

The credit models we discussed in Chapter 3 and the impact of macro factors discussed in Chapter 4 give us a basis to develop a forward-looking measure of performance that helps achieve both the objectives for capital allocation listed in the introduction to this chapter and the objectives of the credit risk process outlined in Chapter 1. This approach is independent of which credit model the user prefers, be it the Merton model, the STV model, the Jarrow model or some other model. The keys to success are the forward-looking nature of both risk and return.

The risk-adjusted performance measure that the authors recommend for strategic asset selection is as follows:

Risk-Adjusted Performance Advantage

$$= \frac{\text{Expected Return } [i] - r}{\text{Standard Deviation of Non - Diversifiable Return}}$$

Risk-Adjusted Performance Advantage (RAPA), is the incremental expected return on an asset class in excess of the risk-free rate, divided by the standard deviation of that component of return that is non-diversifiable. This risk measure has powerful links to the financial theory of both fixed income and equity markets. It is closely related to the well-known Sharpe ratio used in equity markets and to the condition for 'no arbitrage' in term structure models of interest rate movements.

Using RAPA for Shareholder Value Creation and Capital Adequacy Measurement

RAPA can be used for shareholder value analysis and asset selection with or without debt being assigned to business units. When looking at the return on a 'security' (such as a bank with liabilities or a business unit with both assets and liability), the RAPA analysis can be done for any level of capital (and for a range of capital levels) to set the optimal risk and return trade off for both management and regulators. There are many attractive aspects of this form of analysis:

- It is consistent with any credit model;
- It is consistent with any interest rate risk model;
- It is consistent with any model of loss given default;
- It is consistent with any model linking the macro factors we studied in Chapter 4 with asset values (as in the Merton and STV models) and default (in the Jarrow models and by implication, in the Merton and STV models since default probabilities are driven by company asset values);
- It is consistent with both single period (VAR) and multiple period modeling of values, cash flows, defaults and losses;
- It is a more general and transparent implementation of what the Basel Committee is attempting to do by an undisclosed approximation.

At the same time that we note that this approach is consistent with any credit model, it is important to note that the assumptions of reduced form models are best suited to this approach. Reduced form models are multi-period models consistent with a full valuation framework. By using this approach, we can use the procedures below to value Collateralized Debt Obligations (as in the next chapter) and the financial institution itself. We turn now to the calculation of the RAPA process.

Benchmarking the RAPA Calculation Using Observable Market Prices

Modern finance and modern computer technology make a higher accurate RAPA calculation within the reach of almost every financial institution, either through software they install and operate themselves or via a service bureau processing arrangement that brings modern computer power to management without the need to operate the software at the institution itself.

Most importantly, the same calculation process can produce the following output:

- The capital adequacy of each business unit and the financial institution itself;
- The probability of bankruptcy of the institution itself;
- Both statistics at multiple dates in the future.

This is the ultimately regulatory tool, for every financial institutions regulator should know the probability of default for every institution within its regulatory purview.

The steps in calculating RAPA are set out below:

Set the proper assumptions for the current market environment:

- **Risk-free yield curve**: the simulated yield curve should be completely consistent with observable yield curve and securities traded on it (caps, floors, futures, etc.);
- **Financial institution's cost of funds**: the simulated 'own yield curve' should be consistent with market prices, both in terms of new issuance and observable secondary market prices. There are more than 120,000 bond issues with observable prices internationally, so many institutions have access to the price of their own debt;
- **Exchange rates and commodity prices** should match observable market prices;
- **Macro factor values** should be collected and be consistent with current market conditions (including interest rates, exchanges rates, etc. but also equity price indexes, building price indexes, single family home price indexes, etc.).

Link movements in credit spreads to macro factors for all possible classes of borrowers:

- **Corporate borrowers'** credit worthiness usually depends on obvious macro factors. As we saw in Chapter 4, Exxon depends on oil prices, Korean Development Bank depends on the value of the Korean won/US dollar exchange rates, Daiei depends on the yen-dollar exchange rate and so on;

- **Commercial real estate** clients depend on building prices;
- **Mortgage borrowers** depend on home values and interest rates;
- **Small businesses** depend on economic conditions that depend on lagged changes in stock indexes and (in open economies) exchange rates.

This analysis can be done internally or by third party vendors.

Credit models should be adjusted to fit observable market prices to the maximum extent possible:

- **Bank counterparties'** default probabilities should be consistent with observable bond prices and credit derivatives;
- **Corporate counterparties'** default probabilities (if they are very large) should be consistent with observable bond prices and credit derivatives;
- **Corporate counterparties'** default probabilities (if they are smaller companies but have listed common stock) should be consistent with historical default experience in the country and default models benchmarked in that history, such as the Chava-Jarrow model outlined in Chapter 6;
- **Mortgage counterparties'** default probabilities should (a) be updated to reflect current macro factors and (b) be consistent with current pricing on new mortgages;
- **Auto loan counterparties'** default probabilities should (a) be updated to reflect current macro factors and (b) be consistent with current pricing on new mortgages.

Much of the adjustment to pricing models that will need to be done involves capturing expenses that drive up the cost of consumer lending but doesn't reflect default risk, per se.

Loss given default estimates for each borrower class should be consistent with (a) the credit model used, current market prices, and historical experience

Publicly traded securities should have assumptions set so that no risk- free arbitrage is possible

The financial institution's entire portfolio should be loaded and described accurately on a transaction-by-transaction basis. Transactions should not be summarized in any way unless they are truly identical.

If the system does not allow transaction level processing, the system should be replaced. Transaction level processing is essential for accuracy, and lack of this capability is a major concern. The Basel 'granularity' adjustment for diversification of a portfolio is a very rough approximation that would not be acceptable to management teams at most financial institutions because of its lack of accuracy.

Checking the benchmarking process:
A quick mark-to-market of the financial institution's balance sheet provides clues to the accuracy of the benchmarking process:

- **Calculated prices of traded securities** should be identical or nearly identical to observable market prices;
- **Calculated value of the financial institution's equity** should bear a fairly stable relationship (usually lower) than the implied market value of stock price x number of shares outstanding.

The RAPA Calculation

Before running the RAPA calculation, the output of the processing should be set:

- **Multi-period modeling should be done**. The length of all the periods combined should be at least five years, and the length of each period should be monthly or quarterly at most. Many institutions use daily periods for the early days of the five-year time horizon. The Basel approach, by contrast, is based on a single period modeling process; the single period assumption has never been popular for modeling total balance sheet risk because of the inconsistency of that assumption with even the simplest of bank instruments, almost all of which have multiple payment dates.
- **All calculations should be reported for each period**, not just the total length of all periods combined.
- **Standard reports** that are designed to achieve all of the objectives of the credit risk process should be produced. These objectives are summarized in Chapters 1 and 5.
- **The financial institution's probability of bankruptcy** in each period should be calculated.

The calculation process for RAPA involves a very efficient monte carlo simulation process. Monte carlo simulation is done only to simulate the environment, not to calculate market values. Market values can normally be calculated very rapidly using formulas that are consistent with financial theory, given the state of the environment in any given scenario. Major financial institutions are processing millions of transactions using this methodology. Distributed processing and the ability to link chips of increasingly high calculation speed in diverse machines are removing long-standing barriers to accurate risk measurement.

The number of scenarios that needs to be used depends on the nature of the portfolio and the accuracy desired in any given calculation. . Most sophisticated institutions are using 5,000 to 200,000 scenarios, but this number is increasing as computer chip processing speed increases.

Steps in the RAPA calculation process

It is very important to structure the RAPA calculation process so that the impact of macro factors that we analyzed in Chapter 4 can be correctly modeled and measured. The calculation process that captures the impact of macro factors on credit risk, rather than simply using historical correlation, goes like this:

1. Simulate the multiperiod-correlated changes in the key macro factors driving credit risk, interest rate risk, and foreign exchange risk for the institution;
2. Given these macro factors, derive the probability of default and loss given default for every counterparty in every period in every scenario. Default probabilities will be correlated among counterparties because they are functions of common macro factors;
3. In each scenario, given the probabilities of default, simulate the infinite numbers of default times that can occur for that counterparty, given the multi-period evolution of its default probability in that scenario;
4. Calculate the value, cash flows, and financial accruals for each transaction the financial institution has with each counterparty;
5. Generate the standard reports and distribute electronically to end users.

Output from the RAPA calculation process

The RAPA calculation is simple to summarize from this output:

- Expected return is the average return, over all scenarios, of each asset or each asset class

---

As noted earlier in this volume, National Australia Bank has announced in a press release that it is processing over one million transactions per day. A mid-sized Korean consumer lender is processing two million transactions per run.

- The variable r is the return on a risk-free investment in government securities over the simulation horizon;
- Standard deviation of non-diversifiable return is the standard deviation, over all scenarios, of the return on the asset or the asset class;
- Probability of default for the financial institution itself and each business unit;
- Market value of the financial institution in each period for every scenario.

RAPA gives a clear, forward-looking measure of the risk-adjusted returns on each asset class. This approach has some very important advantages over the Basel approach, detailed as follows:

- Macro risks such as the level of interest rates, exchange rates, key commodity prices, and so on, affect the market value of the assets owned by each business line in the bank and the default probability of each asset, business line, and the bank itself;
- The sensitivity of bank capital (or the capital of any financial institution) to changes in these asset values depends on how much debt and equity capital the bank has funding these businesses;
- The market value of the sum of line unit capital should equal the market value of the bank as a whole;
- The risk (and cost) of debt lent from the bank's central treasury unit to each line unit should be the same as the risk (and cost) of debt issued by the bank itself. This insures that all line units have the same risk as the bank as a whole;
- The amount of capital needed in each line unit to equalize risk to the bank's level will depend on:
  - ♦ The volatility of the value of the assets the line unit holds;
  - ♦ The correlation of asset values with interest rates;
  - ♦ The level of interest rates;
  - ♦ The volatility of interest rates;
  - ♦ The effective maturity of the assets held.

A number of calculations are an important set of by-products to this approach to capital allocation and performance measurement:

- Calculation of performance relative to benchmark portfolios (i.e. all government securities, etc.) for any desired naïve strategy;
- Mark-to-market of the entire bank balance sheet;
- Impact of changes in major risk factors on the bank balance sheet, bank capital, and bank default probability;

- Impact of changes in major risk factors on the bank's probability of default and the probability of default of all counterparties;
- Impact of acquisitions on bank share price, bank risks, and bank risk-adjusted return on capital.

The RAPA Approach: In summary

The RAPA approach produces the market value of the bank and its default probability as a by product. Any difference between the calculated values and observable market values (i.e. the stock price multiplied by the number of shares and quotes on credit default swaps for the bank) can and should be reconciled. One of the keys to successful implementation is to use a calculation that is fundamentally sound and yet analytically simple enough that any interested banker can confirm the calculations. Each step of the calculation outlined above is transparent and can be confirmed by an interested third party, be they the audit committee of the board of directors, the regulatory agencies, or an internal risk management audit unit. This is the heart of the RAPA approach. Many of the rules of thumb to risk-adjusted capital allocation are too simple to provide accurate guidance to management on shareholder value. If the signals sent to management are simple but incorrect, then

- shareholder value can be destroyed if the signals are followed;
- bonuses are misallocated and capable managers may depart;
- the capital allocation system may be discredited and ignored.

The RAPA approach is a tried and tested variation of financial theory originally developed by Robert Merton, William Sharpe, John Lintner, Robert Jarrow, and many others. We believe that the advantages over the Basel approach are significant, and indeed, the Basel approach is a rough approximation to the direct RAPA calculation. In that sense, the Basel approach is a special case of the RAPA methodology. There are no constraints in financial theory or computer science that prevent the RAPA approach from being implemented.

The first ten chapters have focused on achieving the objectives of the credit risk process that we outlined in Chapter 1 and again in Chapter 5. We now turn to special topics in credit risk management that deserve special attention.

Impact of Collateral on Valuation Models

Almost all bank lending, from retail to small business lending, involves some collateral. The presence of collateral adds a number of fascinating complexities to the evaluation of the market value of a particular transaction, regardless of whether one is using a structural model of credit risk or a reduced form model.

The impact of collateral on the valuation of the transaction is an obvious one. It is also obvious that the evaluation of the loss given default is dramatically affected by the presence of collateral. It is less obvious, but just as important, to note that the probability of default is impacted by the presence of collateral too, because the costs of seizing and liquidating or managing the collateral are different for the lender than they are for the borrower who owns the collateral. A classic example of this fact is the example of the Mexican banks in the mid 1990s which had a large floating-rate retail mortgage portfolio.[1] As interest rates rose over 100%, the banks faced a dilemma. If they exercised their legal rights to increase the floating-rates on the mortgage, the default of the borrowers became much more likely. This confirms the link between macro factors such as interest rates with default, as we discussed in Chapter 4. Similarly, the Mexican bankers found that if they seized the home as collateral, the only potential occupant of the home was the current occupant, the borrower who has just been forced into default by the increase in interest rate on the loan. Once the default rate on mortgages in Mexico hit 50% of all mortgage loans in the country, bankers reached the conclusion that it was less costly to them to forego their real option to raise the interest rate on the mortgage loan and also to forego their real option to seize the underlying collateral.

[1] The authors wish to thank Dr. Fausto Membrillo Hernandez, Regional Director for the Global Association of Risk Professionals for Mexico, for this anecdote.

We now turn to a survey of the way these kinds of collateral-related issues can be handled in various credit models.

Collateral: The Practical Issues in Valuation

For a financial institution that often uses collateral in its lending practices, there are a number of critical information-management issues to be addressed.

The most obvious and yet frequently overlooked issue is to insure that the lender's right to seize the collateral is 'perfected' in a legal sense.[2] The second issue is to maintain a high quality estimate of the value of the collateral. This issue has been ignored by nearly all financial institutions except for those collateral types for which market values are readily available (marketable securities and derivatives are an example).

Two approaches to valuation of collateral positions can be used: the financial instrument-style valuation and benchmark pricing valuation. The former valuation is simply the normal transaction-by-transaction valuation of portfolio positions like that which we described in the previous chapter (which may include the valuation of credit-risky bonds, for example). The latter valuation, benchmark valuation is based on one or more benchmark pricing variables, which typically would be a price index for the collateral (e.g., commercial property prices in a geographical region, home valuation in a particular post code-defined region, etc.). Benchmark pricing assumes that a collateral value was obtained at the time the collateral was pledged and that the issue is to adjust that value to reflect current market prices for that type of collateral. This is accomplished by determining the ratio of the current value of each benchmark pricing variable to its value at the pledge date, then taking a linear combination of the ratios and multiplying the result by the original pledged value. Either way, one should end up with a good approximation to the current market value of the collateral position.

Benchmark valuation is frequently necessary because lenders rarely measure the value of collateral that is non-financial until they need to, i.e. when the borrower is in default or near default. For good risk management purposes, however, it is important to constantly monitor this value and the benchmark pricing methodology is essential to do this in an efficient manner. Consider the example of Japan, where the value of homes has declined for many years and is approaching the principal value of the loan or is now below it. Retail prices in Japan, at the time of this writing, have

---

[2] As obvious as this may seem, Chinese banks are finding it almost impossible to seize collateral of delinquent borrowers because their legal rights to do so are unclear (*New York Times*, September 26, 2002).

declined for 36 months in a row on a year-on-year basis.[3] For this reason, the real option that mortgage borrowers have is more likely to be exercised—they can 'put' the now cheap home to the lender and 'walk away' from the loan. While this option is often exercised selectively (like an option to prepay a mortgage), there is no question that it is exercised more often when it is rational to do so.

To value the pledge of collateral, the collateral pledge rights can be also be thought of as an option that the lender holds on the collateral value that can be exercised only in the event of default. The borrower, by contrast, owns the option to default or not. Suppose we have a loan to a credit-risky counterparty that has a face amount of $100. If we disregard credit risk, this loan might have a current market value of $98 because market rates are higher than the loan rate. Taking into account the default likelihood of the counterparty, credit-adjusted valuation will price the loan at say $95. So this would be the appropriate value if we didn't pay attention to the collateral. Let's say the counterparty pledged some collateral against the loan that was originally worth $105, but the market value of the collateral has declined so that it is only worth $101 currently. If default occurs in the short-term, then the lender would receive the greater of the value of the loan ($95) and the value of the collateral ($101) or $101, less the lender's costs of managing and disposing of the collateral. These are often very significant and may in fact drive the value of the collateral to the bank below $95 as in the Mexico case cited above.

There are multiple approaches to modeling this collateral issue and we summarize a few approaches in the following sections.

Modeling Collateral in the Structural Model Framework

In the Merton or STV structural model framework, there are a number of approaches to modeling collateral values. They are all ad hoc with varying degrees of precision and have pros and cons versus each other and the collateral modeling approach for the Jarrow models:

- **Make the collateral the value of 'company assets' in the Merton model, and ignore the corporate legal entity**. In the case of a home loan, the value of 'company assets' would be the value of the house. The mortgage loan would be assumed to be a zero-coupon loan. If the value of the house is less than the value of the loan at maturity, the bank gets the collateral. This is not a bad assumption for retail credits

---

[3] *New York Times*, October 26, 2002.

since there is no legal entity and no 'business' except for the earning power of the borrower. The cash flow structure of the loan, however, is very crude. The virtue of this approach is its simplicity and its close parallels to the assumptions of the Merton model.

- **Assume the collateral is completely different from company assets with an arbitrary degree of correlation**. At maturity, the value of the loan is the greater of two assets. If the value of company assets is less than the amount due on the loan, the value of company assets or the value of collateral then we would require an extension of the Merton model. However an option on the greater of two assets has a known valuation formula. We could simply use this 'greater of the value of two assets' options formula instead of the Black-Scholes options formula in implementing the Merton model.
- **Assume the collateral is $X\%$ of company assets and has a value 100% correlated with company assets**. This analysis is only applicable if there is a senior debt and subordinated debt element of the company's zero-coupon debt. This is a simple extension of the Merton model, and it is very helpful in distinguishing between the valuation of the senior debt and the valuation of the subordinating debt even in a model as simple as the Merton model.

The Merton model's fundamental assumptions are consistent with the existence of collateral, but the sacrifice is a very high degree of simplification on the cash flow assumptions of the underlying loan.

Modeling Collateral in the Reduced Form Model Framework[4]

There are also multiple approaches to modeling collateral in the Jarrow reduced form framework and a wide array of closed form solutions is available. We introduce just a few variations here.

Method 1: Model the Collateral In The Same Way As Joint Default Insurance

In the Jarrow model, there is a closed form solution to the payoff upon 'joint default'—i.e. a dollar is paid if both companies default prior to time T.[5] This formula can be used directly with multiple interpretations. The simplest interpretation is that the collateral has only two values (high and low, with

[4] The authors want to thank Robert A. Jarrow for his contribution to this section.
[5] Robert A. Jarrow, Reduced Form Models: Technical Memorandum, Kamakura Corporation, 1999.

low being the 'default' value). For the 'high value' of collateral, collateral is in excess of principal and the bank has no loss. The bank has a loss only if:

(a) the company defaults and;
(b) the value of collateral is at its 'low' or 'default' value.

This known solution can be applied to the collateral problem.

Method 2: Linear Adjustment to Recovery Rate

Collateral can be interpreted as changing the random recovery rate δ in the Jarrow credit risk model, *to a potentially higher random value reflecting the additional value of the collateral.*

We just need to model a random recovery rate that is dependent on the value of some asset or pool of assets. This can be done by making δ depend on the spot rate and an index that reflects the collateral value, e.g. $\delta(t) = \delta_{old} + b_1 r(t) + b_2 I(t)$ where δ_{old} is the value of the recovery rate without collateral.

Method 3: Non-linear Adjustment to Recovery Rate (using the option approach)

The recovery rate can also be thought of as the sum of the unsecured recovery rate plus any gain on the disposal of collateral, if it is positive:

$$\delta(\tau) = \frac{\max[CP_\tau - v(\tau, T:i), 0]}{v(\tau-, T:i)} + \delta_{old}$$

where

CP_τ = value of the collateral pool at the time of default τ

$v(\tau, T:i)$ = value of the credit risky portfolio position at the time of default τ

$v(\tau-, T:i)$ = value of the credit risky portfolio position just before default τ

Note that if the collateral always has significant value, then the above option is always in the money, the 'maximum' operator disappears, and the recovery rate is again a linear function of the variable CP.

In all of these approaches, the Jarrow model has the analytical power to handle the collateral issue and the major concerns of a portfolio modeling effort is to clearly track the nature and value of collateral for mark-to-market considerations, hedging considerations, and credit-adjusted value-at-risk considerations. In all of these approaches, the RAPA methodology outlined in the previous chapter is unchanged, but the valuation methodology becomes more sophisticated.

In the Japanese mortgage example that we mentioned previously, this kind of sophisticated approach to collateral valuation would reflect more clearly the fact that bank valuations are a function of home prices, as we found for Australia in Chapter 4.

12

Pricing and Valuing Revolving Credit and Other Loan Agreements

B esides the issue of collateral discussed in the previous chapter, perhaps the biggest issue in the application of credit models to financial institutions is the valuation of loan commitments. In this chapter, we summarize some of the institutional detail regarding loan commitments and highlight some of the difficult issues in valuation. We then examine how one might model these issues in a structural modeling and reduced form modeling framework.

Practical Considerations in Modeling Loan Commitments

Loan commitments are an agreement between a borrower and a lender with the following typical features:

- **Amount**: the borrower can borrow and repay in any amounts subject to a cap on borrowings during the life of the loan commitment;
- **Pricing**: the pricing is specified in advance, although it sometimes is priced in advance as a function of the borrower's rating from one of the major international rating agencies;
- **Fees**: the borrower typically pays a commitment fee and an on-going fee on the undrawn amount on the loan commitment;
- **Borrower's option**: the borrower, of course, always has the real option (a) to borrow from other sources if it's cheaper and (b) to try to renegotiate the credit line if the borrower's credit quality improves during the life of the loan commitment;
- **Lender's option**: the lender frequently has the option not to lend based on 'material adverse changes' in the borrower's financial

condition and under other circumstances. These clauses are much
discussed and rarely invoked but still very real considerations;

- **Collateral**: loan commitments often include pre-specified collateral
  for smaller borrowers.

For small borrowers, who normally pledge collateral, loan commitments
are normally drawn down when there is an explicit cash need and repaid
from liquidation of collateral (collection of an account receivable) or from
payment on a project or sale where the expenses typically are incurred
before the revenue is received.

For larger borrowers, loan commitments are often unsecured commercial
paper 'back up' lines. The lines would almost never be drawn down if the
commercial paper credit ratings of the borrower are at the highest levels. By
the time commercial paper ratings drop to A3/P3, however, the number of
investors willing to buy commercial paper is sharply reduced, meaning
almost every issuer of commercial paper would need to draw on their back
up lines if they are downgraded to this level unless they could find some
other way to repay their commercial paper borrowings.

For all classes of borrowers, there are a number of features of draw-
downs on loan commitments that need to be captured for a realistic
modeling effort:

- **Partial draw down**: Credit lines are almost never drawn down
  completely. Borrowings are almost always less than the full amount.
- **Random variation in amount outstanding**: Once drawn, the amount
  outstanding varies up and down frequently.
- **Multiple draw downs**: once drawn, there are multiple draw downs,
  consistent with the first two points.

While these two real world considerations seem simple, they
dramatically complicate the modeling effort.

Modeling Loan Commitments in the Structural Modeling Framework

In the structural model framework, the value of the assets of the company is
the only random variable. Similarly, as we explained in Chapter 3, both the
Merton model and the STV model are single period models. While there are a
number of variations on these models where the value of assets can drop to a
'barrier' and trigger default at some time other than the beginning or end of
the period, modeling of managerial decisions is still largely restricted to time
zero (the beginning of the single period) or the end of the period.

Both Merton and STV models also assume that the value of the equity of the company is an option on the assets of the company. More specifically, they are assumed to be a European option on the assets of the company, which is exercisable only on the maturity of the other debt outstanding of the company.

This presents a number of complications for modeling loan commitments in the structural model framework. First, there is only one option exercise date: at maturity, when the equity holders either receive the value of company assets in excess of the amount of debt due or they don't. Second, exercise of the equity holders' option is 'all or nothing'—they either take all the remaining assets of the company or they don't have the option to get anything (bankruptcy occurs).

Therefore, it is difficult to use the structural framework for loan commitments. Does management decide to put the commitment in place at time zero and exercise it at the end of the period? If so, what are the terms and how do we model the draw down since the model is only a one period model and we know nothing about what happens after that? Even if we do adopt that structure, draw down will most likely be 'all or nothing' contrary to the empirical evidence on what loan commitment borrowers actually do.

Another alternative is this: We put two debt issues in place at time zero in the structural model framework, one drawn and the other undrawn until maturity. At maturity, the company has the option to either increase its loan outstanding or not.

We are still left with a number of unanswerable questions in the one period modeling framework:

- How does management decide at time zero whether to have a loan commitment or not?
- Under which conditions would it be rational to draw down at the end of the period? How do we specify their incentives to draw down as a function of company assets?
- If loan commitments are put in place at time zero and partially drawn at time zero, why are they used instead of zero-coupon debt, the standard assumption of the Merton and STV models?

The frequent draw-down and partial draw-downs of loan commitments makes their valuation in a structural model context particularly complex. This is a subject for future research, and it will require a considerable amount of creativity.

Modeling Loan Commitments in the Reduced Form Model Framework

The reduced form model framework has a number of advantages as a modeling framework for loan commitments. First of all, it is a multi-period, no arbitrage valuation framework with considerable analytical advantages, given the nature of loan commitments. Secondly, it has already been used on a similar problem, the valuation of non-maturity deposits (such as savings deposits and checking accounts) which are liabilities of banks which have much in common with loan commitments on the asset side. This problem has been addressed by Jarrow and van Deventer [1998] in a deposit context and charge card context. Like loan commitments, the amount of money a consumer puts in a savings deposit or draws down on a credit card varies over time at the consumer's option. The bank's only option is to stop accepting the deposit or to get out of the credit card business. While there is no cap on the amount the consumer can put in on the deposit, there is a cap on the amount the consumer can draw down on the charge card. There is also pricing formula on both a savings deposit and a charge card in a sense that the consumer and the bank have both observed a long history of how the bank's rates will change over time as open market rates have changed.

The authors expect that there will be considerable breakthroughs in loan commitment pricing in this modeling framework in the near future because of its flexibility and the parallels with existing problems like Jarrow and van Deventer [1998] with a known solution.

13

Credit Derivatives and Collateralized Debt Obligations

The rapid growth of Collateralized Debt Obligations (CDOs) and related variations on the CDO structure has highlighted the need for the kind of advanced credit-adjusted valuation and risk measurement that we discussed in Chapter 10. In that chapter, we outlined the proper calculation methodology for any credit-risky portfolio. To reiterate, there are five key steps:

1. Simulate the multi-period correlated changes in the key macro factors driving credit risk, interest rate risk, and foreign exchange risk for the institution;
2. Given these macro factors, derive the probability of default and loss given default for every counterparty in every period in every scenario. Default probabilities will be correlated among counterparties because they are functions of common macro factors;
3. In each scenario, given the probabilities of default, simulate the infinite numbers of default times that can occur for that counterparty given the multi-period evolution of its default probability in that scenario;
4. Calculate the value, cash flows, and financial accruals for each transaction the financial institution has with each counterparty;
5. Generate the standard reports and distribute electronically to end users.

This calculation methodology goes the farthest in meeting the objectives of the credit risk process that we outlined in Chapters 1 and 5. This level of valuation technology is used by the most sophisticated participants in the CDO market, but the vast majority of CDO market participants are using methodology which significantly understates the potential degree of correlation in the underlying CDO portfolio. This kind of methodological problem also makes it impossible to hedge correlated movements in credit risk and valuation, since the underlying drivers of risk (the macro factors) are not incorporated in the analysis. We turn to these methodologies in the next section.

Simple Approaches to CDO Evaluation

There are three basic approaches commonly used by investors in the CDO market, all of which have a high degree of overlap in the approach they use:

- Transition matrices, which measure the probability that a given borrower moves from one ratings class to the next;
- Rating agencies' published models, which do not require simulation;
- Basel-related approaches, which assume a high degree of homogeneity among the reference names in the CDO structure.

In this section, we will discuss all three approaches in order to contrast the simpler approaches and the recommended approach in Chapter 10.

Link Between Macro Factors and Default

In Chapter 4 and many other chapters in this book, we have been able to measure the impact of macro factors on credit spreads and the probability of default. It is impossible to specify a model that assumes no correlation among individual borrowers that can replicate the waves of corporate defaults that have been experienced in the United States and Japan. There is a high degree of correlation among corporate borrowers because of a common dependence on the same set of macro factors. In Japan, a fall in the Nikkei stock index from over 39,000 in December, 1989 to under 9,000 at the time of writing is consistent with a very weak economy that makes defaults much more likely. The same is true in the U.S., where the 75% fall in the NASDAQ technology-oriented index was consistent with a much higher level of bankruptcies among high technology firms. High interest rates in the U.S. in the late 1970s and early 1980s led to the well-known collapse of the savings and loan industry.

All three of the modeling approaches mentioned above ignore this link between specific macro factors and the default probability of each reference name:

- **Transition matrices** completely ignore the correlation among borrowers and base the probability of default probability movements on a specific historical period, which may or may not be consistent with the current environment.

- **Rating agency** models base correlation among corporations in all industries on one schedule based on historical experience in the U.S.. No macro factor drivers are specified.
- **The New Basel Capital Accords** assume, in the Internal Ratings-Based Approach, that all borrowers have a 20% correlation between the value of their corporate assets in the Merton approach. No justification of this correlation is given, and no macro factors are linked to default.

The result of these omissions is that we cannot answer the three key objectives of the credit risk process outlined in Chapter 1 that the RAPA risk measurement process can answer:

- What are the major risk factors driving the value of my loan, bond or derivatives portfolio?
- Am I as diversified as I could be? What change in risk-adjusted shareholder value added results from a change in my current level of diversification?
- How can I hedge the risk of my portfolio?

This means that as CDO transactions are proposed, or as CDO transactions purchased deteriorate in value, market participants using the three approaches above are unable to measure their risk or hedge the changes in value. This is more than a theoretical concern—it is a critical flaw from a fundamental business management point of view.

Interest Rate Assumptions

In Chapter 4 and later chapters, we saw that interest rates drive the probability of default. Interest rates are assumed constant in all of the three simple approaches to CDO valuation and risk management that are outlined in this chapter.

This leads to a simple conclusion: all three approaches significantly understate the risk in a CDO transaction because they ignore one of the most critical macro factors that drives correlated changes in the probability of default for almost all counterparties.

Over-simplistic Correlation Assumptions

Simplicity is a beautiful thing, as one of the authors pointed out in another risk management book,[1] urging that risk managers following the '80/20'

---

[1] Dennis Uyemura and Donald R. van Deventer, *Financial Risk Management in Banking*, Irwin, 1993.

rule. This rule states that on any complicated problem, 80% of the benefits of a perfect answer can be achieved with only 20% of the effort needed for a perfect solution. Unfortunately, in a highly-complex financial instrument such as the CDO, this is a recipe for a short career in asset management. A well-known story from the Tokyo market illustrates the risks. In the mid-1980s, Salomon Brothers was earning more than $500 million annually in its Tokyo office. One of the tools of the firm was good sales talk on modeling. Salesmen regularly asked clients which models they were using for options valuation. This was part of the relationship-building exercise that leads to more sales, but more than that, the salesman for Salomon Brothers could then take that knowledge to their structured product group, which had a model it felt was more accurate. Knowledge of the client's model allowed the firm to propose an over-the-counter derivative transaction to the Japanese client that looked good to the client using the client's models, while at the same time effectively transferring value from the client to Salomon Brothers. This process is the nature of the complex structured products business on Wall Street. In the CDO market, these are the 'beware' signals:

- The transactions are normally not registered with the Securities and Exchange Commission, and transaction documentation is subject to extremely limited circulation;
- The transactions are structured so that the sum of the value of their tranches is 'worth' more than the underlying transactions.

This is the proverbial 'making of a silk purse out of a sow's ear'. Some argue that there are pools of investors who strongly prefer low-risk pools of credit and the value difference comes from structuring transactions for those investors. Veterans of the securities industry, like the authors, think model error, like that described in the Tokyo market above, might explain more of this value difference than investors would care to admit. What are the model risks inherent in the simple modeling approaches outlined above?

- **Transition matrices** implicitly assume that correlation among borrowers is zero.
- **Rating agency models** make more implicit assumptions. They assume that correlation among the borrower class is exactly the same as correlation among defaults over a long period of history in the United States. Moody's Investors Service 'diversity score' assumes further that correlation among all firms in an industry is the same in all industries, and that correlation between industries is zero.
- **Basel Internal Ratings-Based Approach** implicitly assumes that the correlation among the value of company assets is 20% for all pairs of companies.

A sophisticated CDO structurer, knowing which of these models is used by a potential buyer, can easily structure a transaction which looks good to the buyer but which in fact has much more risk than the buyer thinks. This results in a transfer of value from the buyer to the seller, as we saw in the Salomon Brothers example.

Over-simplistic Homogeneity Assumptions

All of the three modeling approaches commonly used do not deal directly with the exact composition of the underlying CDO portfolio in terms of concentration. They all implicitly assume that the size of the exposure to each reference name is identical in size in order to use the binomial probability distribution to easily calculate the number of defaults that will occur over time. The Basel approach makes a modest adjustment for 'granularity' or concentration, but it is based on a numerical approximation which is much more complex than a direct simulation of the results, the topic to which we now turn.

Lack of Transaction-Level Valuation

None of the three modeling approaches commonly used in the CDO market use transaction-level valuation of the borrower's promise to repay. All of the borrower's promises are valued as if they were simple 'bullet' maturity bonds. What if the bonds are callable? What if they are floating-rate with caps and floors? All of the modeling approaches ignore this 'market risk,' but in reality these market risk considerations are not separable from credit risk. A 10-year bond callable after five years has considerably less credit risk than a non-callable bond, because the possibility of a call reduces credit exposure. Similarly, the existence of credit risk makes it less likely that the bond is called, since the company may (a) default before the call can be exercised or (b) not have the cash to exercise the call option even if it is rational to do so. Only a risk management process like that in Chapter 10, with transaction level valuation, addresses this concern.

Why Not the Best? Monte Carlo Simulation

All three of the simple approaches to CDO risk assessment and valuation have the same thing in common—they are structured so that a monte carlo simulation is not needed. In Chapter 10, by contrast, the risk assessment that is recommended relies very heavily on simulation, because we know that risk assessment has to be forward-looking, not backward-looking, to correctly assess value and probability of default for a CDO, a financial institution, or any other collection of assets and liabilities.

Monte carlo simulation is no longer a mystery. It is a technique that comes in the form of add-ins to common spreadsheet software and it is sold for only about $500. 'Crystal Ball' and '@Risk' ('at risk') are two of the most popular products in use in major financial institutions around the world. For an institution to invest billions of dollars in CDOs without the willingness or the knowledge to invest $500 in monte carlo simulation is, honestly speaking, an inconsistency that is hard to imagine. Every CDO investor should be doing monte carlo simulation for both buy-sell decisions and portfolio risk management. Any institution that does not take this step is taking undue risks in CDO trading. This reluctance should be a major concern to both the audit committee of the board of directors and to the company's regulators.

While the steps outlined in Chapter 10 are comprehensive, an institution can do most of the steps on its own very cost effectively, and vendors of risk information and software have generated cost-sharing benefits that makes CDO risk assessment an investment that any participant in that market can make. The three modeling approaches outlined earlier in this chapter are, at best, an expository tool for senior management that are supplements for, not replacements for, the approach we outlined in Chapter 10.

Future Developments in
Credit Modeling[1]

As we have outlined in the first 13 chapters of this book, the successful implementation and practical use of a credit model involves critical choices. In making these choices, financial institutions management and regulators have a fiduciary responsibility to shareholders and liability suppliers to completely 'vet', or audit, all models used. This is one of the most important prescriptions of the New Basel Capital Accords. A 'black box' approach to modeling fails this test. All credit models used should be subjected to critical analysis and review, either publicly or privately. Many of the most exciting developments in credit modeling will come in the area of model performance assessment. We are learning more every day using model testing techniques such as those outlined in Chapter 6.

Advances in Model Testing

All models should be tested 'out of sample' by the user (or an auditor employed by the user). The most sophisticated tests involve using historical periods with substantially different market conditions (for example, the 1979–1985 high interest rate period in the U.S.) or tests in other countries with different market conditions. Japan and the rest of Asia over the last decade, for example, provide a much better testing ground than just using the most recent twenty years of prosperity in the U.S.. Similarly, models tested on the wave of defaults in the U.S. since 2000 is a much richer testing ground than testing during the more benign middle 1990s.

All models have weaknesses, and it is better to aggressively seek them out rather than to identify them after a problem has occurred. An ideal credit

---

[1] Parts of this chapter are adapted from Jarrow and van Deventer [1998].

risk management system should utilize multiple credit models to help diversify this model risk. Such a system would allow the user full control of the model audit and performance testing process. This kind of system ends the debate about relative model performance, because it is 'agnostic.' Through its usage the user will obtain definitive proof of 'best model performance.' This is perhaps the area of most rapid advances in the practical use of credit models.

Despite their inherent difficulties, credit models provide the key ingredient to a successful credit risk management system. This is because they can be used to estimate true credit-adjusted valuations that correctly reflect the risk-adjusted value of a borrower's promise to repay. Such credit adjusted valuations can and should be used for:

- all major derivative exposures;
- callable bonds;
- stand-by letters of credit;
- other contingent credit lines;
- all value at risk calculations;
- all risk-adjusted capital calculations;
- middle office exposure management,
- mark-to-market real time trade authorizations,
- net income simulation with default adjustment.

Steady progress in sophisticated valuation of defaultable instruments is another area where tremendous advances are being made, as we discuss more fully below.

Recent Research on Credit Modeling with Applications to Retail and Small Business Credit Scoring

Ironically, small business and retail credit-scoring were the hottest areas of credit risk research until the development of reduced form modeling in the last five years. Now a major new area of research is the merger of reduced form modeling with the advanced hazard rate modeling that is taking over the credit-scoring function. The Chava Jarrow approach is an example of the benefits from this merger. Using this merger of reduced form and credit-scoring technology, advanced credit rate modeling can be done equally well for a diverse class of borrowers, namely:

- retail borrowers;
- small business borrowers;
- large private companies;

- companies which issue equity but not debt;
- institutions which issue debt but not equity;
- institutions which issue both debt and equity.

Many of these developments are contained in work that has not yet been published. We summarize the major contributions of a few key papers, some of which we discussed in earlier chapters, by quoting from abstracts of these papers.

'Bankruptcy Prediction Using Hazard Rate Estimation: Industry Effects,' by Sudheer Chava and Robert A. Jarrow

'This paper investigates the forecasting accuracy of bankruptcy hazard rate models for U.S. companies over the time period 1962–1999. The contribution of this paper is threefold.

One, the authors validate the superior forecasting performance of the bankruptcy hazard rate model of Shumway (2001) as opposed to the models of Altman (1968) and Zmijewski (1984). Two, the authors demonstrate the importance of including industry effects in hazard rate models using a new bankruptcy database that is unique to this paper. Industry groupings are shown to significantly affect both the intercept and slope coefficients in the forecasting equations. Three, the authors extend the standard hazard rate model to apply to financial firms. Modified but analogous forecasting variables to those used with non-financials, both balance sheet ratios and market, provide equally accurate forecasts to those obtained for non-financial firms.'

Perhaps even more importantly, the authors demonstrate that the hazard rate derived from this process can be used in the Jarrow or other reduced form credit models without modification. It is a powerful valuation technology with equal application to all of the kinds of institutions mentioned in the previous section.

'Bankruptcy Prediction, Market versus Accounting Variables, and Reduced Form Credit Risk Models' by Sudheer Chava and Robert A. Jarrow

'This paper investigates the bankruptcy prediction model of Chava and Jarrow (see above) for U.S. companies over the time period 1962–1999. The contribution of this paper is threefold. One, the authors investigate the performance of this bankruptcy hazard rate model using monthly data. The existing academic literature employs only yearly observations. The authors show that bankruptcy prediction is improved using this shorter observation interval. Two, they demonstrate that accounting variables add predictive power, although the increase is modest, when market variables are already included in the bankruptcy model. This supports the notion of market efficiency with respect to publicly available accounting information. Three, the authors compare the default probability estimates obtained from this hazard rate model (explicit estimates) with those obtained implicitly from debt prices using the reduced form model contained in Janosi, Jarrow, Yildirim (2000). Consistent with the diversification argument of Jarrow, Lando, Yu (2000), the authors find that one cannot reject the hypothesis that the explicit and implicit default intensities are identical.'

From a practical bankers' point of view, this paper shows how to use logistic regression (the basis of credit scoring) for large private companies, small businesses, and retail clients with and without market variables. While Chava and Jarrow focus on equity and its volatility in this paper, other market-based variables (even if the counterparty is not an equity issuer) can be powerful explanatory variables. There are various ways to incorporate these types of variables in credit scoring analysis:

- The default probability of the employer of a retail borrower;
- The average default probability of the industry of the employer of a retail borrower;
- The average default probability of the industry of a small business;
- The average default probability of the industry of the clients of a small business.

'Estimating Expected Losses and Liquidity Discounts Implicit in Debt Prices,' by Tibor Janosi, Robert Jarrow and Yildiray Yildirim

'This paper provides a comprehensive empirical implementation of a reduced form credit risk model that incorporates both liquidity risk and correlated defaults. The model implemented is from Jarrow [2000]. The time period covered is May 1991–March 1997. Monthly bond prices on 20 different firms' debt issues are studied. The firms are chosen to provide a stratified sample across various industry groupings. Five different liquidity premium models are estimated, no liquidity premium being the simplest. First, on a relative basis, unit root tests for the time-series stationarity of the estimated parameters, and both in- and out-of-sample goodness-of-fit tests support the existence of a non-zero liquidity premium. Second, on an absolute basis, the best performing liquidity premium model fits the data quite well with stationarity of the estimated parameters, an average R^2 of .87, and an average percentage pricing error of only 1.1 percent.'

This paper provides a comprehensive empirical test of the Jarrow reduced form model, consistent with the highest standards of academic work.

'Estimating Default Probabilities Implicit in Equity Prices,' by Tibor Janosi, Robert Jarrow, and Yildiray Yildirim

'This paper uses a reduced form model to estimate default probabilities implicit in equity prices. The model implemented is a generalization of the model contained in Jarrow (2000). The time period covered is May 1991–March 1997. Monthly equity prices on fifteen different firm's debt issues are studied. The firms are chosen to provide a stratified sample across various industry groupings. Four general conclusions can be drawn from this investigation. First, equity prices can be used to infer a firm's default intensities. This is a feasibility result. Second, due to the noise present in equity prices, the point estimates of the default intensities that are obtained are not very precise. They have large standard errors and they exhibit time series non-stationarities. Third, equity prices do appear to have a bubble component, not explained by the Fama-French (1993, 1996) four-factor model and proxied by a P/E ratio. Fourth, the authors compare the default probabilities obtained from equity with those obtained implicitly from debt prices using the reduced form model contained in Janosi, Jarrow, Yildirim (2000). Due to the large standard errors of the equity model's intensity estimates, the authors find that one cannot reject the hypothesis that these default intensities are equivalent.'

Perhaps the most important bankers' conclusion from this work is that the default intensities derived from debt prices have a much higher degree of statistical significance than default intensities using the best available equity-based model of default.

Maintaining a 'Model Independent' Portfolio Modeling Capability

In Chapter 10, we outlined a modeling approach that allows a financial institution to maintain a model-independent credit risk management capability, using any variation of the models studied in Chapter 3:

- fixed-interest rate Merton model;
- random interest rate Merton model [Shimko, Tejima and van Deventer, 1993];
- Jarrow basic model with company-specific default intensity;
- Jarrow advanced model with interest rate-driven default probabilities, and;

- Jarrow advanced model with interest rate and market index-driven default probabilities.

With this capability, the user can test relative portfolio modeling performance using a hedge test like that discussed in Chapter 7 to see how each model would have performed using the data and time period most relevant to the user. Financial institutions are implementing these models so that users can evaluate their relative performance on a common data set of the user's choosing.

This kind of model independence is essential for meeting the model testing requirements of the New Basel Capital Accords.

Valuation Methodologies for Different Instrument Types

As mentioned in the early chapters of this book, first generation models assume that the counterparty is in effect risk-free and the only random variable is the variable that determines the payoff on the security. The second generation modelers use ad hoc Monte Carlo simulation to model default/no default in order to estimate the difference between the value of a security where the counterparty will not default (often called 'replacement value') and the value of the specific counterparty's promise to pay given that default may in fact occur (this is 'credit-adjusted value'). The difference between these two values is the loss in value (versus the equivalent risk-free transaction) due to the credit riskiness of the counterparty.

Third generation models include more than one random variable and allow for an explicit closed-form solution for some (but not all) security structures for which default is a possibility. This section summarizes selected published or known valuation formulas associated with the Merton, STV and Jarrow models. Perhaps the greatest area of credit risk research in the next decade will be research that adds substantially to the valuation formulas listed below.

Selected Valuation Formulas in the Merton Model

The two principal valuation formulas commonly mentioned in the Merton framework are related to variations on the Black-Scholes options model:

- Value of defaultable zero-coupon debt;
- Value of a call option on equity of a defaultable company (Geske 'Compound Option' formula).

Generally speaking, these formulas do not cover the majority of financial institutions assets, and considerable original theoretical work would be necessary to make the Merton model framework apply more broadly. Its principal liability as a model is the assumption that the risky company has only one debt issue, a zero-coupon debt issue, outstanding. When this is not the case, the model requires a complex dynamic programming-oriented numerical. Some researchers are addressing the single period nature of the model by allowing the amount of company debt relevant to the model to vary with the maturity of the debt. While this is a simple adjustment, it enhances the ease of practical application.

Selected Valuation Formulas in the Shimko, Tejima and van Deventer Extension of the Merton Model

Shimko, Tejima and van Deventer extended the Merton model framework to random interest rates in 1993. The principal valuation formula they derive is the value of defaultable zero-coupon debt.

Any other valuation formula would be more complex than the Merton framework because of the randomness of interest rates within the model. The same kind of Black-Scholes-related extensions in valuation can be made.

Selected Valuation Formulas in the Jarrow Model

The following valuation formulas are known for the Jarrow model but many have not yet been published. This list is growing daily because of the power of the reduced form modeling technology:

Zero-Coupon Bonds;
Coupon-Bearing Bonds;
Callable Coupon-Bearing Bonds (European or American);
Credit Derivatives:
- Credit Derivatives on Coupon Bonds;
- Default Insurance;
- Bond Insurance;
- Credit Swaps.

Options on Bonds: . . . . . .
- European Options on Zero-Coupon Bonds;
- European Options on a Coupon Bond;
- Callable Coupon Bonds;
- Putable Coupon Bonds;
- Collateralized Borrowing.

Lattice Computations for Valuation;

Credit Derivatives on Portfolios (Baskets):

- Joint Default Insurance;
- Default Insurance of a Basket;
- A Portfolio on Default Insurance Contracts;
- Credit Swap on a Basket;
- Default Insurance on a Basket (The General Case).

A Forecast of the Future

The tremendous advances in the reduced form modeling technology has occurred just prior to a substantial increase in the number of defaults in the U.S. market, of which Enron and Worldcom are the most prominent names to date. The authors feel that this fortunate correlation of modeling capability and modeling need will lead to a very rapid increase in the ability of financial institutions world-wide to better manage credit risks in the years ahead. We hope that this book has been helpful in showing the potential that lies ahead and best practice at the time of this writing.

Index

A

Accuracy Ratio 101, 102, 105–107, 109–112, 114, 123–126, 130, 131, 137, 138, 196, 197
ANZ Banking Group 7, 67
Asia 7, 16, 17, 19, 21, 26, 70, 74, 83, 193, 212, 259
Asset and Liability Management 22, 23, 117, 190, 217
Australia 66, 67, 84, 202, 239, 248

B

Bank Insurance Fund 8
Bank of Tokyo-Mitsubishi 67, 69
Basel Accord 119, 123, 199, 204, 217
Basel Capital Accord 2, 119, 137, 138, 181, 193, 199, 203, 204, 206–208, 217, 255, 259, 264
Basel Committee 5, 6, 85, 117, 119, 163, 181, 190, 197, 199, 200, 202–211, 213, 215–217, 219, 220, 223, 224, 226, 235
Basel Committee for Banking Supervision 5
Black 1, 26, 28–32, 34, 39, 40, 50, 117, 146, 158, 181, 190, 218, 234, 246, 259, 264, 265
Black-Scholes 1, 26, 28–31, 34, 40, 146, 158, 181, 218, 246, 264, 265
Board of Governors of the Federal Reserve System 5, 200, 215

C

Camel 8
capital 1, 2, 5, 8, 11, 14–16, 18, 19, 22, 24, 27, 32–36, 38, 39, 43, 44, 48, 51, 59, 61–63, 73, 85, 86, 94, 117–119, 137, 138, 144, 146, 154, 155, 161–163, 181, 182, 190, 191, 193, 197, 199, 200, 202–206, 209, 210, 212, 213, 215–236, 240, 241, 255, 259, 260, 264
Chava 3, 27, 54, 55, 61, 94, 96, 115, 117, 119–126, 128, 130, 131, 133, 135–137, 139, 194–197, 201, 202, 205–207, 210, 237, 260–262
Chi-Squared 97–100, 112, 114, 195
Commonwealth Bank of Australia 67
Continental Illinois 54
correlation 11, 13, 17, 20, 35–39, 43–45, 47–49, 67, 69, 74, 80, 152, 153, 170, 181, 193, 194, 197, 208–210, 212, 215, 218–222, 239, 240, 246, 253, 254–256, 266
Cox 38, 41, 49, 63
credit adjusted valuation 260
credit derivatives 13, 15, 22, 23, 26–28, 50–54, 56, 60–62, 93–96, 122, 135, 154, 205, 237, 253, 265, 266
Credit Scoring 54, 95, 96, 130, 211, 260, 262

D

Daiei 69–73, 230, 231, 233, 234, 236
debt prices 26–28, 60, 69, 72, 93, 117,
    135, 142, 143, 172, 173, 181, 190,
    205, 226, 262, 263
default probability 9, 10, 18, 19, 21,
    23, 25, 28, 29, 37, 44, 45, 52, 54,
    87, 92–96, 102, 110, 111, 115, 116,
    130–136, 146, 147, 152–154, 201,
    202, 205–208, 210–212, 219, 226,
    234, 239–241, 253, 254, 262
delta 18–21, 32, 33, 56, 57, 158
Dennis Uyemura 13, 255
deposit insurance 15, 16, 50, 201, 223
Duffie 26, 30, 52, 62, 117, 201

E

Empirical Probabilities 34, 35
expected return 34–37, 44, 173, 221,
    233, 235, 239
Exxon 52, 56, 73, 174, 176, 236

F

Federal Deposit Insurance Corporation
    16, 201
Federal Reserve System 5, 200, 215
Financial Institutions Monitoring System
    8, 201
Financial Risk Management in Banking
    13, 14, 50, 255

G

Goldman, Sachs 73, 74

H

hazard rate 16, 50–52, 54, 95, 96, 120,
    260–262
Heath 26, 50, 53, 62, 155, 218
hedge 7, 10, 13, 14, 18, 20, 21, 23, 32,
    33, 47, 56, 57, 61, 62, 86, 156–158,
    160, 161, 163, 164, 254, 255, 264
hedging 10, 11, 13, 14, 20, 21, 32, 34,
    37, 51, 55–58, 61, 63, 87, 89, 91, 93,
    94, 96, 139, 155, 156, 158, 160–163,
    181, 193, 247
Hokkaido Takushoku Bank 8

home mortgages 19
Hong Kong 18, 19
Hosmer 101, 110, 112, 116, 117
Hull 41, 53, 117, 173, 190, 218

I

Ingersoll 38, 40, 41, 49, 50
Interest rate derivatives 21, 53, 56, 57

J

Jamshidian 28
Japan 2, 5, 8, 15, 54, 66, 67, 69, 77,
    79, 80, 84, 130, 137, 210, 212, 230,
    244, 248, 254, 256, 259
Jarrow 1–3, 26–28, 30, 33, 36, 50–56,
    58–63, 72, 85, 87, 93, 94, 96, 115,
    117, 119–126, 128, 130, 131, 133,
    135–137, 139, 140, 142, 147, 148,
    150, 152–158, 160–163, 165, 172,
    173, 181, 182, 190, 191, 194–197,
    201, 202, 205–207, 210, 218, 234,
    235, 237, 241, 245–247, 252,
    259–265
JP Morgan 1, 17–20, 22, 23, 25, 54
JP Morgan Chase 17

K

Kiefer 54
Korean 18, 19, 24, 69, 74, 76, 236,
    239
Korean Development Bank 69, 74, 193,
    194, 236

L

Lehman Brothers 16
Lemeshow 101, 110, 112, 116, 117
LIBOR 10, 11
Likelihood Ratio 111, 112, 114, 116,
    123
liquidity 11, 25, 26, 28, 52–54, 56, 59,
    74, 117, 147, 153, 162, 163, 190,
    219, 224, 262
loan loss reserve 15, 86
logistic 61, 95, 96, 101, 110–112,
    114–117, 121, 123, 125, 136, 137,
    194, 195, 201, 205, 206, 208, 262

logistic regression 61, 96, 101, 110–117, 121, 123, 125, 136, 137, 194, 195, 201, 205, 206, 208, 262
Long Term Capital Management 11, 163
Long Term Credit Bank 8, 77, 79, 80, 130
Long Term Credit Bank of Japan 8, 77, 79, 80, 130
Longstaff 26, 38, 41, 155

M

macro factor 11–14, 18, 20, 21, 23, 25, 26, 29, 52, 53, 55–57, 60, 61, 65–67, 69, 72, 76, 83, 84, 91, 93, 94, 137, 160, 208, 210, 212, 234–237, 239, 243, 253–255
Macro Risk 13, 14, 17, 27, 52, 55, 59, 89, 91, 207, 212, 225, 240
Malaysia 18, 21, 83, 84
Mann-Whitney U test 101, 102, 105–107
Merrill Lynch 63, 73, 74, 176, 178
Merton Model 29, 30, 33, 34, 36, 37, 40, 42, 128, 142, 145, 152–154, 157, 161, 171, 173, 174, 264, 265
Merton model 2, 25–27, 30, 32–34, 36–39, 42, 44, 45, 49, 51, 54, 55, 58–61, 69, 72, 77–85, 87, 122, 123, 126, 128, 130, 135, 136, 142–144, 146–148, 152–155, 157–165, 167, 168, 170, 173–179, 181, 182, 201, 205, 209–211, 215, 218, 221, 224, 234, 245, 246, 250, 263, 265
Mexico 20, 243, 245
Miller 31, 32, 39
Modigliani 31, 32, 39
Moody's Investors Service 58, 89, 124, 126, 137, 256
Morton 26, 50, 53, 62, 155, 218

N

National Australia Bank 67, 202, 239
Nippon Credit Bank 8, 77, 80, 82, 130
North American Asset and Liability Management 22

O

of Internal Ratings 86, 87, 98
Office of the Comptroller of the Currency 16
oil prices 12, 14, 20, 52, 56, 57, 94, 236
Ordinal rankings 87
Outram 85, 91, 93, 95, 96, 111, 116

P

Petronas 73, 83, 84

R

Receiver operating characteristic 101, 105, 196
reduced form 2, 16, 26–28, 41, 50, 51, 53, 58, 60, 70, 83, 85, 87, 93–96, 119–121, 124, 130, 133, 135–138, 142–144, 146, 154, 156, 160, 162, 164, 181, 182, 194, 201, 210, 211, 213, 215, 216, 235, 243, 246, 249, 252, 260–263, 265, 266
Reduced form models 2, 26–28, 41, 50, 51, 53, 58, 60, 70, 83, 87, 93–95, 124, 133, 136–138, 142–144, 146, 160, 164, 181, 182, 201, 215, 235, 246
Relative rankings 87
risk factors 10, 12, 13, 17, 18, 24, 52, 59, 86, 212, 225, 240, 241, 255
Risk-neutral 34, 36
ROC 101, 102, 105–112, 114, 123–126, 130, 131, 137, 138, 196, 197, 202
Ross 9, 14, 32, 38, 41, 49, 55, 57, 67, 87, 123, 157, 163, 212, 217, 262, 263

S

savings and loan institution 7, 15, 19, 20, 26
scenario-specific 19, 21
Scholes 1, 26, 28–32, 34, 39, 40, 117, 146, 158, 181, 191, 218, 246, 264, 265
Schwartz 26, 38, 41, 63

Security Pacific Corporation 14, 57
Shareholder Value 6, 9, 10, 12–17,
    21–23, 48, 144, 154, 182, 199, 200,
    217, 224–226, 228, 232, 233, 235,
    241, 255
Shimko 1–3, 25, 27, 30, 37, 38, 49, 50,
    55, 58–62, 85, 87, 91, 118, 155, 161,
    173, 191, 216, 218, 263, 265
Shumway 54, 120, 131, 261
Singleton 26, 30, 52, 62, 117
SK Securities 17, 65, 67
Southeast Asia 7
Standard and Poor's Corporation 89
structural approach 26, 27, 58, 96

T

Tejima 2, 25, 27, 30, 37, 38, 49, 50,
    55, 58–62, 85, 87, 91, 118, 155, 161,
    173, 191, 216, 218, 263, 265
term structure 2, 26, 28, 29, 37, 38, 41,
    44, 49, 50, 53, 58, 62, 63, 117, 118,
    146, 155, 191, 218, 235
Thai 7, 18, 19, 21, 23–25, 226–228
Thai baht 7, 18, 19, 23–25, 226–228
transfer pricing 22, 23
Turnbull 2, 3, 26, 30, 33, 51, 62, 63,
    155, 158

U

Uyemura 13, 14, 40, 50, 255

V

value at risk 260
value of company assets 27, 30–34, 36,
    37, 40, 47, 49, 55, 58, 59, 61, 69,
    93, 142, 146, 155, 162, 165, 167,
    221, 251, 256
Vasicek 3, 38, 41, 42, 49, 50, 53, 58,
    218, 219
Vasicek model 38, 41, 42, 53, 218, 219
volatility 25, 31, 33, 34, 37–45, 47, 48,
    49, 52, 53, 96, 117, 122, 123, 125,
    126, 146, 152–154, 157, 162, 172,
    173, 181, 190, 194, 195, 217–223,
    226, 228, 234, 240, 262

W

White 41, 53, 66, 117, 173, 190, 218

Y

yield curve 28, 38, 41, 53, 117, 140,
    164, 190, 218, 223, 236
yield-curve smoothing 140, 164
Yildirum 26, 54, 72, 93, 117, 190